With the Spanish against Napoleon

Sanford Whittingham

Sir Samuel Ford Whittingham, K.C.B., K.C.H., G.C.F.

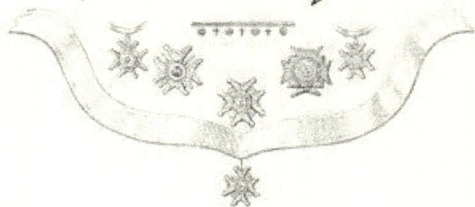

With the Spanish against Napoleon
The Peninsular War experiences of a British Officer

Sir Samuel Ford Whittingham

LEONAUR

With the Spanish against Napoleon
The Peninsular War experiences of a British Officer
by Sir Samuel Ford Whittingham

FIRST EDITION

Leonaur is an imprint of Oakpast Ltd
Copyright in this form © 2016 Oakpast Ltd

ISBN: 978-1-78282-555-5 (hardcover)
ISBN: 978-1-78282-556-2 (softcover)

http://www.leonaur.com

Contents

TO
HIS ROYAL HIGHNESS
FIELD-MARSHAL
GEORGE DUKE OF CAMBRIDGE, K.G.
COMMANDER-IN-CHIEF,
THIS VOLUME IS
BY THE GRACIOUS PERMISSION OF HIS ROYAL
HIGHNESS,
MOST RESPECTFULLY DEDICATED

Preface

By graciously consenting to accept of the dedication of this volume, the illustrious field marshal who commands the British Army has conferred upon the memory of Sir Samford Whittingham an honour, which can hardly fail to convince military readers that his services and conduct are worthy of being recorded. As regards civilians, it is probable that they may be interested in the career of an officer, who, although a *thorough* was yet not a *mere* soldier: for statesmen, and ambassadors, as well as generals, have testified to his merits, in the most eulogistic terms, and his services were, on several occasions, of a civil as well as military nature.

In consequence of the services of Sir Samford Whittingham having been principally performed in the Spanish Army, and also because nearly the whole of his military career was passed abroad—in America, in the Peninsula, and in the East and West Indies,—it was his misfortune, as regarded his countrymen to be ignored by the many, although most highly appreciated by the illustrious few; whose recognition of merit forms its surest test, as well as its most valuable recompense.

It does not appear that the subject of this *Memoir* ever contemplated making any record of his services. His brother-in-law, however, Mr. Richard Hart Davis, successively member for Colchester and Bristol, always preserved as much as possible his letters and papers; in the belief that such a publication as the present, would sooner or later occur.

Unfortunately, many valuable letters have been lost, including the greater part of General Whittingham's correspondence with two successive military secretaries at the Horse-Guards. The editor was not, however, greatly surprised, when the letters in question were found missing from their registered places, as he had long believed that their contents had, for the most part, been embodied in Southey's *History of the Peninsular War*. Indeed, a number of details in that work

9

could hardly have been collected from any other source. At the Battles of Baylen and Medellin, for instance, only one Englishman appears to have been present, and yet he is not mentioned by his brother Bristolian, Southey; although from him only could the latter have learned the speeches which Castaños and Alburquerque addressed to that Englishman. This personal silence confirms the fact in question to those who know how General Whittingham was wont to leave to others the task of recording his merits and services.

In consequence of the loss of the letters addressed to Colonels Gordon and Torrens, the private letters to his brother-in-law, Mr. Hart Davis, form the chief basis of this *Memoir;* and their frank and unreserved style is particularly suited for such a purpose. But from their voluminous nature, it has been possible only to give brief extracts, as a general rule.

The editor first projected this work in 1845. Aware that the late heroic Earl of Fife had been the friend and admirer of Sir Samford Whittingham, he wrote to his Lordship to inform him of, and to consult him on, his intentions. The following (omitting only some irrelevant private matters) was the reply of Lord Fife:—

Duff House: Tuesday, (post-mark 28 March, 1845), Dear Whittingham,—I was very happy to have the pleasure of receiving your interesting note regarding the memory of your excellent father, my late intimate and worthy friend. I, of course, am acquainted with much information about Sir Samford, and all that I can possibly do, to forward your views and wishes, shall be with much good will executed; to do justice to the gallant soldier, and talented gentleman, your father.

Suchet, with whom I was well acquainted, often conversed with me regarding different officers who had opposed him; and particularly mentioned the merits of your father which, he said, might have been followed with bad results to the French, had the war continued much longer. He said, "Whittingham's corps was the best disciplined, and if the example had been followed in many other instances, in different parts of Spain, the French army would have felt the effects in a remarkable manner."

General Reeves, an intimate friend of mine, who was in Catalonia, often spoke most honourably of your father, although he did not much like those English who were with the *Espagnolles.* There are two points to be noticed about your father's conduct, which party and other reasons have rendered obscure: his commanding the troops that marched to Madrid, when the Cortes were assembled; and also at the Battle of Barrosa. I shall afterwards make some observations and references about both; and also give some details of his services in the early part of the war with General Cuesta, and the Duke of Alburquerque, the importance of which were passed over or little known. . . .

I took your father from Talavera, and, I think, saved his life, in having a very good surgeon of the Guards every day, and by having fed him with tea, coffee and butter, which were then of more value than gold; and I obliged him to go from the field in the evening, and made a doctor go with him to my quarters. My brother. Sir Alexander Duff, knew your father well, and came home with him from Buenos Ayres. I was nearly being his second in a duel between him and J—— of the Guards. Sir Charles Felix Smith, his second and I made it up; which was fortunate for J——, as your father was a capital shot.

Believe me, most truly, yours

Fife.'

Major Whittingham, 26th Cameronians, Manchester.

★★★★★★

The goodness mentioned of the surgeon, *in a medical sense*, is disproved in this *Memoir*.

No record of this duel will be found in this volume, owing to want of details on the subject. The editor believes that, either at Cadiz or Seville, the quarrel arose from some expressions on the part of the guardsman, which were deemed insulting to the Spanish officers.

★★★★★★

In consequence of the increasing infirmities of Lord Fife, the editor did not again trouble his Lordship, nor did the latter ever send his promised information. By his letter, however, he had confirmed to the son, that valuable testimony regarding Marshal Suchet, which in 1814 he had spontaneously sent to the father, (see chapter 11). But the effect of his letter was to delay the writing of this *Memoir*. Regimentally the editor was then only a captain; and he had not the means or leisure for acquiring that completeness of information, necessary to do justice to a case, which party spirit and ignorance of details, had rendered obscure, in the opinion of a good and friendly judge. Indeed, some important facts only came to the knowledge of the editor, after the death of Sir William Napier and the publication of his life.

The editor, however, delayed chiefly on account of his roving and unsettled life. He waited therefore till he should have both leisure, and a fixed habitation, to enable him to study the voluminous correspondence of Sir Samford Whittingham and the *Wellington Dispatches*. At length he has accomplished his task to the best of his ability; amidst the difficulties of selection, rejection, and condensation, and of the loss of many valuable papers; and having also considerably to curtail the MSS. when finished, as too bulky.

The delay brings with it, however, this advantage, that it has facilitated candour and plain speaking; and has also probably given time for the decay of that party spirit, and professional jealousy, by which some facts were formerly greatly misrepresented.

The editor also trusts that the letters of distinguished persons which are published in this volume, may be interesting in themselves, as well as from their being strong testimonies to character and conduct. Next to those of the Duke of Wellington, and of the Marquis Wellesley, the letters of the Honourable Sir Edward Paget, and of Lord William Bentinck, furnish the strongest proofs of the merits of Sir Samford Whittingham. Lord William has an established reputation as a good officer and enlightened statesman; but Sir Edward Paget has not perhaps been sufficiently appreciated. How highly the Duke of Wellington esteemed him, his *Dispatches* have proved: but what Sir Charles Napier thought of him is probably less known, and is, therefore, here recorded; on the authority of a living eye—and ear—witness of the circumstances.

In 1848 Lord Frederick Fitz-Clarence, then Lieutenant-Governor of Portsmouth, accidentally met, in the streets of that town, the two soldier-sons of Sir Edward Paget, and asked them to lunch with him that day, as he was expecting Sir Charles Napier, on his way to Osborne to see the Queen. This was at the time, when, at the general call of the country, Sir Charles was about to proceed to India to save that empire from what was then considered as impending ruin. Lord Frederick introduced the young men to his distinguished guest, who, taking them each by the hand, said: 'Ah! if poor Sir Edward had had the health for it, he would have been the man to send to India.' (As this circumstance occurred some years after the death of Sir Samford Whittingham, it is recorded here instead of in the body of the work).

During his last visit to England Sir Samford promised at the request of his eldest niece (Mrs. Harford of Blaise Castle) to commit to writing some of those Peninsular anecdotes with which he had amused his relatives. This promise he fulfilled on his last voyage to Madras in 1840; and the Editor has made use of nearly all these *Recollections*; placing them in this volume, as far as possible in the order of their proper dates.

Finally, as far as is consistent with the sacred claims of justice to the memory of a beloved and honoured parent, the Editor has endeavoured to justify the confidence placed in him by the highly estimable gentleman, who may be deemed to represent the interests of his celebrated connection—Sir William Napier. This task has been greatly facilitated by the fact that six of the seven grand-children of Sir Samford Whittingham are related to that family, one of whose most distinguished members did him a great, even if unintentional wrong.

The confidence in question was expressed in a note concluding with the following words:—

> I greatly respect your sense of honour and justice and am sure that in vindicating your distinguished father you will not forget what is due to others.'

Chapter 1

1772–1805

For more than sixty years the subject of this *Memoir* and his sons have passed the best part of their lives in the public service of their country, in various parts of the world, and without a settled habitation. Owing to this fact, to the local changes in his native town, and to the circumstance that all the early contemporaries of Sir Samford Whittingham have long since departed this life, it is no easy matter to trace in accurate detail the antecedents of the family. Nor is this necessary in a case where the distinction gained by personal merit, unaided by aristocratic connections, is one of the chief justifications for holding up as a useful example to others the career of a military officer.

The father of Sir Samford Whittingham was a respectable citizen of the ancient and honourable city of Bristol. Mr. William Whittingham appears to have retired from business, with an independent, though not large, fortune, and thenceforward to have lived on his means as a gentleman in his native city. He had early married a young lady, who lived in the neighbourhood, who was of Warwickshire extraction, and who was called 'the beautiful Miss Richardson.' They had three children. The eldest, a girl, Sarah, married in 1789 Richard Hart Davis, a prosperous merchant in the Spanish wool trade, who, in 1806, became member for Colchester, and in 1812 was returned for his native city of Bristol (which he represented in six successive Parliaments), and was succeeded at Colchester by his eldest son. Hart Davis, afterwards Deputy Chairman of the Board of Excise.

The third child, James, eventually obtained a small post under Government. The elder of the two sons, Samuel Ford, the subject of this work, was born on the 29th January, 1772. When he grew up, his father desired to train him to the law, in its less brilliant but more probably remunerative branch; but his son revolted at the very idea.

From the first he was resolutely determined to be a soldier; and nature had fitted him for the profession of arms.

Tall and broad-shouldered, with a fine figure, and an excellent constitution, he possessed an open fearless disposition, and an enthusiastic impetuosity, with much ambition, all tempered by the most generous and chivalrous feelings. In addition to this, Samford (for into that one word the names Samuel Ford were soon contracted by himself and his friends) possessed much natural ability, very great energy, and a truly wonderful power of application. A bright and winning smile, a large and powerful forehead, neutralized the irregularity of his features, and, coupled with his strong and commanding figure, formed a prepossessing exterior, which manners, always allowed to be singularly charming, rendered very attractive even to strangers, and completely fascinating to relatives and friends.

★★★★★★

One of Sir Samford Whittingham's nieces thus describes her uncle's appearance:—'If by the word *handsome* is simply meant beauty of feature and profile, it does not apply to him. But if eyes of matchless brilliancy, and the whole heart and soul animating a countenance beaming with talent and affection, be the test, then his countenance was eminently fascinating and delightful to look upon; as were his manners and powers of conversation, by which he won the hearts of all who approached him.'

To this may be added another peculiarity, which may interest the reader. One of the medical officers called in when Sir Samford Whittingham was dying afterwards declared that he had '*the largest forehead* he had ever seen.'

★★★★★★

His respectful and disinterested deference and attentions to the fairer half of the creation was ever one of his most striking characteristics; and he truly was the knight without fear and without reproach. His natural impetuosity was calculated to make great friends or great enemies. If in his career the former greatly preponderated; if the latter were indeed very rare, as is believed to have been the case; this must be attributed to those winning qualities, that never lost a friend, but often won over an enemy. But his father would not hear of his entering the army; and his filial piety was such that he gave up the cherished object of his life till he became his own master.

★★★★★★

According to the *Bristol Times* (in its review of this work) Samford Whittingham was one of the mounted volunteers composed of the richer citizens, who were enrolled in Bristol in 1797, on a threatened French invasion. No doubt this episode increased his warlike tendencies.

★★★★★★

He even allowed his brother-in-law, Mr. Hart Davis, to persuade him to give a trial to the wool trade, so far as to agree to travel into Spain, and visit the connections at Bilbao of the Bristol House. The desire to travel and see the world attracted him. He proceeded to Spain; there, with his wonted application and energy, he speedily acquired a perfect knowledge of the Spanish language and people. But he preferred the society of the military to that of the merchants, and the ruling passion only became stronger and firmer than ever.

Mr. William Whittingham died at Earl's Mead, Bristol, on the 12th September, 1801, aged sixty; a man much respected by his relatives and acquaintances. The part of the town in which he lived has undergone such changes as to be no longer recognizable, thus adding to the difficulties of all researches into the past.

By his father's death, Samford Whittingham became independent. He did not, however, immediately return to England; probably waiting till he should learn if there were any prospect of his being at length able to obtain a commission in the army. Fortunately, the rule that prevented anyone above twenty-six years of age from obtaining a commission did not then exist. But it is probable that the further unfortunate delay was occasioned by his respect for his mother, who might have been shocked at the earnest wishes of the father being disregarded too soon after his death. The son appears to have remained abroad till he received the news of his approaching appointment. At all events it was not till the 3rd of January, 1803, that he arrived at the house of his widowed mother, in College Green, Bristol; and on the 20th of the same month he was gazetted to an ensigncy. But he was bent on being a cavalry officer, and immediately proceeded to London to negotiate the exchange.

The following fragment of a letter (which must have been written from London about the middle of February 1803, as it is recorded that he left the Green on the 3rd of that month) was carefully preserved by his mother, and found in her pocket-book, after her death:—

My dearest Mother,—I have almost concluded the business of the Lieutenancy in the 1st Life Guards. Lord Harrington, the colonel, is to give me a positive answer on Monday; and Mr. Greenwood, (later called Messrs. Cox and Co., the *par excellence* Army Agents of England), has no doubt it will be favourable. The price is 2,000 guineas; but out of this will be deducted the price I have already paid for the Ensigncy, &c.

Samford Whittingham was now thirty-one years of age. At that period, men usually obtained their first commissions at sixteen or earlier. He had thus lost at least fifteen years, and started in the army at a most lamentable disadvantage. If such a thing were possible now, it would be sufficiently disadvantageous. But sixty years ago it was worse. It is true that, thanks to that 'Soldier's Friend,' the Duke of York, the days were past in which English colonels might be seen in long clothes, or Scotch majors be heard 'greeting for their porridge.' But the road to promotion for the noble and wealthy was still wonderfully quick; and many men scarcely out of their teens were often found in actual command of regiments. Mr. William Whittingham's obstinacy had done irreparable injury to his son, rendering it almost impossible for him to expect to live to attain to the higher posts and rewards of the profession of arms, especially as he had nothing but his own merit to rely on in the struggle.

He did not return to Bristol, but proceeded immediately to the military college, then situated at High Wycombe. Although in those days science was not much encouraged in the army yet the zealous soldier was determined thoroughly to fit himself for the duties which he had undertaken to perform. He determined to endeavour to make up for lost time by extra exertions. It is recorded that, whilst at college, he lived on vegetable diet, in order to be able to study *sixteen hours a day!* And his constitution was able to bear for about a year and a half this trying strain upon its powers. He left an impression at High Wycombe, which, in the memory of more than one professor, was transmitted to Sandhurst College, when the scholastic locality was changed; and of which impression, the editor was an ear-witness nearly thirty years later.

Samford Whittingham appears to have joined the 1st Life Guards in London towards the latter part of 1804. He had made, probably in Portugal, the acquaintance of Mr. Thomas Murdoch, a wealthy and influential wine merchant. This gentleman appears to have been the means of introducing Lieutenant Whittingham to the notice of the Right Honourable William Pitt, the Premier, who was then projecting an expedition against the Spanish South American colonies, and was desirous to secure for that purpose the services of a certain Englishman, named Captain Rogers, then in Madrid, in the service of Spain. Rogers was probably the captain of an English merchant ship, though this is a matter of conjecture only. The Life-Guardsman's knowledge of Spain and of the language, and his High Wycombe education no doubt were considered good qualifications for the negotiation in question: and he was of course delighted to be of service to the great minister of the day.

As Mr. Pitt entered into his last period of office in May 1804, and as Lieutenant Whittingham belonged to the 1st Life Guards only from the 10th March, 1803, to the 14th February, 1805, there is no difficulty in filling up that part of the date of the following note, which is left blank in the original:—

> Greenwich, 18th December 1804.
> Dear Sir,—Mr. Pitt will be glad to see Mr. Whittingham to-morrow morning at any time he will call and send in his name. The sooner he calls after eleven o'clock the less chance there will be of his being kept waiting.
> I have written, by his direction, for leave of absence to Lord Harrington.
> > Yours faithfully,
> > > Wm. Eliot.
>
> Thomas Murdoch, Esquire,
> No. 1 Fitzroy Square.

There is no doubt that the above note was written by the honourable William Eliot, brother to the first Earl, and afterwards himself the second Earl, of St. Germans. The ensuing correspondence has been lost, in consequence of the box in which it was deposited in the care of Mr. Richard Hart Davis having been stolen a few years later. A certain Captain Richards was, it appears, employed by Lieutenant Whittingham to proceed from Lisbon to Madrid in the disguise of a smuggler, and to bring over Captain Rogers to England, and nothing more is at present known of the transaction itself. As regards Lieutenant Whittingham, he obtained the thanks of Mr. Pitt, but declined at the time all remuneration. The premature death of the minister, on the 23rd January, 1806, was one of Samford Whittingham's earliest misfortunes, preventing his deriving at that time any advantage, either from his services or his disinterestedness. But the Ministry took these services, amongst others, into consideration when, many years later, a small pension was granted to him.

In the *United Service Journal* for April, 1841, this affair with Mr. Pitt is thus noticed in the account of the services of Sir Samford Whittingham:—

> In 1804, Lieutenant Whittingham, at the desire of Mr. Pitt, was selected to proceed to Portugal on a secret mission. This service detained him in that country about twelve months, and during his residence at Lisbon, he was promoted to a company in the 20th Foot.
>
> Captain Whittingham, on his return to England, was complimented by Mr. Pitt on the very able manner in which he had executed the commission entrusted to him by that minister; and shortly after a troop in the 13th Light Dragoons becoming vacant, he was removed into that regiment.

The article from which the above was taken was (there is every reason to believe) written by Mr. Hart Davis, Junior, late Deputy Chairman of the Board of Excise, who was better acquainted than any person then living with all that concerned his uncle, Sir Samford Whittingham. The exchange into the 13th Light Dragoons must have cost a large sum of money; but the amount has not been recorded.

In that same year, 1805, in which Samford Whittingham was promoted to be captain, his future greatest friend and patron—then wholly unknown to him, and two years younger than himself—was gazetted a Major-General. This was the honourable Edward Paget (whose brother, Lord Paget, afterwards became Marquis of Anglesey).

CHAPTER 2

1806–1807

Towards the close of 1806, when the secret expedition against Lima, under the command of Brigadier-General Robert Craufurd was organised, Captain Whittingham was appointed Deputy Assistant Quartermaster-General to that force. Early in October, he joined it at Portsmouth, and sailed from England on the 12th November of the same year. From the day of his embarkation to that of his return to England, he—notwithstanding his many official duties—kept a copious journal, which completely filled two small manuscript volumes. From these alone a full and graphic history of one of the most disastrous expeditions, that England ever embarked in, might easily be written. And surely with profit: for the study of defeats, by teaching us how to avoid them, is as profitable, though not as agreeable, as the study of victories is to teach us how to gain them. But as this work is not a history, but only the memoir of an individual, the quotations from these voluminous journals will be limited to such matters as regard the character, conduct, and fortunes of Captain Whittingham, although to do this clearly must entail the narration of many general details of the expedition.

The fleet and convoy touched at St. Iago, the capital of the Verde Islands, on the 14th December, 1806. There Captain Whittingham's knowledge of languages was very useful to the brigadier-general, in official matters, and very agreeable to the donna and to her lovely daughters at whose house the captain was quartered during the few days the fleet remained in the harbour. As the staff officer of the force, he had also to settle a serious affair, the result of the wanton midnight freaks of some wild British officers, who had finished by insulting the guard of the Governor Don Antonio Continho. (The ring-leader of these rioters was the Hon. Captain ——, who was madly determined to force the governor *into a bag*, which he had obtained for the purpose; and he was with difficulty dissuaded from carrying out his scheme).

But the generous governor was satisfied with an apology, interceded warmly in favour of the offenders, and finally ended by hospitably entertaining them and their mediator to dinner. 'Sorry I am to say,' says the journalist about this business, 'I never saw my countrymen appear to less advantage.'—

On the 11th June the expedition left the islands. On the 29th, it passed the line, and reached the Cape of Good Hope on the 15th March. The secret of the expedition had been well kept even from the staff officer. But fresh instructions received at the Cape caused an entire change of the original plan. Meantime the stay at the Cape was enlivened by putting the troops ashore for some days; on one of which there was a grand review of the united forces under Generals Grey and Craufurd. The second of the two following extracts shows the penetration of the writer of the journal:—

> *6th April* 1807.—The gale having subsided about half past four in the morning, we got under way. The weather was beautifully serene, and a few hours took the whole fleet out of the harbour. In the evening we were becalmed.

> *7th April.*—Yesterday evening the Admiral Murray made the compass signal to steer north-west during the night. This has decided my opinion as to our present destination: we are certainly going to St. Helena, and thence to Buenos Ayres.

The fleet sighted St. Helena on the 19th April. On the 20th, Captain Whittingham left the *Warre* transport to take the orders of the general, who was on board the admiral's ship. He then proceeded ashore to call on the governor, with whom he breakfasted; a clever crotchety man, who started a long and tedious discussion in the vain endeavour to prove to *the pupil of High Wycombe* the value of some very doubtful improvements in gunnery.

On the 25th, the fleet and transports again started; and cast anchor near Montevideo on the 13th June, where they found Sir Samuel Achmuty (who had taken it by storm) with some 7,000 men. General Whitelocke had also arrived; and now Craufurd's division was incorporated with the rest, and Captain Whittingham lost his Staff post. But General Whitelocke appointed him his extra *aide-de-camp* without delay, and ever afterwards treated him with kindness, and with a flattering appreciation of his abilities.

16th June. . . . At five, we were going to sit down to dinner at General Whitelocke's, when a flag of truce arrived. It proved to be an *aide-de-camp* of General Liniers, a captain of hussars, named Don Pedro Joseph de Pendo. He came to propose an exchange of prisoners . . . General Whitelocke rejected the proposal altogether. He (the captain) was invited to dinner; and in the course of the evening, the general desired him to say to General Liniers that he could not, after the abusive letters which had been addressed to his predecessor Sir Samuel Achmuty, enter into any correspondence whatever.

On the 18th June, the order of battle was given out to the troops as follows:—

In the first line Brigadier-General Achmuty was to command the left brigade, consisting of the 5th, 87th, and 28th Regiments of Foot; Brigadier-General Lumley was given the command of the centre, composed of the 36th and 88th Foot, and a part of the 17th Light Dragoons dismounted. To the right brigade, commanded by Brigadier-General Craufurd, were attached the 95th Regiment, and the Light Battalion.

The right of the first line was to be supported by two batteries of artillery of six guns each.

The second line, or reserve, was supported on its left flank by a six-gun battery. Then came, successively, the 9th Light Dragoons on foot, the 45th and 40th Regiments, the 6th Dragoon Guards on foot, and finally the remainder of the 17th Light Dragoons mounted.

The whole force considerably exceeded 10,000 officers, non-commissioned officers, and men, from which might be deducted about 400 sick, and less than 50 absent.

The embarkation at Montevideo was successfully carried out; and the landing, 'a little to the westward of Barragan,' which began at ten a.m. on the 28th June, was effected without opposition.

Previous to leaving Montevideo (where Colonel Brown was left in command). General Whitelocke made an offer to Captain Whittingham, which, however kindly intended, and however flattering, yet proved how little he understood the character of his *aide-de-camp*. The journal records:—

He (the general) began by saying that, if my views in this country were those of pleasure and amusement, he feared that what he had to propose would not merit my approbation; but that, if, on the contrary, my desires and wishes were to render myself useful to my country, and to make unto myself a name, he thought he had an opportunity of placing me in a situation of honour, of emolument, and of much utility to the public good. In a word, he wished to make me a sort of commandant, and to place under my care the police of Buenos Ayres, and of all the surrounding country, giving me the direction and control of all the force, whether native or English, that should be employed for that purpose. He did not entirely explain himself on this head, but as far as I understood him, he intended to appoint one officer under me, and he wished me to recommend another.

Under the direction of the first the military branch might be immediately placed; under the orders of the second, the civil branch; both, of course, to be immediately under my command. Soon afterwards Major-General Gower repeated nearly the same offer. I told them both and more particularly General Whitelocke, that I could not sufficiently express my gratitude for the confidence with which he was pleased to honour me; that I felt highly honoured by the offer he had made me: but that, as he had condescended to enquire into my views and wishes as a soldier, I hoped he would excuse the liberty I took in stating that, if the employment he intended to confer on me must of necessity confine me to Buenos Ayres, and prevent my following the army to the field, I should feel myself called upon to refuse it, if left by him a right of election.

"For, sir," I added, "I would rather be a common hussar in the outposts in an active campaign than enjoy the most honourable and the most lucrative situation which should deprive me of the chance of seeing service." I had the satisfaction of finding my sentiments were not disapproved of.

In his journal of the 3rd July, Captain Whittingham narrates the first of the most important faults made by his kind but inefficient commander:—

It appeared that General Gower had passed the Richuelo (rivulet) the day before at the Paso Chico, had fallen in with the enemy's advanced guard at the Miserere, and had taken nine pieces of cannon and a howitzer. This trifling advantage unfortunately changed the original plan of attack; which was to have gained the north-west side of the town, and to have taken up a position from the Ricoleta to the Plaza de los Toros. From this commanding situation it would have been in the General's power to have laid the town in ashes, or to have dictated to the inhabitants the terms of a capitulation. It was now determined to attack the town from our present position, which was behind it, upon a line nearly parallel to the bank of the river.

4th July.—I was sent with a flag of truce to offer terms to General Liniers. They were refused, and the attack was ordered for the next day.'

He then gives in his journal all the orders for the attack in great detail. The chief mistake was the division of the troops into many separate columns, too distant to support each other, and having to penetrate narrow streets, the windows and housetops of which were crowded with armed militiamen. The troops were ordered to advance to the proposed point of union or post which they were to reach, not only without firing, but also unloaded. The wisdom of the latter part of this order at least may be doubted, but the general was acquitted at his court-martial of all blame in this respect; and this acquittal of part of one charge was the only exception to the universal verdict of guilty, on four charges. The words of the order in question were '*The whole to be unloaded, and no firing to he admitted on any account;*' an order not calculated to encourage troops exposed to murderous street-firing, and not sanctioned by the example of more recent times in Paris and elsewhere.

5th July.—The signal agreed upon was made at thirty-five minutes past six. The commander-in-chief was stationed in the rear of one of the centre streets. The fire was very heavy, but more particularly on the left. In consequence of having observed some considerable bodies of the enemy's cavalry hovering about, I was sent to reconnoitre them with ten dragoons and a small body of infantry. I was joined soon after by Colonel Torrens, and we pushed our reconnaissance to some miles distance. However, in spite of every stratagem we could make use of, we could never get the enemy to stand the charge, though their numbers exceeded at one time 200. The dragoons came up with them once, and despatched five in less than as many minutes.

On our return we found that the carabineers had advanced up the centre street to take some guns, and that they had behaved with great gallantry, though they had not succeeded. Colonel Kington was wounded and taken prisoner, and Captain Burril killed. The 9th Dragoons had got into much confusion, and had lost some men. No account whatever had been received from either wing, and all communication with the right and left was entirely cut off.

A little before three o'clock, General Whitelocke began to be uneasy at having heard nothing from Sir Samuel Achmuty, or from Brigadier-General Robert Craufurd, and General Whitelocke said that, although it was a service that he would not press upon any man, yet he should feel himself infinitely obliged to any of his staff who would undertake to penetrate to the Plaza de los Toros, and find out the state of Sir Samuel Achmuty and his brigade. I immediately said I should be most happy to have an opportunity of rendering myself useful, and at three o'clock I marched off with a sergeant and ten dragoons, and thirty infantry. I neglected no precaution as to the proper distribution of my little force.

The whole country about Buenos Ayres is intersected with hedges. I divided the infantry into two separate bodies, to act as flankers, one on each side of the road; and I had, moreover, a corporal and two mounted dragoons as an advanced guard, and two private dragoons at some distance as a rear guard. I had good reason to be satisfied with having taken these necessary precautions, for our whole route was one continual skirmish, and the enemy was constantly on the watch to surprise us.

Captain John Brown, J.D. and A.D.C., joined me, as a volunteer. My directions for finding the Plaza de los Toros were to keep the Ricoleta on my left, and whenever this church should bear nearly west, the Plaza de los Toros would be nearly east. Notwithstanding, when we got within about a mile, being desirous to come to it by the most private road, I ordered the flankers, instead of firing upon the next armed people they should meet with, to endeavour to make them prisoners. They presently brought me three, and I gave them to understand that, if they wished to avoid the gallows, they must take care to conduct me safely to the Plaza de los Toros; where, in fact, I arrived after a march of one hour and a half.

I found Sir Samuel Achmuty in complete possession of the Plaza de los Toros. He had taken thirty-three pieces of cannon, an immense quantity of ammunition, and 607 prisoners. The slaughter of the enemy had been considerable. Sir Samuel had under his command his own brigade, which had suffered considerably, and the 36th Regiment, which had joined him, under General Lumley. The 88th Regiment, which formed part of General Lumley's brigade, was missing. The communication with the navy was opened. Sir Samuel expressed his desire that the commander-in-chief should, if he thought proper, effect a junction with him without loss of time with all the force which he could draw from the centre.

But, at all events, he requested that some artillerymen might be sent immediately to work the guns which had fallen into his possession. As it appeared of importance to communicate Sir Samuel's report as soon as possible to the commander-in-chief, I left the infantry at the Plaza de los Toros, and effected my retreat with the dragoons. I got to headquarters in less than an hour, and, in consequence of my report, eighteen artillerymen were forthwith sent to Sir Samuel.

We were still ignorant of the fate of General Craufurd's brigade, and of that of the 45th; and that of the 88th Regiment appeared very doubtful. It was very necessary that the general should know as soon as possible the state of affairs on the right, and I again volunteered my services to penetrate to the position which General Craufurd might be in possession of.

6th July.—At daybreak I was on horseback. My instructions were to make about one mile southing, and then three miles easting. At the moment of my departure, one of the *peones*, (native scouts or spies), arrived with the intelligence that Colonel Mahon had passed the bridge with the column under his command of the 40th Regiment, the 17th Light Dragoons dismounted, two companies of the 45th Regiment, and one hundred men of the 88th, and waited for further orders.

Colonel Mahon had been left at La Reduction, with the above-mentioned force, to act according to the orders he might subsequently receive. A letter had been sent to him to advance, but he had not received it, and had passed the bridge only in consequence of the firing he heard, and as concluding naturally that he should, at all events, make his force more disposable, by getting rid, as soon as possible, of the obstacle of the bridge.

With the usual precautions, I advanced within half a mile of the Residencia, when, finding the enemy's parties falling back on the same point, and collecting in great numbers, I thought it right to endeavour to communicate to Colonel Mahon the order to advance to headquarters, before I attempted to force the road to the Residencia. I inclined, therefore, to the right, and in about half an hour fell in with the advanced pickets, and waited upon the colonel at his headquarters. With Colonel Mahon, I left the party of thirty infantry I had brought with me, and received in return 100 men of the 40th Regiment, under the command of Captain Gilles. A little after one o'clock, I joined Majors Nicols and Tolly at the Residencia. Major Nicols had under his command seven companies of the 45th Regiment.

Major Tolly, of the 71st Regiment, who was one of the prisoners under General Beresford's capitulation, but had made his escape, led this column on the day of attack, and had taken possession of the Residencia with the loss of only seven men. They had had no communication with General Craufurd. On the morning of the attack, an English flag had been seen flying about 700 or 800 yards in advance towards the north-west, or the direction where General Craufurd was expected to be. At three o'clock p.m. of the same day, it was struck. (An almost sure proof of the surrender of that brigade and of its most gallant leader.)

Colonel Gerard, of the 45th, had advanced with his company of grenadiers, soon after his regiment had taken possession of the Residencia, to endeavour to open a communication with General Craufurd, and had been seen no more. Whilst we were in conversation on the top of the building, a cannon-shot went over our heads; the guns were advancing up the street. In a moment, Major Nicols was at the head of his men, and in less than five minutes a howitzer, with the timbers, was in our possession. Major Nicols and Major Tolly having given it as their opinion that it would be in vain for a small force to attempt to penetrate in search of General Craufurd, and that a large force could not be spared without risking the safety of the Residencia, we were constrained to give up all hopes of opening a communication with the Light Brigade; and at four o'clock p.m. I began my retreat.

At seven o'clock p.m. I arrived at headquarters, without having lost a man; a little skirmishing had taken place on the road, and the enemy lost two men killed, and two taken prisoners. I found that the commander-in-chief and Major-General Gower had gone to the left, and that Colonel Mahon had occupied with his brigade our former position at the Miserere. I reported to the colonel the strength of Majors Tolly and Nicols' position, the abundance of the provisions they had found in the convent and adjacent houses, and the two guns and the howitzer they had taken; the proximity of the river, which was not 300 yards distant, and the ease with which a communication might be opened with the navy. I added the want they had expressed of an artillery officer, and the advantage they would derive from a reinforcement. The colonel immediately decided that a reinforcement of 300 men, under Major Gwyn, should be sent to them next morning, with an artillery officer.'

7th July.—At daybreak, I was on horseback, to proceed with a small detachment to the commander-in-chief on the left; and the party for the support of Majors Tolly and Nicols was already paraded, when a flag of truce arrived with orders from General Whitelocke to suspend all hostilities till further orders!

At nine o'clock, I joined General Whitelocke, and reported upon the state of the Residencia, Colonel Mahon's brigade, &c. I then learned to my infinite sorrow that soon after my departure a flag of truce had arrived from General Liniers to inform the commander-in-chief of the capture of General Craufurd, Colonel Duff, Colonel Gerard, Colonel Pack, and Colonel Cadogan, together with the 95th, the Light Battalion, and the 88th; and to offer all the English prisoners in South America to return if the general would agree to evacuate the territory of Buenos Ayres in ten days, and the River Plate in the course of two months. This offer was rejected without hesitation. The flag of truce was sent back, and the commander-in-chief and Major-General Gower repaired without loss of time to the Plaza de los Toros.

★★★★★★

Note:—Colonel Duff was the younger son of the Earl of Fife and afterwards General the Honourable Sir Alexander Duff. He was brother to the gallant Lord Macduff and father of the present Earl of Fife.

★★★★★★

On my return from Sir Samuel Achmuty on the evening of the 5th, I had reported the position of the Plaza de los Toros to be extremely good; that from it we might lay the town in ashes; that no force the enemy could bring forward would ever be able to take it from us; that the head-quarters of the army might be established in the Ricoleta, a short distance to the rear; that a few mounted dragoons would clear the country . . . and, consequently, ensure our *peones* being able to supply the camp with beef; and that, finally, our communication with the navy being opened, we should be enabled to obtain an ample supply of salt provisions, biscuit and spirits.

When the two generals came to the Plaza de los Toros, Major-General Gower's opinion of the position by no means coincided with my report, and I understand he expressed himself so strongly as to say that nothing more could be done, and that it would be better to accept General Linier's terms. I have since, however, had the satisfaction to find my report of the position completely supported, *in all its extent*, by the chief engineer, Captain Squire, and the commanding officer of artillery, Captain Fraser.

On the morning of the 6th, a very short time after his arrival at the Plaza de los Toros, Major-General Gower went himself with a flag of truce to General Liniers, and agreed upon the preliminaries of the treaty. This took place about the time I was returning from the Residencia.

At twelve o'clock, the 7th of July, I was sent to General Liniers, who returned with me to wait on General Whitelocke. The preliminaries were finally agreed upon. In the evening, English and Spanish patrols of cavalry were established in the town. It was determined that the Residencia and Miserere should be evacuated, and that all the troops should reunite at the Plaza de los Toros. At eight p.m. the treaty arrived, signed by General Liniers. General Whitelocke signed it the same evening, and Admiral Murray the next day.

The journal of Captain Whittingham contains many pages of sharp criticism and of indignant commentaries on the facts which led to this shameful surrender, which will not be dwelt on in this *Memoir*. One passage, however, is here given; and this chapter will conclude with a few more extracts from the journal, personally concerning its writer.

7th July.—History will record, and posterity with difficulty will believe, that such an army as ours capitulated with the rabble of a South American town, and sold the interests of the country, and gave up the hard-earned conquests of their brother soldiers, in order to secure a retreat which it was most amply in their power to have made at their good pleasure; or, at best, to procure that liberty for their countrymen which under such circumstances was scarcely worth their acceptance. But enough of this subject. I am sick of it! Would to God the waters of Oblivion were as near at hand as are those of La Plata!'

11th July.—Generals Whitelocke and Lumley, with their staff, dined with General Liniers at the fort. The dinner was excellent, and very well served. "God save the King" was played, and the healths of the Kings of England and Spain drunk. The meeting went off as well as the nature of the affair could admit, and certainly nothing could exceed the modesty and propriety of General Liniers's behaviour . . . Liniers is an emigrant, an ex-baron, and a *ci-devant* captain of a ship of the line in the French Navy.

12th July.—I waited upon General Liniers for the last time relative to the hostages. They are three volunteers—Captains Stanhope, 6th Dragoon Guards, Carroll, 88th Regiment, and Hamilton, 5th Regiment . . . .At two o'clock, I got on board the *Aurora* packet. We went under the stern of the *Nereide*, and, having received the general's final instructions, made sail for Montevideo.

14th July Montevideo.—I cannot express what I have felt this morning, at having been informed by Brown, Blake, and Forster, that upon many of the corners of the streets was written, "General Whitelocke is either a coward or a traitor! Perhaps both!"
All the English merchants are in an uproar. They say their losses will be immense; that upwards of three millions worth of property is on its way to this country, and that, if it is given up, half the merchants in England will be ruined. God knows what will be the result of this most unfortunate affair. It appears to me

one of the most severe blows that England has ever received,'

15th July.—Lieutenant-General Whitelocke landed about seven o'clock a.m. at Montevideo.

By a return written by Captain Whittingham, but evidently copied from the official one, dated 5th July, 1807, there were 16 officers killed at the attack on Buenos Ayres, and 56 wounded; and of non-commissioned officers and men, 289 killed, and 592 wounded; 207 was the total amount of the missing.

The following extract from the journal is inserted from a feeling of justice and compassion to poor General Whitelocke, since many a man unfit for the trying post of a military commander in war may yet be excellent in other positions, and worthy of love and regard.

17th July,—The head of the *Cavildo*, (local governing council of Montevideo), waited upon the general, to request he would sign certain papers relative to their justification, which the General promised to do. The head of the *Cavildo* begged leave to return his most sincere thanks to General Whitelocke for the honourable and generous treatment which the magistrates and people of Montevideo had experienced at his hands, and at those of his predecessors. He added that he was well aware that under the mild and benign influence of the British Government alone could they have hoped to meet with such strict and impartial justice, tempered with mercy. He spoke of the mob of Buenos Ayres in much the same terms as I have done heretofore, (in a part of his journal not published in this work), and seemed to think the period of a revolution not far distant.

Before dismissing the subject of the Buenos Ayres expedition, it must be stated that the journal of Captain Whittingham contains a long and interesting conversation that he had on the 26th July, at Montevideo, with Captain Cormero, the *aide-de-camp* of General Liniers; or rather, it was the questions of the Englishman that drew out the information from the Spaniard. Captain Cormero (at the hospitable table of Captain Squire) appears to have been very frank in his communications. They were of a nature completely to confirm and verify the criticisms which had previously been entered in Captain Whittingham's journal; though also imparting much new and valuable information. One only of the answers will be here inserted.

Captain Cormero said:

In possession as you were, of the two important posts of La Plaza de los Toros, and the Residencia, we were convinced from the very instant that you indicated a wish to treat of a capitulation that your general must have been influenced by the tenor of his instructions, which, we conceive, must have directed him, in the most positive manner, to avoid all harsh measures with the inhabitants of South America. *In no other way could* we account for his conduct; though we had no idea at that time that the whole British force had ever exceeded 5,000 men, including all the losses in killed, wounded, and prisoners, sustained in the attack of the 5th.

Captain Whittingham was eager to leave Buenos Ayres, and return to England. He had lost his paid Staff appointment, and was only an extra *aide-de-camp* to a general going home. He wished to obtain some new appointment, or, failing that, to rejoin the 13th Light Dragoons. Accordingly, having obtained leave from the General, and a passage from the admiral, and taken leave of both those functionaries, he sailed from Montevideo for England, on the 30th July, 1807.

Whilst on the staff of General Whitelocke, in South America, Captain Whittingham contracted many durable friendships amongst his brother officers, and more especially with Lieutenant-Colonel Henry Torrens, and Lieutenant-Colonel the Honourable Henry Cadogan. The former was destined soon to become the military secretary of His Royal Highness the Duke of York, and under the name of Sir Henry Torrens to acquire a reputation at the Horse Guards, honoured and respected in the army; the latter, a younger son of the Earl of Cadogan, gallant, chivalrous, and generous-minded, was destined to an early, but glorious, death, whilst leading his regiment to victory under the great captain of the age. But before this sad event was to occur, Lieutenant-Colonel Cadogan and Captain Whittingham were to renew their friendship in the Peninsular War, although their meetings there were to be brief and rare.

The letters of Cadogan have not reached the author's hands. It is possible that they may have been returned to his friends at his death, although of this there is no proof. Fortunately, two copies of letters written to him by Captain Whittingham have been preserved, and will appear in their proper places. It is enough here to say that they give sufficient proof of a warm and almost romantic affection, rarely to be met with in these calm and civilized days.

It is probable that Captain Whittingham divided the few months that he remained in England (which were not occupied with the long trial of General Whitelocke) in doing duty with the 13th Light Dragoons, in which he was a captain, and in visiting his sister and brother-in-law. The famous court-martial commenced its proceedings on the 28th of January, 1808, at the Royal Hospital, Chelsea, under the presidency of Sir William Meadows, K.B.

Captain Whittingham was one of the most important witnesses; and to him (from the uniform kindness which he had received from the unfortunate prisoner) the task he was compelled to perform must have been truly painful to his feelings. The trial lasted till the 18th of March; about six weeks from which time Captain Whittingham re-embarked for foreign service, having obtained a new Staff appointment.

General Whitelocke was tried on four long charges, most of them implying want of judgment and of capacity. The third charge was the most disgraceful, accusing him of being wanting in personal exertion, in a manner that appeared to comprehend a still graver charge, which it is needless to specify. The prisoner was sentenced to be 'cashiered,' and was declared to be 'wholly unfit and unworthy to serve His Majesty in any military capacity whatever.'

Short as was the time that Captain Whittingham had at his command, during his present stay in England, it is certain that he then had the high honour of attracting the notice of that great admirer of military merit, and indeed of all merit. His Royal Highness the Duke of Kent. This was, no doubt, due to the reputation which Captain Whittingham had acquired by the publication of his (and other corroborative) evidence on Whitelocke's court-martial.

The first of the following two letters was written by General Robert Craufurd, one of the best and bravest of soldiers, who was afterwards mortally wounded at the siege of Ciudad Rodrigo on the 19th January, 1812, and died on the 24th of the same month.

The date of the note, unfortunately, does not fix the time; but it must have been in the autumn of 1807:—

Brigadier-General Robert Craufurd to Captain Samford
Whittingham
Mickleham, Sunday evening 1807.

My dear Whittingham,—A visit from a brother, whom I have not seen for a long time, and who can only pass two days with me, and some other circumstances, have occasioned my deferring this answer to your last letter, in which you expressed a desire that I would write to Gordon. You may *perfectly depend* upon my sending you, by *tomorrow's* post, a letter both to him and to General Brownrigg; and I beg you to be assured that to have an opportunity of expressing the very high opinion which I entertain of your military merit, or of proving my very sincere personal regard and friendship for you, will ever afford me the most real pleasure and gratification.

Believe me always, your sincere friend,

Egbert Craufurd.

P.S.—I hope my letters will not arrive too late. If you have not been with Gordon or Brownrigg, Tuesday will, I suppose, be as good a day as Monday. At any rate, pray send my letters to them if you do not get them in time to deliver them in person.

★★★★★★

Lieutenant-Colonel Gordon was Military Secretary at the Horse Guards, and afterwards for very many years Quartermaster-General of the army, as Sir Willoughby Gordon, G.C.B., and who survived to an extreme old age.

★★★★★★

Lieutenant-Colonel Gordon to Richard Hart Davis, Esq. M.P,

Horse Guards, 30th September, 1807.

Sir,—I have the pleasure of your letter of yesterday, with its enclosures, which I will give to Mr. Murdoch as soon as he comes to town.

It has given me great satisfaction promoting the views of Captain Whittingham, of whose good conduct every officer under whom he has served speaks in the highest praise. I remain, with great truth, sir,

Your faithful servant,

J. W. Gordon.

Richard Hart Davis, Esq. M P.
Clifton; Bristol.

CHAPTER 3

1808

Captain Whittingham was appointed in the spring of 1808 Deputy-Assistant-Quartermaster-General on the Staff of the army in Sicily. This was a post not at all to his taste, for he conceived himself much better fitted by his antecedents for service in South America; to which it was then believed that another expedition was soon to be despatched, to recover lost prestige by new and better organised plans. In 1806 his brother-in-law had been elected member for Colchester, and he was no longer in the friendless state in which he had entered the army; whilst his conduct at Buenos Ayres had gained him some friends, who were attracted to him both by his military merits and by his agreeable manners.

Captain Whittingham to Richard Hart Davis, Esq. M.P.
(Extract.)
(*As nearly all the letters in this work from Samford Whittingham to his brother-in-law, Mr. Davis, will be extracts, the word extract will be omitted in future in such letters*).

Sunday morning (probably April 1808).
I dined yesterday with Colonel Gordon, who received me in the kindest manner. He has promised to endeavour to procure me a passage in a frigate which will sail in a few days. To-morrow I go to the Duke of Kent's, and from thence to Fulham, so that I shall not be able to see you. Tuesday I am to see the Duke of York and Colonel Gordon. But I will not fail to call upon you previously to my going to the Horse Guards.

As Captain Whittingham had no official connection whatever with His Royal Highness the Duke of Kent, his going to take leave of that prince previously to embarking for foreign service is a proof of the favour he enjoyed in that quarter. Then, doubtless, was arranged that correspondence the existence of which will be proved; although the letters themselves, with one exception, are unfortunately lost or mislaid. This correspondence was a great and valuable tribute to the merit of a captain of brief standing in the army, and possessed of neither military nor aristocratic connections.

Captain Whittingham to his Brother-in-law.

Portsmouth, 28th April, 1808.

General Oake's *aide-de camp* has just been here to announce that we weigh anchor at eight o'clock tomorrow morning. I shall not, therefore, be able to receive your letter of tomorrow. There seems to be a strange kind of predestination in my going to the Mediterranean; and a soldier is more particularly bound to believe that whatever is, is right. It is to me most grievous to think that all my hopes of being once more employed where best I could have served my country are done away with. The die is cast, however, and there is no remedy. For as to my recall from Sicily to join the army in South America after the affair is over, I cannot even wish it. For that would be completely reducing one to the situation of a civil agent, whose knowledge of the language might be considered convenient.

Captain Whittingham, however, sailed without effecting his object of a change of destination. After his arrival at Gibraltar, (where, as in duty bound, he waited on the governor, Lieutenant-General Sir Hew Dalrymple,) he wrote on the 2nd June:—

You will see by the enclosed letter for Mr. Murdoch the present state of things, and will judge of the heavy heart with which I shall, in a few days, embark for Sicily. When you have read it, have the goodness to send it to him. I have seen Maitland. He is well, and going into Spain with Captain Dalrymple. The King and Queen of Spain, the Prince of Asturias, and several of the first nobility have been arrested at Bayonne, where they went to meet Buonaparte, and have been sent into the interior of France.

Captain Whittingham, it appears, now acted as Sir Hew's Military Secretary in the absence of Captain Dalrymple on leave. He thus discovered that the Governor was in correspondence with Lieutenant-General Don Xavier Castaños, commanding the Spanish camp near Gibraltar, relative to the plan of a projected campaign against the French. He, therefore, entreated Sir Hew Dalrymple to give him permission to join General Castaños as a volunteer. As his perfect knowledge of the language and people of Spain especially fitted him to cement the alliance of the two nations, the Governor does not appear to have thrown any difficulties in his way. How delighted this consent made him, let his own pen demonstrate:—

To his Brother-in-law.

Gibraltar, 5th June, 1808.

My dear Davis,—It would be in vain to attempt to express to you the feelings of my heart upon this most delightful occasion. I feel thankful to God for all things; and I bless that fate which has been so singularly propitious to all my soul's best wishes. This very morning, my own dear brother, I proceed to San Roque, to meet the Spanish General Castaños, and to accompany him to the advanced guard of the Spanish army, which is at present near Ecija. I saw General Castaños yesterday, and he was highly pleased at Sir Hew Dalrymple's offer to send me to remain with him during the campaign. My instructions from Sir Hew are to send him a faithful and exact account of the state of the Spanish Army, its numbers, its positions, the marches that may be made, and the battles that shall take place! This, of course, during His Majesty's pleasure; and I have now only to beg and entreat that you and my dear Mr. Murdoch will, *if Colonel Gordon approve,* use your utmost endeavours with Lord Castlereagh to get my present appointment from Sir Hew Dalrymple confirmed.

He concludes a long letter by requesting his brother to get him put on half-pay, if his request could not otherwise be granted. The reply from the Horse Guards was long in reaching him, in his opinion; and yet the authorities could hardly have answered quicker, or, practically speaking, in a more flattering manner. But, meantime, he was exceedingly anxious on the subject. Full of hope, nevertheless, he joined General Castaños, whose headquarters were soon after established at Utiera.

The following extract from a letter speaks for itself. It is written with the kindness and in the spirit of an affectionate elder brother:—

Richard Hart Davis, M.P., to Captain Whittingham.

London, 12th July, 1808.

My dear Samford, . . . Your most welcome letter of the 5th has come to hand. We share all your feelings in regard to your appointment . . . Prudence requires that your communications with Mr. Murdoch and myself should only embrace transactions that would be interesting to us in as far as you are personally engaged in them, and not embracing, as your letters to government undoubtedly will, the secrets of the Spanish Army, and the general policy of the country.

In short, ours must be an interesting correspondence, because it regards you, but not as politically regarding Spain. *Trust no one* with information but through the regular channel of government. Suspect all men around you; and depend alone on your own clear and unbiased judgment. Inspire enthusiasm in others; but do not be led into acting by it yourself. Never push yourself unnecessarily into danger: *my caution shows how ready you will be to meet it.* (His relations ever feared that his chivalrous eagerness for distinction might lead him into acts of rashness).

Never send information home as certain and to be depended on but on the clearest evidence. Always speak cautiously as to future events, but without desponding. Recollect that it is a new system of warfare that will be required to make volunteers beat the troops that have conquered all Europe. Perhaps the Fabian system of delay, though the least magnanimous, will be of the most efficacy. I want in some degree to temper your enthusiasm, by suggesting that *you may be uselessly sacrificed by your ardour* in leading on young troops who may be panic-struck, and desert you. Excuse this advice which may be, nay, probably is, unnecessary, but which the warmest affection for you suggests. You must, at all events, make up your mind to a long struggle, if Spain is to be successful; God grant that she may.

If an early battle is fought, and the Spaniards are defeated, I fear that it will break the energy of their measures, and the unanimity of their councils. France has possession of the government, and the centre of the country, and can march to any part of the circle, and separate the force that is forming against her. She has, besides, possession of the passes into the country, and can, therefore, reinforce her army to any extent. The salvation of Spain, in my opinion, will not depend upon her own efforts only, nor on our assistance, powerful as it will be; but it must be connected with other hostile movements in other parts of Europe. (A true prophecy: for except for the invasion of Russia by

Napoleon, the Peninsula could scarcely have been delivered).
Be cautious in writing your dispatches. Use your own short and
nervous language. Cultivate the good will of the Spanish commander-in-chief. You will be the link to unite the two armies,
nay, perhaps the two countries; and to be successful, they must
be harmonious. Besides, what the Spanish commander says of
you in his dispatch will have great weight. I am most anxious to
hear of the expected engagement with Dupont. Wellesley has
probably sailed from Cork with his armament.

The following letter was not communicated to Captain Whittingham till sometime after the Battle of Baylen, though written more
than a fortnight before it:—

> Colonel J. W. Gordon to Lieutenant-General Sir Hew
> Dalrymple.
> (Extract.)
>
> Horse Guards, 2nd July, 1808.
> Sir,—Captain Whittingham, of the 13th Light Dragoons, hav-
> ing been appointed a Deputy-Assistant Quartermaster-General
> to the forces under the command of Lieutenant-General Sir
> Arthur Wellesley, I am directed to acquaint you that Captain
> Whittingham has the commander-in-chief's permission to re-
> main with General Castaños.

Had this post been given to Captain Whittingham a few weeks
sooner, he would undoubtedly have joined Sir Arthur Wellesley without delay, and thus have been attached to that illustrious hero for
the rest of the Peninsular War. In after years, he often regretted the
decision that he now made to adhere to the career which he had,
in the first instance, embraced mainly to escape proceeding to Sicily. He would certainly have been spared many disappointments and
mortifications, occasioned by the misfortunes and misconduct of the
Spaniards, if his service in the Peninsula had all been performed on
the staff under the eye of the great duke; and he would have personally
shared in more of his victories.

But, on the other hand, the very subordinate rank he would have
held would have deprived him of the opportunity of displaying the
military ability that he undoubtedly did display with the Spanish
troops, the wretched condition of which ennobled the task of commanding them by increasing its difficulty. Still less, had he adhered to
his English Staff Captaincy, could he have gained the confidence and

respect of Marquis Wellesley, and of Lord Cowley, or have earned the flattering praises of an accomplished Marshal of France; all of which advantages fell to his lot in the service of Spain.

From Sir Samford's *Recollections*.
(Mentioned in the preface)

The army of Castaños was composed of 10,000 regular infantry, 25,000 rabble, twenty-four pieces of horse artillery, and about 1,500 cavalry. The French force at that time in Andalusia exceeded 25,000 men. (The French, however, at Baylen had only 17,500 men, including cavalry; but that number should have easily routed the undisciplined troops of Castaños).

Our first point of assembly was at Utiera, from whence we advanced to Baylen in four divisions, the three first commanded by Major-General Reding, (a Swiss officer of considerable ability). Lieutenant-General the Marquis de Compigny, and Lieutenant-General La Pena, (destined later to be the involuntary cause of the greatest mortification that ever befell the subject of this *Memoir*). The fourth division formed the reserve. Previous to the memorable battle that took place some days afterwards, Reding and Compigny, by a flank movement, got to the rear of the French position; whilst Castaños, with two other divisions, attacked it in front.

Dupont, in the battle, committed the fault of successively attacking the Spanish position at four different points, instead of concentrating and repeating his efforts upon one and the same point. The Spanish troops behaved nobly; and the Spanish artillery was eminently successful. Victory, after a hard-fought day, declared for the Spaniards; and the French *remained prisoners of war*. Nothing could excuse or palliate the conduct of Dupont; for he had not only surrendered himself and his army to a far inferior force, but he obliged General Vedel to counter march on his route to Madrid, and to come to Baylen to be included in the capitulation.

(After describing how the disgraceful conduct of Dupont was mainly owing to his desire to save his effects, and the plunder he had accumulated, the *Recollections* continue.)

On the following day, when Dupont advanced at the head of his staff to deliver up his sword to General Castaños, the Spaniard dismounted, and approaching the carriage in which

Dupont and his Staff were seated, he addressed him in a kind and consolatory speech: calling his attention to the inevitable vicissitudes of human life, and attributing his victory over one of the most renowned of Napoleon's generals more to his good fortune than to any superiority of talent. 17,500 men, of which 3,000 were cavalry, and a brilliant and numerous train of horse artillery, filed off before our ragged ranks, and laid down their arms.

By joining La Pena, Captain Whittingham shared personally in this victory, and had thereby the honour of being the first Englishman who fought for Spain in the Peninsular War. Two days later, 20th July, 1808, Sir Arthur Wellesley, having preceded his troops, landed at Coruña, from His Majesty's ship *Crocodile*, commanded by Captain the Hon. George (afterwards the late Earl) Cadogan, the younger brother of Lieutenant-Colonel Cadogan, the intimate friend and correspondent of Captain Whittingham.

In his *History of the Consulate and the Empire*, M. Thiers says:—

Such was the famous capitulation of Baylen, the name of which, in our childhood, resounded in our ears as often as that of Austerlitz or of Jena. (*Telle fut cette fameuse capitulation de Baylen, dont le nom, dans notre enfance, a aussi souvent retenti à nos oreilles que celui d'Austerlitz ou d'Iéna.*—Vol. i.)

In one of his letters to his brother-in-law. Captain Whittingham writes:—

General Castaños deserves the highest honour for his well-conceived plan, and for the cool determination with which he carried it into execution, in spite of all the popular clamours for an immediate attack upon the position of Andujar. The general was so kind as to allow me to advance with General La Peña's division.

After Baylen, he travelled in various parts of Spain on General Castaños' missions, who himself, it appears, went to Seville.

To his Brother-in-law.

Cordova, 15th August, 1808.

You forgot to enclose the note from Sir Thomas Plumer. I will not attempt to express the delight with which I have heard Sir Thomas's opinion upon my conduct. I will not run into unnecessary danger; but in the day of battle I cannot remain at headquarters. General Castaños permitted me, with some difficulty, to move with the advanced guard at the affair of Baylen.' I trust that he will never refuse his permission in future. It is the only point upon which I shall differ in opinion with my beloved general, whose kindness to me is that of a father to a son. Charles IV. has lost Spain for ever. He and his infamous queen are detested, and the hopes and wishes of the people are fixed upon Ferdinand VII.

. . . I have bought four horses, three for riding, and one as a bat horse; and a travelling carriage. I have made upwards of a thousand miles post since the Battle of Baylen; and in this country we are obliged to travel with four horses. A number of little purchases made at Gibraltar for officers of General Castaños' staff I have requested them to accept, because even in the veriest trifle at present I would wish to see liberality the order of the day. . . . . On the 29th July, I delivered my letter for you to Lord Collingwood. I explained to his Lordship the reasons which induced General Castaños to grant such favourable terms to General Dupont, "namely, the impossibility of preventing the retreating of General Vedel upon Madrid." In the evening, I waited upon General Morla.

★★★★★★

Note:—Lord Collingwood had not been satisfied with the terms granted to General Vedel. He was not sufficiently acquainted with the circumstances to understand why an inferior division should have been allowed to capitulate after the principal force had been defeated.'—Southey's *Peninsular War,* vol. i. Don Thomas de Morla, whose treacherous surrender, afterwards, of Madrid has covered his name with perpetual infamy.

★★★★★★

31st July, I left Cadiz, and on the morning of the 1st August arrived at Gibraltar. Sir Hew received me with the greatest kindness. 3rd August, returned to Algeciras; 5th, to Cadiz; 6th, went again on board the fleet to see Lord Collingwood, where I learned the news of the augmentation of the British Army of Portugal and the appointment of Sir Hew Dalrymple to the chief command. In the evening General Morla informed me that the French evacuated Madrid on the 31st July. On the 7th, I dined with Mrs. Gordon, at Xeres, and on the 8th, arrived at

Seville at nine in the morning.

I do not conceive I am wanting in my duty by communicating to you the very satisfactory conversation I had with General Castaños on my return to Seville.' (After mentioning a number of military arrangements that he had made in the province, Castaños added,) 'that he had sent the chief of his staff to General Moreno to Madrid, where he intended to go himself within a few days. The general then informed me that a battle had been fought in the neighbourhood of Rio-Seco between General Cuesta and General Bessières; the French force consisted of 15,000 men; the Spaniards, including the army of Galicia, amounted to 50,000. The Spaniards had no cavalry. The battle was fought in a plain. The French horse turned the left wing of the Spanish line; the defeat was complete; 5,000 or 6,000 men were killed, and the whole army dispersed. General Cuesta retreated to Salamanca, and General Blake, with the army of Galicia, to the frontiers of that province.

If I might be allowed to give an opinion upon matters of such high importance, this Battle of Cuesta, evidently fought without a proper attention to the nature of the ground, or the composition of the army, will ultimately tend to much good. In all probability it will lead to giving the chief command of the whole Spanish Army to General Castaños, who will, I have no doubt, follow up the excellent system which he has begun, and prove himself the Fabius of Spain.'

11th August.—I had a long conversation with the general, relative to the affairs of this Government. It appears that disputes had run high in the Junta Suprema of Seville upon the subject of Granada. Count Tilly threatened that a division of the army of Andalusia should march against Granada, and force them to obey the orders of the Junta of Seville. General Castaños then arose from his seat, and, striking the table with his hand, he said, And who is the man that will dare to lead a division of my army, contrary to my orders? I do not consider the army I have the honour to command as the army of Andalusia, but as the army of Spain, and never will I stain the laurels which it has won by suffering it to become the vile instrument of civil discord. The affairs of Granada may be amicably and easily settled." As soon as the general had done speaking, Don Vincento Ori stood up, and, taking off his *banda*, threw it upon the table, saying that "he would never be a member of any body where such words as those which he had just heard from Count Tilly were tolerated."

The discussion ended by an apology on the part of the count for what he had said, and a recantation of his ideas upon the subject of civil war.

For his services at the Battle of Baylen, Captain Whittingham was made a Colonel of Cavalry in the Spanish army by General Castaños, subject to confirmation by the *Junta*. Colonel Whittingham, soon after the above letter, accompanied his beloved and excellent chief to Madrid, and here we will quote from his manuscript *Recollections*:—

On our passage through La Mancha to Madrid, I was taken to the house of a woman, who had obtained great celebrity by the murder of a number of French soldiers. In the courtyard of her dwelling, there was a well of very good water, but the rope for drawing it up was very short, and you were obliged to stoop forward in order to be able to drink out of the bucket. Whenever an incautious soldier came to the well, and bent over to drink, she came behind him, and, seizing him by the legs, tumbled him into the well. She had, I understood, put eight men to death in this manner.

The triumphant march of General Castaños to Madrid far exceeds my powers of description. On entering the gates of Atocha, our steps were directed to the chapel to hear mass. The crowd was immense; and at the church door, one of the Manolas, a stout handsome young woman, threw her arms round my neck with such affectionate violence that down we came at full length together on the floor, she exclaiming all the while, "God bless the Englishman, the delight of my soul." "*Bendito sea el Inglesito de mi alma*). The burst of laughter was not quite in harmony with church gravity, but Castaños long enjoyed the joke, and the Englishman's fall became a standing dish at his table.

To appreciate the joke, the reader must bear in mind that Colonel Whittingham was about six feet high in his boots, and stout and broad-shouldered, even more than in proportion to that stature; and he was a fine figure in the dress which he still wore, of Captain of the 13th Light Dragoons. He was, from early date, however, obliged to guard against a too great *embonpoint*, and at times lived very abstemiously for that purpose.

Whilst at Madrid, Captain Whittingham (for so by the Horse Guards authorities he was still styled) must have received the letter of which the following is an extract, and which was found amongst his papers;—

Lieutenant-Colonel Gordon to R. H. Davis, Esq. M.P.
(Extract.)
Horse Guards, 23rd August, 1808.

You may assure Captain Whittingham that his conduct has given great satisfaction, and that, whenever the rules of the service admit of it, the commander-in-chief will immediately recommend him to the king for promotion. He is in the meantime to continue with Castaños, and to hold his appointment as Deputy Assistant Quartermaster-General to the army, under Sir Hew Dalrymple. It is perhaps unnecessary for me to repeat to you the high opinion I have long formed of Captain Whittingham; but you may rely upon me for every aid in my power to the advancement of his interest, convinced that in so doing I am assisting an officer whose zeal and talents will be eminently useful to his country.

★★★★★★

Note:—The Supreme Junta of Seville, by a decree in the name of King Ferdinand VII. of 20th July, 1808, had made Don Santiago Whittingham a Colonel of Cavalry, 'for the zeal and known valour with which you have distinguished yourself in the campaign of Andalusia, which terminated with the glorious battle of Baylen.'

★★★★★★

A letter from Samford Whittingham to his brother-in-law, dated Madrid, 2nd September, 1808, concluded with this commission:—

On the part of General Castaños, pray ask Mr. Knight to order one of the machines for making lint for the use of the army, to be forwarded immediately to Coruña. *Adieu*, God bless you. The French have pillaged Bilbao. The slaughter has been great.

This commission for Mr. Knight led to a graceful act of courtesy on the part of the Duke of York to General Castaños, which Mr. Knight thus explained in a letter to Mr. Hart Davis, dated Weymouth, 30th October, 1808:—

I accidentally mentioned to the Duke of York the commission of General Castaños, and His Royal Highness has taken advantage of the circumstance and the opportunity to pay His Excellency a suitable compliment, by directing me to accompany the machine with a present from His Royal Highness of a portable medicine chest and complete set of instruments, finished after the manner in which they are furnished for service, for the duke's personal use . . . I think this is a most handsome trait of the duke, and it is like himself.

It may be easily imagined what pleasure it gave to Colonel Whittingham to be the first to announce to his respected and kind chief the coming present from the Royal Commander-in-Chief of the British Army.

General Castaños, whilst at Madrid, despatched Colonel Whittingham on a special mission, which the latter thus announced to Mr. Davis in a letter, dated Madrid, 7th September:—

I leave this town for Saragossa tomorrow. General Castaños sends me to examine into the real effective forces and condition of the armies of Aragon, Valencia, and Castile. I shall return with a faithful account of the state of things to our divisional headquarters, which are about to be established at Soria. My old friend and commander, Lieutenant-General La Peña, commands there, and is extremely anxious to receive a report on the subject from me.

On the 22nd September of this year, Sir Arthur Wellesley, unfortunately for the Peninsula, embarked at Lisbon to return to England. He arrived in London on the 6th October. There he was detained by the long enquiry into the convention of Cintra, and received the warm thanks of both Houses of Parliament. It was not till the 22nd of April, 1809, that he returned to Lisbon. During his absence occurred the defeat of the Spaniards under Castaños at Tudela, and the death of Sir John Moore at Coruña, followed by the abandonment of that coast of Spain.

In a long letter to Mr. Stuart, the Minister, dated Madrid, 22nd September, 1808, Colonel Whittingham defends the conduct of General Castaños after the Battle of Baylen. The last sentence alone is here quoted:—

The terms of the treaty, it is very clear, cannot be fulfilled. The

Spaniards have neither ships, men, nor money to send these men to France, and by the capitulation they can only be sent home in Spanish vessels manned by Spaniards. They must, therefore, of necessity remain prisoners in Spain at least for some years.

Colonel Whittingham to Lieutenant-Colonel the Hon. Henry Cadogan, 71st Regiment, 2nd Battalion.

Madrid, 6th October, 1808.

My dear Cadogan,—It would be difficult for me to express the pleasure which I have received from your truly friendly letter. Believe me, few things in this life could have given me greater satisfaction. I love to cherish the hope that you will be with us. We have much yet to do, and great indeed is the assistance which we stand in need of. I have been detained in Madrid longer than I had wished or expected. The proposed march of the English army to this country has been the cause of it. Everything is now settled, and tomorrow I go off to the army. We occupy the right bank of the Ebro, and the French the left. Their right is at Miranda, and their left at Milo. Pampeluna is in their possession, and the other day they again entered Bilbao. They expect strong reinforcements by the 15th of this month. Their present force is 45,000 men.

The centre of our army, commanded by General Castaños, occupies Logrono, Calahorra, Corella, Cascarte, and Tarragona. The left under Blake is at Frias and Orduña. The right, under Palafox, is at Saragossa, with a detachment advanced towards Sanguera. Our whole force may amount to 100,000 men. But at least 30,000 of them are not yet near the scene of action, having been detained by a complete want of clothing. Yet there is no time to be lost if we mean to attack the French before the arrival of their reinforcements. The orders to this effect from government are positive, and I shall probably have to communicate an account of a general action in less than ten days. *For the first time in my life, my dear Cadogan, my heart misgives me, and forebodes no good. I fear the result of this action.*

(The editor has placed these words in italics, as proving that the victory of Baylen had not blinded the judgment of Colonel Whittingham to the inferiority of the Spanish to the French troops. The subsequent constant defeats of the Spaniards only too well justified his prognostications).

The French are concentrated, and we are considerably scattered. Their troops are all equal; ours, some bad, and some good. They have the advantage of unity of command; we are directed by three generals, all independent of each other. I trust in God that nothing will delay the march of the English Army to Burgos. It will be an excellent rallying point for us in case of disaster; but no time must be lost. The enthusiasm of the Spaniards is worthy of their cause, and their bravery such as you would wish your best friend to possess. But we are not yet organised; and as we are now to move in large bodies, and with combined operations, I cannot help entertaining some doubts of the issue of the first battle.

As I shall probably not have time to write to anyone again before the action, I pray you, should anything happen to me, to let Colonel Gordon see this letter. It is not, however, with one or with twenty battles that Buonaparte will. conquer Spain. Every town will become another Saragossa; and when his brother reigns in Spain, women and children will be his only subjects. I have General Castaños' order to join my old commander, General La Pena. His outposts are generally engaged with the French, and hitherto the Spaniards have uniformly had the advantage.

When I returned about ten days ago from a reconnaissance of the line occupied by our troops, I sent my horses forwards; so that I have nothing to do but to pass into the saddle of a good post-horse, and hasten to the scene of action. I have a famous stock of cigars, a pocket-compass, and some excellent horses. So that, you see, your old friend is well provided for the campaign. God bless you, and grant that you may soon be with us.

> Yours ever,
>
> Samford Whittingham.

His prophetic anticipations of failure were too soon realised, and the reputation of General Castaños was eclipsed on the 23rd of November at the fatal Battle of Tudela. The blame, however, entirely lay with the Spanish Government. The battle was fought by order of the commissioner, whom the Supreme Junta attached with full powers to the army, and who compelled Castaños, against his will, to assault the army of Marshal Victor. But by these remarks we are anticipating, and must now return to our story.

To his Brother-in-law.

Headquarters, Calahorra, 30th October, 1808.

Have the goodness to direct all your letters to me as follows:—
Á *Don Santiago Whittingham, Coronel de Cavalleria, en el Quartel General del Excellentisimo Señor Don Francisco Xavier de Castaños, Capitan General y General in Xefe del exercito centro. Adonde se halle.*

(From this time forth, he was usually addressed by his Spanish rank during the Peninsular War, except in official letters from the authorities in England, in which he was generally addressed by his rank in the British service).

I have paid every trifling debt, and I left Madrid without owing a shilling to anyone. On the other hand, my contingent account, which will be paid to me by the Commissary-General of the British army—at least so Sir Hew Dalrymple informed me—amounts to 708 dollars; all for expenses of different journeys and messengers on government account. My carriage, horses, and personal expenses, of course, I have paid myself, and should not think of charging. Doyle has a *carte-blanche* for his expenses from Lord Castlereagh. You will see by the enclosed copy of a commission which I have received from General Castaños that they have made me a Colonel of Horse, with full rank and pay. But what I most esteem is the cause or motive which they state for having conferred the honour upon me, *viz.* my good services in the campaign of Andalusia.

As His Royal Highness has approved of the rank given to Doyle, I flatter myself that he will have no objection to my holding the commission in the Spanish service. I understand that it is General Castaños' intention to give me the command of a regiment of hussars. This will not prevent his continuing me upon his staff, and he has appointed me his first *aide-de-camp*. In regard to my promotion in the British service, Lord Castlereagh has remitted to General Castaños a very handsome letter from His Royal Highness the Duke of York, in which he is pleased to say that His Majesty will be glad to promote me as soon as I have my standing.

On the 6th November, a week after the above letter was written. Colonel Whittingham was attacked in Tudela by rheumatic fever, which totally deprived him of the use of his limbs. He was thus compulsorily absent from the battle near that town which took place on the 23rd of the same month; and was saved the chagrin of witnessing the defeat of his gallant chief and comrades on that unlucky day. But let him speak from his *Recollections*:—

Before the Battle of Tudela, I had been attacked by rheumatic fever, and confined to my bed for many days. Towards the close of the action, General Graham called on me to say that all was lost, and that I must be moved forthwith, or I should be taken prisoner. As all my horses were too gay and unsteady for a sick man, the general had brought one of his own, a strong steady horse, quite equal to my weight. A pillow was placed on the saddle, and I was carried downstairs, and lifted into it. But my sufferings were beyond human endurance; and after proceeding about three miles to the village of Ablitas, I was taken off the saddle, and thrown on a mattress.

★★★★★★

Note:—From this it would appear that General Graham (afterwards Lord Lynedoch) was present at the Battle of Tudela; no doubt as a volunteer. No English troops were then in Spain, and Sir A. Wellesley was in London giving evidence on the Court of Enquiry regarding the Convention of Cintra.

★★★★★★

About ten o'clock at night. General Castaños and the principal officers of his Staff arrived. We had been completely defeated, were in full retreat upon Cuença, and the French pursuing. The general directed that I should be carried downstairs, and placed on a mattress in a little covered cart, which had been secured; and that, without a moment's loss of time, I should proceed on the road to Cuença. The whole of my body was at that time so inflamed with rheumatism that I could only be turned in bed by lifting up the sheets on which I was extended. Yet in this dolorous state I was forced to make a journey of three hundred miles in a cart without springs, in the depth of winter, and over abominable mountain roads.

Castaños had kindly directed his principal medical officer to accompany me to Cuença; and one very cold morning before daylight. Doctor Turlan (that was his name) requested that I would permit him to enter the cart, and share my mattress with him. I readily consented. But we had not proceeded half a mile when the cart was overturned, and pitched down a precipice. In the fall, the unfortunate medico got under the mattress, and as Santiago (S. W.) with his feather weight remained upon it, the poor doctor was nearly suffocated. His cries and screeches were quite terrific. "For the love of God, Señor Don Santiago," shouted he, "I am stifled, I am suffocated! For the love of the most Holy Virgin, I beseech you to get up, or I shall die!"

"Dearest Turlan," I replied, "you see that I am totally incapable of movement; so that, if it should appear that your last hour is arrived, recommend yourself to God; for from human aid you have nothing to expect."

The arrival of a few straggling soldiers put off the doctor's evil hour. They dragged me out by the feet, and again set the cart upright, but nothing could induce Turlan to reoccupy a share of my mattress.

On the loss of the Battle of Tudela, Castaños was superseded, and directed to appear at Seville before the Supreme Junta. (The *Junta* performed the supersession gently and politely; pretending that they wanted the aid of General Castaños as a counsellor).

The Condé of Montijo, a *grandee* of the first class, but a man of infamous character, and a personal enemy of Castaños, preceded him by some days on the road to Seville, and spread the report throughout La Mancha that Castaños was a traitor, and deserved to die. At Miguel Turra, Castaños was billeted at the house of a curate, to whose firmness and presence of mind he owed his life. Deceived by the lies of Montijo, an infuriated mob assembled before the house of the curate, and demanded their victim. But Castaños had already passed through the garden by a back door, and had been conveyed to a secret spot; where his horses and servants were waiting.

A few weeks after this occurrence, I was sent by the Duke of Infantado to Seville, and had to pass through Miguel Turra. An immense crowd was assembled in the *Plaza*, and I advanced on horseback into the midst. They asked, "What news of the traitor Castaños?" and I was happy to have an opportunity of speaking on the subject.

"Gentlemen," said I, "I am grieved, astonished, and deeply afflicted, to see so many good and worthy men so easily duped and led astray by the lying inventions of one of the vilest of men. Castaños commanded the Campo de Gibraltar before the present struggle commenced. The French did everything in their power to gain him over to their party. But he met their intrigues by assembling the forces of Andalusia, and gaining the battle of Baylen. I saw 17,500 French soldiers lay down their arms, and surrender themselves prisoners of war to this very General Castaños.

"He then proceeded to Madrid, and organised and command-ed the army which a superior French force has now defeated at Tudela. But, be it known unto you, gentlemen, that the general was obliged to fight this battle, against his own better judgment, by orders from the Supreme Junta.

"For he was well aware that an army of newly raised levies could ill compete with the veteran troops of Napoleon. This same Castaños, your best, your most devoted, friend, you, gen-tlemen, have wished to murder, because an infamous and lying coward, for such is Montijo, has fled from the field of battle to denounce him here." (If the conduct of the Count de Montijo was actuated by a partiality for the French, it has met with an unlooked-for reward to his family, in the elevation of the fairest and best of the Montijos to the throne of France).

The boldness of my address evidently surprised them. A mur-mur of consultation ran through the assembly; when a voice from one of the leading men exclaimed, "*When the English-man says so, it must be true.*" ('*Quando el Ingles lo dice, verdad será.*' No doubt, the fluency with which the English dragoon offi-cer addressed them in their own language—by surprising and pleasing the mob of Spaniards—greatly facilitated the success of this well-timed oration)' A tremendous shout of applause confirmed this opinion; and I was carried in triumph to my quarters, proud indeed of the honour done to my countrymen's integrity by so impartial a tribunal.

But many things which are agreeable as *Recollections* are unpleasant enough when actually occurring, as the following letter, written at the period in question, will demonstrate:—

Headquarters, Cuença, 16th December, 1808.
My dear Davis,—A rheumatic fever attacked me on the 6th of last month in Tudela, and totally deprived me of the use of my limbs. I will not now enter into a detail of my sufferings. My

escape was miraculous. In a covered cart, I have followed the retreat of the army. My servants were daily obliged to lift me in and out of the cart. I had no powers of motion, and the pains which I suffered were intolerable. The army retired to Calatayud, Siguenza, Guadalaxara, and Cuença. Our rear was warmly pursued by the French. Madrid has capitulated. Buonaparte is now collecting all his force to attack Sir John Moore. We shall probably soon advance towards Madrid. I can scarcely hold the pen. Let this plead in excuse for not writing to Colonel Gordon, to whom you will please to communicate this letter. I shall not abandon the Spanish army as long as I consider that my communications with Mr. Frere can be useful to the service of my country.

The prospect of affairs in Spain in the absence of Sir Arthur Wellesley, and with General Cuesta as chief of the principal Spanish army, were now gloomy enough to excite very serious apprehensions of many coming disasters and defeats.

At some period in 1808, which the Editor is unfortunately unable to particularise, Colonel Whittingham certainly met Lord William Bentinck for the first time at Aranjuez, and assisted his Lordship in certain negotiations with the Spanish Government in that town, for the fact (as the reader will find) is recorded by him more than twenty years afterwards, after having, for the third time, acted officially under that distinguished and excellent nobleman.

CHAPTER 4

1809

The commencement of a new year found Colonel Whittingham at Seville recovering his health, having been sent there by the Duke of Infantado. We continue the fraternal correspondence:—

To his Brother-in-law.
Seville, 13th January, 1809.
I have the pleasure to inform you that my health is tolerably re-established, and that I shall again set off for headquarters in a few days. You are not to imagine that I should have quitted the army for anything relative to myself. The Duke of Infantado requested that I would go to Seville on a particular commission, which, I am happy to say, I have executed to his satisfaction; and I have now no other anxiety but that of again entering the field of Mars with all possible expedition. I shall enter into no details upon our late unfortunate campaign, because I have to remit to Colonel Gordon by the next post General Castaños' defence of his conduct as laid before the Supreme Junta.

To the Same.
Seville, 20th January, 1809.
My dear Davis will rejoice to hear that this fine climate has operated a most favourable change on my health. I am, thank God, once again fit for the field; and I love to flatter myself that fate will throw in my way some opportunity to distinguish myself.

21st.—On the 13th and 14th, the advanced guard of the Duke of Infantado, at Tarancon and Uccles, was attacked by the French in force, and obliged to retire upon Cuença, our headquarters. For the last three days, we have received no news from the army. It is sadly to be lamented that the Duke had not quitted the position of Cuença long since. It was proposed and strongly urged that the army should immediately advance to Ocaña and Toledo as early as the 29th of last month. The advantages of this movement were clearly pointed out, (by himself, no doubt, all his Spanish commanders appear to have listened to his counsels; but few, except the Duke of Alburquerque, followed them), and the duke appeared determined to advance. Cuença is in itself a bad position, and the retreat towards Andalusia impracticable, at least for the artillery.

Twenty-six leagues is the distance from Cuença to Manzanares, the first town on the high-road to Seville. The road is so excessively bad and heavy that I was ten hours making three leagues in a light carriage with five mules, I set off for the army on Thursday next. My health is quite re-established. Be assured, my dear Davis, that, however we may be beat for the present, we shall ultimately drive the French out of Spain. I cannot tell you with what delight I look forward to my return to the army. I really am never quite happy but in active campaign.

When the Duke of Infantado left Madrid on 2nd December, 1809, to join the army commanded, since the departure of Castaños, by Lieutenant-General La Peña, the latter most generously caused the Duke to be elected to the chief command. Infantado had been accompanied from Madrid by the young, patriotic, and chivalrous Joseph Maria de la Cueva Duke of Alburquerque; (the spelling of Spanish names by Colonel Gurwood is adopted, as he took much pains to acquire accuracy in that matter; whilst compiling the *Wellington Dispatches*), a man beloved by his officers and soldiers, and having for enemies only the baser and meaner of his countrymen, who were governed by their jealousies or other malignant passions.

If, as was the case with the Spanish nobility generally, his education had not been neglected, he might have made a greater figure in history; and as it was, he left a name second to none amongst his countrymen at that period. Colonel Whittingham, from the first, admired and loved him, and all the more because the duke rarely displayed the obstinacy so common amongst his countrymen, and only required to hear in order to take good advice. What follows is from the already quoted *Recollections*;—

On my return from Seville, I was attached to the *corps d'armée* under the Duke of Alburquerque in La Mancha, where we had many affairs of cavalry, as the duke had under his command 3,500 horse and two troops of horse artillery.

At Mora, the French had a detachment of 600 cavalry. The duke advanced to surprise the post with 1,500 horse. We bivouacked a few miles from their outposts without being discovered; and before daylight we were upon them. The surprise was complete. They lost 160 men, and fled at full speed.

Amongst the foremost of the pursuers was a servant of mine, a young Irish lad, named Charles, whom I had dressed up as a hussar. He fixed his eye upon a well-dressed middle-aged man, well mounted and apparently well fed. Charles was satisfied that he would turn out a good prize. Both horses were excellent; and both were urged to the top of their speed by the pursuer and the pursued. But my hussar had the advantage of a lighter weight, and was gaining fast upon his adversary, when the Frenchman turned round upon his saddle, and fired a pistol at him; which was soon followed by a second shot.

Both shots, however, missed their object, and the old soldier was reduced to his last shift, which was, however, a good one. Judging from the appearance of his pursuer that his object would be plunder, he drew a knife from his pocket and cut the straps which fastened his portmanteau. The portmanteau then fell to the ground, and Charles immediately reined up, and secured his prize, which contained a brace of pistols and a good stock of clothes.

Amongst the variety of incidents of this exciting day, an occurrence took place which we all deeply lamented. A remarkably fine young woman, apparently about seventeen or eighteen years of age, was making her escape from Mora in an open carriage, belonging to the French general commanding. Some of our cavalry attempted to arrest her progress. She immediately fired a pistol at the nearest soldier, and in return received from him *a coup de sabre* which almost divided her head from her body. In a moment she was stripped with that dexterity peculiar to soldiers, and her body left on the road.

On our return to Mora, we were quartered in the house of the Countess de ——, whose previous guest had been the French general commanding. The enthusiasm of the lady was beyond description. She thanked the Blessed Virgin for her miraculous escape from perdition, and declared her determination to avail herself of the happy opportunity of returning to the paternal house, which our arrival afforded. Her gratitude to Heaven and to us knew no bounds. Orders were immediately given to pack up all her plate and jewels. A splendid dinner was prepared by the major-domo. The only carriage in the place and six mules were employed by the duke's order for her conveyance, and the hour of departure was fixed for four o'clock on the following morning.

Our party consisted of the Duke of Alburquerque, Alava, (afterwards General Alava—a favourite of Lord Wellington and on his personal staff—eventually Spanish ambassador in London about thirty years later), and myself. The duke retired to rest at nine. But I felt uneasy that our departure should have been put off till the morning, and I submitted to Alava that it was always a point of honour with the French to return a surprise with the least possible delay.

I added that their force in cavalry and horse artillery in our immediate neighbourhood was very considerable; and that to effect our retreat, we must pass through a long and narrow defile, which commenced at the entrance of Mora, and that, if attacked during the passage, confusion and complete defeat would be the inevitable consequences, and the duke's character as a soldier lost. I proposed, therefore, that we should awake the duke, and submit to him the expediency of our commencing our retreat forthwith. Alava coincided in my view of our position. We awoke the general, and orders were immediately given to put the troops in motion.

The chivalrous feelings of the duke and of Alava did not permit their forgetting the perilous position of the disconsolate countess. The carriage was ordered to the door, and her servants were directed to finish the packing with all expedition. But, alas! the countess had fainted; and when she came to herself, she broke out into the most bitter lamentations against her cruel destiny. "Alas!" she exclaimed, "by this time tomorrow I shall have ceased to exist. For the French, on their return, will assuredly put me to death as a traitress and a spy. But, happen what may, how is it possible that a poor little delicate thing like me should be able to suffer the privations, the miseries, the hardships, of a camp follower? It cannot be. I am well aware of the cruel death that awaits me on the return of the French; but there is no remedy, and if my last hour is come, it is better for me to die in my own house and bed than in the fields!"

A more complete humbug I never saw! Thus ended a comedy worthy of *Camilla* and *Don Rafael;* and the countess, laughing secretly at the simplicity of our hearts and heads, dedicated herself forthwith to the preparation of an excellent breakfast for the French general on his return.

Our accelerated retreat was fortunate. We had scarcely cleared the defile when our rear-guard was attacked.

Thus was the gallant Spanish duke and his party saved by the vigilance of their English comrade. (Doubtless this was one of Samford Whittingham's 'services in the early part of the war, the importance of which was passed over or little known,'—See the Earl of Fife's letter in *Preface*).

On the 30th January, 1809, he relates to Mr. Davis the particulars of the defeat at Uccles of General Venegas, and adds, 'The Duke of Infantado's want of decision was the cause of this misfortune.' The duke had been repeatedly advised to advance and support Venegas, who was sure to be attacked, but took no notice of the warning. In consequence he was ordered to join General Urbina, Count of Cartaojal, and to serve under him as part of the army of the Carolina. This supersession took place on the 18th February. But General Urbina proved to be a far worse commander than the duke he superseded, as will be hereafter demonstrated.

To his Brother-in-law.

Headquarters, La Carolina, 12th February, 1809.

The French are advancing against General Cuesta in force, certainly not less than 20,000 men. Their headquarters on the 5th were at Oropesa. Their advanced posts occupied the bridge of the Arzobispo. General Cuesta had his headquarters at Truxillo; his advanced posts at the bridge of Almaraz. A division of Portuguese and English was stationed at Alcantara, a force of from 12,000 to 14,000 men. Cuesta's army is about the same strength. A part of the French Army from Galicia had directed its march upon Ciudad Rodrigo. On the 5th, they had arrived at Martin del Rio, distant from Ciudad Rodrigo ten leagues. The moment you cast your eye upon the map, you will see the danger of General Cuesta's position. Our advanced guard will march tonight upon Toledo, be supported by a second division, and followed by the whole army. The total strength of this army, now called the army of the Carolina, including the remains of the army of the centre, amounts to nearly 30,000 men. Our movement will call the attention of the French; and even if we arrive too late to save General Cuesta, it will prevent them following up the advantage which they have obtained. I have no comments to make on our probable success.

As soon as I receive Mr. (Hookham) Frere's answer, I intend to ask General Urbina's leave to join the advanced guard. (This determination, to be always in front, never slackened. The risk, with such troops as the Spanish then were, was self-evident).

Adieu, my dear Davis, and as I once before told you, if we meet no more on this side of the famous river, don't forget to drink a glass of your best wine to my memory once a year.

To the Same,
Headquarters of the Advanced Guard,
Ciudad Real, 13th March, 1809.

Our headquarters are changed from Manzanares to this place, in consequence of the movements of the enemy.

I cannot account for the long silence of my friends in England. Your last letter was dated November. Since that period I have not heard one word from you, or anyone on that side of the water.

There is too much reason to believe that a great number of letters addressed to Colonel Whittingham, in the course of the Peninsular War, never reached him. But at this time, after the departure of the army of Sir John Moore from Coruña, and during the prolonged absence of Sir Arthur Wellesley from Portugal, the means of conveying English letters into the interior appears to have been equally rare and hazardous.

Colonel Whittingham to the Right Hon. John Hookham Frere, H.M.'s Minister in Spain.
Ciudad Real, Headquarters of the
Advanced Guard, 17th March, 1809.

Sir,—The repeated advices of all the confidential agents employed by the Duke of Alburquerque to watch the movements of the enemy confirm, beyond the possibility of doubt, the march of the French towards Talavera, and the certainty that the expected attack upon General Cuesta will immediately take place.

Our commander-in-chief, General Urbina, has rejected the proposition of the Duke of Alburquerque to allow him to advance upon Toledo with a division of 12,000 or 15,000 infantry, 4,000 cavalry, and twenty pieces of artillery. The general-in-chief considers the organisation of the main body of the army as an object of more importance, and the arguments of the duke to convince him that this organisation would be secured rather than impeded by his proposed movement have been of no effect.

You may rest assured, sir, that there is no time to be lost, and if the Junta Suprema does not come to a speedy determination, and immediately communicate decisive orders in consequence, it is sadly to be feared that General Cuesta will be defeated by the superior force which he will have to contend with, *viz.* from 30,000 to 35,000 men.

You will recollect the effect produced by the expedition to Mora, and the retrograde movement made by the French troops in Estremadura in consequence. Surely, the same arguments which were then made use of by General Urbina, to induce the Duke of Infantado to consent to the advance of the Duke of Alburquerque, exist in the present case in even greater force, inasmuch as our means of offence are greater, and the dispositions of the enemy to attack General Cuesta more formidable.

I shall only add that the confidence of the officers and men in the Duke of Alburquerque affords the best-founded hopes of the fortunate result of the proposed expedition.

I have the honour to be, with the highest respect,

 Sir,

   Your most obedient servant,

     Samford Whittingham.

P.S.—It is scarcely necessary to point out the advantages of the proposed movement, should the fortune of war favour General Cuesta, and the French be repulsed. The unexpected appearance of the duke's division upon the rear or flank of a defeated enemy would probably prove as decisive as the combined march of the columns in the Battle of Baylen.

      S. W.

From the Same to the Same.

Ciudad Real, Headquarters of the
Advanced Guard, 20th March, 1809.

Sir,—In consequence of the orders from the Junta Suprema, the whole of the disposable force of this army will immediately advance upon Toledo, in order to effect a diversion in favour of General Cuesta. The Count of Cartaojal, (General Urbina), at the same time that he communicated this order to the Duke of Alburquerque, directed him to deliver up the command to Brigadier-General Don Juan Bernuy, and with the division of Brigadier Don Luis Bapcourt, and that of Don Pedro Echavari, to march immediately to Guadalupe to cooperate with the army of Estremadura.

Thus, at the moment that the plan proposed by the duke is about to be executed, he is deprived of the command of the vanguard, and exposed to risk his military reputation at the head of a small body of newly raised infantry without cavalry or artillery. It is to be feared that the absence of their favourite general may produce a bad effect upon the troops. At all events little or nothing can be expected in favour of General Cuesta from the small corps entrusted to the command of the duke.

I cannot avoid expressing my sentiments with freedom at this interesting moment. I conceive that the duke has fallen a sacrifice to his too great popularity with the troops; and I sincerely lament that the army should be deprived of the valuable military talents of this officer. It is not to be expected, after what has passed, that the duke will accept any command under the Count de Cartaojal.

According to the advices received today from Sevilleja, the French had passed Estrella to attack a division of the army under the command of General Cuesta, which occupied the position of Valdevilacasa. It is therefore very possible that the movement upon Toledo may be now too late, and should General Cuesta be defeated, much evil, instead of good, may result from it.

On the 13th of this month, the duke proposed to the general-in-chief to make this diversion in favour of General Cuesta. At that moment there could be no doubt that the army of Estremadura would have been saved by our advance upon Aranjuez and Toledo. At present the result is doubtful, and may be fatal. The duke begins his march tomorrow towards Guadalupe, and

I shall take care to inform you most exactly of everything that occurs.

I have, &c. &c.

Samford Whittingham.

The contemptible conduct of General Urbina was not long in bringing deserved retribution upon him, in the form of a disastrous and crushing defeat, which was followed by his supersession in the chief command by General Venegas:—

Colonel Whittingham to his Brother-in-law.

Seville, 4th April, 1809.

You will see by all the enclosed papers the chain of evils, and the gross misconduct, which have completely destroyed our well-founded hopes of soon re-occupying the capital of Spain. General Urbina, Count of Cartaojal, has betrayed his country, and fled in disgrace with 30,000 infantry and 5,000 cavalry before 2,000 French horse.

The Duke of Alburquerque has been sacrificed to the envy and jealousy of General Urbina. Cuesta has fought bravely, but unfortunately. I had the pleasure of being with the duke in this action (the Battle of Medellin). At last the eyes of the Junta Suprema are opened. Urbina is deprived of his command, and the duke appointed temporarily to the command of the army of the Carolina. Things do not look well.

But if I can carry the point which I have in view, *viz.* that our total force, amounting to at least 40,000 infantry and 8,000 cavalry, shall be immediately concentrated, I have yet my hopes. If not, depend upon it, all is lost. We leave this place tomorrow at daybreak for the army. We have been here a few hours to make arrangements with the government. Have the goodness to get Mr. Murdoch to translate the enclosed papers, and lay them before Lord Castlereagh and Colonel Gordon. I have not heard from you since January.

The Battle of Medellin was fought on the 28th March, 1809, and was one of General Cuesta's numerous defeats. That stupid and obstinate, but very brave and indefatigable, old general fought the battle with his usual contempt of tactics and prudence, and yet had nearly won it by the bravery of the infantry but for the gross misconduct of the Spanish cavalry. Colonel Whittingham, being attached to the staff of the Duke of Alburquerque's division, shared his fortunes on that unfortunate day. We will now revert to his *Recollections:*—

Previous to the Battle of Medellin, the Duke of Alburquerque was directed to join General Cuesta in Estremadura with two troops of horse artillery and 1,500 cavalry. On our route we came to a small town which had become notorious for receiving and concealing deserters. The *alcalde, (mayor),* and the *escribano,* (town clerk), were deeply implicated, and the duke was determined on making an example. They were, therefore, both laid hold of, and placed in the grenadier company of a leading battalion (to expose these compulsory soldiers to the greater danger in action). I saw these men the next day, as we were moving upon the enemy in column of companies, and their faces are even at this moment completely before my eyes. I never had a just idea of the personification of Fear till then. Their countenances were literally horror-struck; their hair stood on end. They recognised me instantly, and, dropping on their knees, they shouted out, "Mercy, Señor Don Santiago, for the love of God and of the Holy Virgin, do not permit this sacrifice!" But the hard-hearted Santiago was implored in vain; and the butt ends of the soldiers' muskets soon brought them on their feet again. I never heard what became of them. At the Battle of Medellin, the defeat was complete; and as Victor gave no quarter, they probably perished with the rest. (This appears like a proof that even the gentle-hearted Duke of Alburquerque could steel his heart in active service; but the fact is that, at such a time, no Spanish general would have ventured to show mercy to traitors).

When everything was lost, and the last battalion broken and dispersed, the French cavalry formed a chain in rear of the Spanish troops, and the slaughter commenced. The Duke of Alburquerque, Alava, Bigodet, Nazaro Eguia, and Santiago, with a few orderlies and servants, formed a little group. The chain was closed around us. The duke, turning to me, said, "Santiago, do you see that smart light dragoon, how vain he is? Now, be assured that before two minutes are passed, he will be under my horse's feet;" and putting spurs to his fine Andalusian horse, he charged full speed upon the *chasseur,* followed, of course, by all his little party. (These words—written from memory in 1840—slightly differ from those given by Southey, who at an earlier period doubtless obtained them from the letters written to Colonel Gordon, the Military Secretary at the Horse Guards, by the subject of this *Memoir*).

The *chasseur*, being somewhat of Falstaff's school, held prudence to be the better part of valour, and taking ground rapidly to the right—with half a dozen soldiers who followed his salutary example—a hole was left in the chain, through which we instantly passed at full gallop. The chase after us was long, but vainly kept up.

A wounded artilleryman whom we passed called out to Alava, "Señor Don Miguel, for God's sake, help me, or I am lost! I am badly wounded, and you see the French give no quarter."

"Get up behind me," said the heroic Alava; "we will both be saved, or both perish together."

'It was about ten at night when we arrived at a solitary farm-house; and having made a bonnie fire, and got a dish of chocolate and a cigar, the Spaniards unanimously agreed, "The more we lose the more we gain; the Body Politic will yet require much blood-letting before its health can be perfectly restored!" ("*Quando mas se pierde, mas se gana, y que muchas sangrias eran menester para restablecer la salud del cuerpo politico!*")

We lost at Medelihn 14,000 men. An intimate friend of mine, a colonel of infantry, had two sons with him in the action. The eldest, under eighteen years of age, was most severely wounded by the dragoons late in the day. He was taken to Medellin, and to the quarters of the commander-in-chief, just as Victor was sitting down to supper; who graciously informed the young officer of the fate intended for him by saying, "If my orders had been executed, you would not have been here!"

To his Brother-in-law.

Cordova, 6th April, 1809.

My dear Davis,—In the actions of the Duke of Alburquerque in La Mancha, the troops under his command were covered with glory. All the officers of his staff, including me, were recommended to the government for promotion, (afterwards he was made Brigadier-General by the Spanish Government, with date from 2nd March, 1809). In the last unfortunate action of Medellin, I had an opportunity of particularly distinguishing myself by reforming the routed cavalry and leading them against the enemy. The duke did me the honour to speak of my conduct in the field in the highest terms. You are yourself well aware that since the first shot was fired in Andalusia, I have been constantly with the army, and have sought every occasion of rendering myself useful. Yet I am the only officer to whose promotion the government has objected. The reason is obvious: I was a friend of the unfortunate Castaños, and all his friends are persecuted.

I entreat, therefore, that you will immediately apply to Colonel Gordon for leave to join my regiment. I can no longer be of service to a country to whose government I am become obnoxious, nor am I accustomed tamely to suffer the insults of any man or class of men.

★★★★★★

Note:—Here, no doubt, is another of those little known actions referred to by Lord Fife (*vide Preface*). This passing allusion to his having rallied the cavalry at Medellin is all the editor knows on the subject. The lost letters to the Military Secretaries at the Horse-Guards might tell more of *what Lord Fife knew.*

★★★★★★

To the Right Hon, J. H, Frere.

Cordova, 11th April, 1809.

Sir,—I observe by your letter of the 7th, which has been returned to me from the Carolina, that you consider the Duke of Alburquerque in command of that army, and ready to realize his projected plan of attack against the French force in La Mancha. I am surprised that the Junta Suprema should not have informed you that a division of 7,000 infantry and 3,000 cavalry began its march from the army of Sierra Morena on the 5th, and will enter Seville the day after tomorrow. The force which now composes the army of Sierra Morena consists of 16,000 infantry and 2,000 cavalry, and is commanded by General Venegas.

Had the duke received the command of the army of Sierra Morena before the separation of the above-mentioned division, he might have defeated the French force in La Mancha, and immediately afterwards have reinforced Cuesta with nearly 10,000 men, by the same route which we before followed from Ciudad Real. At the same time that I received your letter, Mr.

Ovalle communicated to the duke the same information; and yet, previous to that date. General Venegas had taken the command of the army, and the division had already begun its march, with orders to the commanding officer, Major-General Count of Orgaz, to report daily to the Minister of War.

I have, &c.

Samford Whittingham.

Most unfortunately, all Mr. Hookham Frere's letters to Colonel Whittingham are lost. The above letter proves how necessary British agents were, from whom alone the English envoy could obtain reliable information and active assistance.

There is no doubt that Colonel Whittingham had the highest esteem for the duke, as well as affection. (These feelings were shared by Mr. Hookham Frere, and, subsequently, by Marquis Wellesley). He had also had cause for gratitude, as will be seen in the following letter to his brother-in-law:—

Seville, 17th April, 1809.

I enclose you two letters from the Duke of Alburquerque, the one addressed to his Royal Highness the Duke of York, and the other to Lord Castlereagh. I am proud to receive these recommendations from the duke, because as a soldier he stands unrivalled in this country.

After detailing the ill-treatment that the duke received from General Urbina and the Junta Suprema, he proceeds:

The duke was further ordered to put himself at the head of a division of troops destined to march from the Carolina to the assistance of General Cuesta as soon as General Venegas should have taken the command of the army of Sierra Morena.

Before the duke joined the army, General Venegas had taken the command, and we are now on our route to join General Cuesta at Santa Olalla and Monasterio. The division commanded by the duke is composed of 2,500 cavalry and 7,000 infantry. General Cuesta's army, after our junction, will exceed 25,000 infantry and 6,000 cavalry. The force left in Sierra Morena under the command of General Venegas is 16,000 infantry and 2,000 cavalry.

In regard to the late shameful flight of the army of Sierra Morena from their cantonments at La Mancha, it is altogether too bad for description. Suffice it to say that folly, or more probably treason, sacrificed an army of upwards of 30,000 men, including 4,500 cavalry. The Battle of Medellin, in Estremadura, was fought with bravery by all the troops excepting the cavalry on the left of the line. Their want of firmness lost the day. The right, where I had the honour of being with the duke, behaved extremely well; and as our orders were positive not to retreat, the whole division of the duke was sacrificed. When everything was completely lost, we opened a passage through the enemy, sword in hand.

The following are translations of the two letters which were enclosed in the above:—

The Duke of Alburquerque to the Duke of York,
Cordova, 6th April, 1809.

Sir,—The special merit which Colonel Santiago Whittingham, (see note following), has displayed during the whole of the present war in Spain—and particularly the great degree in which he has distinguished himself in all the actions in which he has served under my command—affords me the opportunity of having the honour to make this known to your Royal Highness, for the satisfaction of this deserving officer. And for the same reason, I take the liberty of entreating your Royal Highness to make the same known to His Majesty.

I take this occasion to present my highest respects to your Royal Highness, and I pray the Almighty to preserve your valuable life through many extended years.

At the feet of your Royal Highness,
The Duke of Alburquerque.

★★★★★★

Note:—Apparently, though the rank was dated back to 2nd March, 1809, either the government had not yet gazetted Whittingham as Brigadier or the duke had not known it so early as the 6th April.

★★★★★★

The Duke of Alburquerque to Viscount Castlereagh.
Cordova, 6th April, 1809.

Excellency,—I cannot do less than bring to the notice of your

Excellency the distinguished services which Colonel Santiago Whittingham has rendered in the present war in Spain, and especially during the time he has been under my command, under which he still continues, with the most effective desire to distinguish himself daily more and more.

I hope your Excellency will excuse the liberty I am taking in order that this highly deserving officer may obtain the satisfaction he so justly desires of being made known to your Excellency.

This occasion affords me the especial gratification of presenting my respects to your Excellency.

May God preserve your Excellency.

His Excellency the Duke of Alburquerque.

Brigadier-General Whittingham to the Right Hon. J. H. Frere.
(Extract.)

Olalla, 23rd April, 1809.

(*Sir Arthur Wellesley arrived at Lisbon, on his return from England, on the 22nd April, 1809*).

I enclose a copy of the duke's letter of this morning to the Count of Orgaz, who commands the infantry of the division of Andalusia. You will observe by his answer that he does not consider himself under the orders of the duke, and therefore declines sending him the returns he required. In consequence, the duke has determined to proceed to Monasterio, where he will see General Cuesta tomorrow morning.

These contradictory orders appear too nearly to resemble those of our last expedition to the Carolina. The country we have passed over today is not the least fit for the operations of cavalry. From Guillena to Santa Olalla the road is one continued defile; and cavalry, instead of being of use, would only serve, by a precipitate flight, to weaken the effects of the infantry. The total of General Cuesta's cavalry is very nearly 7,000. It appears that the French have attacked his advanced guard at Santos with a division of 6,000 men.

Probably, this will prove a reconnaissance in force—an operation which they seldom omit previous to a general action. General Cuesta will, of course, defend the position of Monasterio as long as possible, fall back upon Santa Olalla, and finally occupy and defend to the last extremity the strong pass of the Herzadura, near to the Venta de la Cruz del Chapaxo, two leagues on the Seville side of Ronquillo . . . .

If 4,000 cavalry were sent immediately to the Carolina, and the command of that army given to the duke, he would either enter into Madrid or force Victor to detach a considerable part of his army towards Toledo. This, in my humble opinion, is the only thing to be done in the present situation of affairs; and should General Cuesta offer to the duke the command of the advanced guard, he would, I should think, do well to accept it. For upon the least further advance of the French, the cavalry at Santos must fall back to the rear of the Monasterio, and continue retreating to Seville; and thus the duke, without the hope of victory, would only have acquired the fame of being a second time beaten.

The present moment is so extremely critical that I feel it my duty to state it to you as my opinion that the salvation of the country will depend upon the success of your endeavours to change the theatre of war once more to La Mancha.

Should this, however, not be approved of by the Spanish Government, they should, at all events, order a camp to be formed of 5,500 cavalry in the neighbourhood of Seville, which would be a rallying point for the infantry should the passes be forced, and might, possibly, if well directed, restore the fortune of the day. I am sure you will agree with me that the command of the force should be given to the duke.

From the Same to the Same.

Santa Olalla, 24th April, 1809.

Sir,—We have been today to Monasterio. General Cuesta has finally determined that the duke shall command only the cavalry of his former division, which he is to canton in the rear of the position of Herzadura. Tomorrow the duke will reconnoitre the ground, and determine upon the distribution of the force entrusted to his command. Major-General Echivari, with the advanced guard of this army, is at Fuente de Cantos, five leagues in advance beyond Monasterio. The outposts are daily engaged with the French. Two leagues in rear of this corps is situated Major-General Enesterosa with 8,000 cavalry; and he is supported by a strong detachment, at the distance of about a league, under the orders of Brigadier Zayas, General Cuesta's headquarters are at Monasterio.

I am convinced more and more by every day's experience that *General Cuesta is not the man to command an army upon which the fate of Spain may depend. His age, his infirmities, his excessive reserve, and his constant ill success, conspire to render him unfit for his situation; and the Junta Suprema will learn, when too late, that good intentions alone are a poor substitute for military talents.* (Perhaps the retreat of Sir Arthur Wellesley, in August, from Talavera would never have been necessary had the advice of Colonel Whittingham in April been acted on, and the stupid and incompetent Cuesta been exchanged for a more rational and practical commander. The editor has placed in italics a prophecy destined to such speedy fulfilment).

Would to God it was possible to give General Blake the command of this army, and the Duke of Alburquerque that of the army of the Carolina! I am convinced that everything would go rightly, and, by a proper co-operation with the army of Portugal, affairs might soon be completely re-established.

Will you have the goodness to send the duke, if you can procure it for him, a map of the kingdom of Seville? I will thank you to direct your letters to me at Gerona, where the duke's headquarters will be established till further orders. He is very much hurt at what has passed, and has written to Mr. Ovalle upon the subject.

I shall have the pleasure of writing to you as soon as we have finished the reconnaissance of the cantonment; and I have the honour to be. Sir,

    Your most obedient servant,

      Samford Whittingham.

The Right Hon. J. H. Frere.

        To his Brother-in-Law.

              Gerona, 26th April, 1809.

You will see by the enclosed letters to Mr. Frere the position and strength of our armies. The headquarters of General Victor are at Merida; his force about 40,000 men. General Sebastiani commands in La Mancha a division of 10,000 men. Of the division of Soult at Oporto and of that of Ney, in Galicia, I conclude that you are well informed.

Our cause is sacred; and in spite of the errors into which we have fallen, we shall, I trust in God, with the cordial assistance of England, ultimately prevail. I am well aware that the conduct of the Government has been in many instances weak and ridiculous; but I love to hope that His Majesty's Ministers will forget and forgive, and only look to the great good that may ultimately result from the success of our endeavours.

I did not lose my horses and baggage at Tudela. They afterwards appeared. But I lost at Madrid clothes, baggage, and a travelling carriage; the total cost of which exceeded £350. What most has grieved me is the loss of all my books and papers. The value of what I lost at Coruña you are exactly acquainted with. (His baggage appears to have been lost in Sir John Moore's retreat having been sent to Coruña from England). I think, in the present state of affairs, you had better not send out the carriage for the Marquis of Benamigi. (This was, no doubt, some intended present from the too generous Englishman to some Spanish gentleman who had formerly shown him hospitality).

On the 28th April, Colonel Whittingham forwarded to Colonel Gordon, Military Secretary at the Horse-Guards, a copy of the following letter which he had addressed to the British envoy, the day before Sir Arthur Wellesley arrived at Villa Franca, and wrote the first batch of his dispatches in Spain:—

To the Right Hon. J. E. Frere.
(Extract.)
Gerona, 27th April, 1809.

I had the honour to accompany the Duke of Alburquerque in his reconnaissance between this place and Santi Penni, and returned to Gerona this day by the way of Guillena. In Santi Penni the duke has left three officers of Engineers to make a plan of the adjacent ground.'

(He then enters into long local details, geographical and strategical, with his wonted accuracy and clearness, and continues).

The more I become acquainted with the Army of Liberation, and the major part of its generals, the more I am convinced that it is not in a state to cope with a French army, unless infinitely favoured by the strength of the position which it may occupy. General Cuesta would already have attacked the French again but for the instructions of the Supreme Junta. Upon so brave and respectable a character as that of the old general, I should not wish to be severe. But the times are too critical to admit of attentions of any kind which may lead to the smallest deviations from truth. The general is so extremely infirm that he is not in a state to fulfil the active duties of his profession, and at the same time so jealous of his authority, or so little accustomed to the treatment of organised armies, that he has no idea of delegating that proportion of his command to others without which the necessary and proper subdivision of labour cannot take place.

In all the engagements which he has had with the French, his mode of attack has been below criticism; and the consequences have been such as might be expected. At General Cuesta's time of life, men are little disposed to change; and experience, however dearly bought, is not sufficient to correct errors, which by long habit have become second nature. Rest assured, sir, that, if General Cuesta is to direct the operations of this army, it is of the first importance to oblige him to remain upon the defensive; not only because he is at a distance of only a few leagues from the capital, and, consequently, the effects of a defeat may be fatal; but that it is almost impossible that he should ever be successful against the French, fighting his battles in the way that he has hitherto done.

This being the case, the proposed expedition to La Mancha becomes doubly necessary. For, at the same time that the greatest good would of necessity result from the appearance of the Duke of Alburquerque at the head of a strong division in a province where his name is idolized, and where public opinion has so great an effect upon the people of Madrid, we should obtain, also, the much-to-be-desired advantage of obliging the Army of Liberation to remain on the defensive, at least till the co-operation of an English Army should afford hopes of success.

I have, &c.

Samford Whittingham.

★★★★★★

Note:—In spite of the lost replies of Mr. Frere, there can be no question that the latter agreed, and sympathized, with his correspondent. It is a pity, however, that he did not send these letters to Sir Arthur, to acquaint him with what the latter learnt only after painful experience—the utter incapacity of Cuesta.

★★★★★★

In another letter to Mr. Frere, dated Gerona, 1st May, Colonel Whittingham enforced the same views, adding more details on the state and positions of the Spanish armies.

The hero of the age had now arrived in Spain, and in a letter dated Villa Franca, 29th April, 1809, acknowledged to Mr. Frere the receipt of a letter from him, and of another from General Cuesta. Sir Arthur stated his intention of communicating with the Spanish Government only through Mr. Frere, and one sentence of his letter may be appropriately quoted here, as confirming the wisdom of the advice given to Mr. Frere by the English captain who was serving so zealously in the arduous and hazardous post of a British agent, and at the same time of a Spanish colonel, in an ill-disciplined, disorganised, and badly commanded army. Sir Arthur, (*Wellington's Dispatches*, vol. iv.), writes:

I hope that the Spaniards will adhere to their determination of acting on the defensive till I shall return to the eastward.

In a letter of the same date to Don Martin Garay, Sir Arthur writes:—

In the meantime, I cannot sufficiently recommend a strict defensive position in all quarters.

If this advice had been strictly carried out, and General Cuesta at once removed from the command, much trouble would have been saved to the English commander. For although many of the Spanish generals were as incompetent as Cuesta, few were so impracticably stupid and obstinate as that old soldier, who, excepting courage, does not appear to have had a redeeming quality of any kind. To the subject of this *Memoir* he was destined to be a constant source of annoyance and disgust up to the very hour of his death, as Captain-General of the Balearic Islands.

The return of Sir Arthur Wellesley to the Peninsula, who was soon to take into his powerful hands the universal management of affairs, naturally lessened in some degree the personal influence of the military agent who was but a captain in the British Army. He continued, however, to enjoy the full confidence of the minister. To gain that of Sir Arthur was a work of time, especially as he had at first no direct communication with the commander-in-chief, but was considered under the orders of Mr. Hookham Frere in his capacity of agent. It may, however, be here remarked that, if the subject of this *Memoir* had not eventually obtained the complete confidence of his illustrious chief, these pages would never have been written; for, though the great Wellington was after all a mortal, and as such liable to error, still it is not too much to say that his opinion of those who served under him must be considered as final both for the present age and for posterity.

The jealousy of Cuesta against the Duke of Alburquerque vented itself in giving that gallant nobleman so reduced a command that 'nothing could induce him, (the duke), to remain but the expectation that a general engagement would take place as soon as Sir Arthur shall return from the attack of Soult.' (Letter from Brigadier-General Whittingham to Colonel Gordon,—Military Secretary at the Horse-Guards—dated Zafra, 20th May, 1800).

Sir Arthur Wellesley to the Right Hon, J. H, Frere.
(*Wellington Dispatches*, vol. iv.).

Oporto, 22nd May, 1809.

My dear Sir,—My letter of the 20th will apprize you of all that has occurred in this quarter since I wrote to you on the 9th instant. I have returned here with the advance of the army, having done all I could, or had to do, northward, and having thought it necessary to move to the southward, in consequence of the invasion of Portugal by the attack and capture of Alcantara

I am much obliged to you for your letters of the 15th and 17th. I acknowledge that I do not consider Lord Wellesley's appointment a subject of congratulation to himself or his friends. I suspect that the task which will devolve upon him will be a most arduous one; and that some time will elapse before he will be sufficiently *au courant des affaires* to be able to form a judgment of its extent. I am truly concerned, however, that your removal should not be so consonant to your wishes.

Believe me, &c.

Arthur Wellesley.

There can be no question that the new appointment did not, and could not, suit Sir Arthur Wellesley. The *marquis*, his elder brother (and former patron, and official superior as Governor-General), was coming out as Ambassador Extraordinary to relieve the minister, Mr. Frere. With such powers, and considering his past career, Lord Wellesley could not be expected to play any but the first part; and Sir Arthur would naturally hold a position relatively inferior to that which he possessed while Mr. Frere was minister.

The advent of Marquis Wellesley in Spain, if no matter of rejoicing to his famous brother, brought with it one of the pleasantest episodes of Samford Whittingham's adventurous life, though his Lordship's sojourn in Spain was as brief as it was brilliant.

The following is the only copy in the editor's hands of the several letters which its writer undoubtedly addressed to the illustrious father of Her Majesty the Queen. (Only a very rough copy, difficult to read, and not apparently in the handwriting of Brigadier-General Whittingham, exists of this letter. The writer was, for the sake of the unhappy country he was so zealously serving, evidently trying to palliate the national errors):—

To His Royal Highness the Duke of Kent.
Headquarters of the Second Division of Cavalry,
commanded by the Duke of Alburquerque,
Zafra, 23rd May, 1809.

Sir,—Since the Battle of Medellin, which cost us the amount of 22,000 men, great changes have taken place. The efforts of this nation are in exact proportion to the difficulties which it has to labour under. Defeated at Medellin, put to a shameful flight in La Mancha, the French advanced to within fifteen leagues of Seville; the whole force which we at that time could collect in the passes of the Monasterio, and St. Olalla did not exceed 8,000 men. General Victor, who commands the French Army in Estremadura, lost the favourable moment for attack, and the energies of the nation were called forth. The present force and distribution of the Spanish and French armies are as follows:—

General Cuesta, 24,000 infantry, 7,000 cavalry, and fifty pieces of cannon. His advanced guard at Merida, sustained by a body of 2,000 cavalry at Almendraligo; headquarters at Fuente del Merthyr. His reserve at this place, (Zafra, from which the letter is dated).

Opposed to General Cuesta is General Victor. His army is about 30,000 strong. He occupies Truxillo and Caceres, and has his advanced guard at Mortanchis. A small detachment of 300 or 400 men still occupies the old castle of Merida, but they are hourly expected to surrender.

General Venegas commands the army of La Carolina, but subject to the orders which he may receive from General Cuesta. His force is 20,000 infantry and 3,500 cavalry, and a large and well organised force of horse artillery.

General Blake is appointed Commander-in-Chief of Aragon, Catalonia, Valencia, and Murcia. *I understand* that he has advanced from Anton towards Cuença with 24,000 infantry and 1,000 cavalry.

General Sebastiani, who commands in La Mancha, against General Venegas, has with him a body of 9,000 men.

General Mortier marched a short time since from Saragossa to Burgos with a division of 11,000 men; and it is said that General Augereau has passed Irun from Bayonne with a body of 15,000 conscripts.

General Ney with a small force occupies Ferrol and Coruña, but as the whole of Galicia is again in arms under the Marquis de la Romana, he may be considered as blockaded.

General Soult has been completely defeated at Oporto by Sir Arthur Wellesley; but of this, I conclude, your Royal Highness is already informed.

I have not sufficient details to be able to state accurately what is passing in Catalonia; but there is no doubt that affairs have there taken a very favourable turn.

The result of this extension of the forces, and distribution of the Spanish and French armies, is that, should Victor fall back upon Madrid, and join Sebastiani, and should the divisions of Mortier and Augereau advance upon the capital, they will concentrate a force of 70,000 men. Cuesta, by effecting a junction with Venegas and Blake (which it is always in his power to do by a flank movement to his right, or by their making a flank movement to their left), will collect an army of 58,000 infantry and 11,500 cavalry.

Sir Arthur Wellesley has promised to advance into Spain, following the right bank of the Tagus, and to cooperate with General Cuesta the moment that he returns from his expedition to Oporto; and he has requested General Cuesta not to compromise himself in any general action till his arrival. Sir Arthur's force between Coy and Portugal is estimated at 50,000 men. It is not for me to presume to give your Royal Highness an opinion on the issue of the present contest. But, at all events, whatever may be the issue, your Royal Highness may rest assured that as long as we can collect a dozen muskets we shall fight, and by dint of fighting, I trust in God, we shall become good soldiers.

I have, &c.

Samford Whittinqham.

P.S.—I have the pleasure to inform your Royal Highness that the Junta Suprema has made me a Brigadier-General of Spanish Cavalry.

S. W.

Brigadier-General Whittingham to the Right Hon. J. H. Frere.
(Extract.)

Zafra, 26th May, 1809.

The truth of what you have so often stated relative to the necessity of a diversion in La Mancha is now most strongly felt at headquarters. General Venegas has received repeated orders to advance and attack General Sebastiani, who has with him not above 12,000 men. But General Venegas pleads the want of spirit in his soldiers, and their reduced numbers. Under such an impression, it may perhaps be better for the country that he should do nothing. But it is sadly to be lamented that, at a moment when such important consequences might, and indeed must, arise from calling the attention of the enemy towards the right, the plan of the campaign should be exposed to ruin rather than employ, in the command of the army of the Carolina, the only man who possesses the full confidence of that army, and to whom the peasants of La Mancha look up with the most enthusiastic admiration, he alludes to Alburquerque).'

★★★★★★

Note:—Those readers who have observed how earnestly the brigadier had suggested to the minister this diversion in La Mancha will be struck with the above passage. Anxious to have what is right properly done, he is indifferent about the credit of the original suggestion.

★★★★★★

The English Envoy and the military agent were evidently working harmoniously together, though we can produce only one side of the correspondence carried on between them. He now meets again with an old friend:—

To his Brother-in-law.

Zafra, 9th June, 1809.

I am just returned from the vanguard, where we had a pretty little action, and carried off from the enemy 700 *fanegas* of corn.

Lieutenant-Colonel Bourke and Cadogan are arrived at head-quarters from Sir Arthur Wellesley, at Alcantara. His whole force may be up in a few days. He has with him a force of 40,000 men, out of which 24,000 are English. General Cuesta has not less than 35,000 men. These armies co-operating must utterly destroy Victor if he awaits the attack. But if, as it is feared, he retreats from his present position in time, it will be absolutely necessary to pursue and harass him in his retreat with the whole body of the united arms.

To the Same.
Villaneuva de la Sirena, 15th June, 1809.
The French abandoned Merida on the 13th. Today they have retired from Miajadas; and it is evident that they are in full re-treat by the bridge of Almaraz. Their position on the other side of the Tagus will probably be at Talavera de la Reyna.

I cannot help expressing my opinion that, if General Cuesta crosses the Tagus, and follows the traces of Victor, we shall be reduced to the necessity of fighting a battle in order to obtain his further retreat; and, in the comparative state of the French and Spanish armies, the result of a general action is always to be feared; whereas by the plan which I have taken the liberty to propose, the desired effect would be produced by a war of movement without the smallest risk.

I have taken advantage of Colonel Cadogan's, (*aide-de-camp* to Sir Arthur Wellesley), departure for the British Army to send you these few lines.

To the Same.
Villar de Robledo, 25th June, 1809.
You will see by the date of my last letter that we are within a league of the Tagus. We marched all last night in order to at-tack the bridge of Arzobispo this morning. It has been delayed in consequence of the artillery not arriving in time. We shall probably cross the Tagus tomorrow. Sir Arthur is marching from Abrantes to Castel Branco, Rosminhal, Sigura, Zarza, Coria, Placencia—distance thirty-seven leagues.

You will be much grieved to hear that the Duke of Alburquer-que has left this army. He has been disgusted by the repeated ill-treatment which he has received; but I hope, when Lord Wellesley arrives, that everything will be set to rights. I remain with the vanguard, or rather with the cavalry of the vanguard, commanded by the Prince of Anglona. I think that we may probably enter Madrid in ten days.

Sir Arthur Wellesley has appointed me to the Staff of his army as Deputy Assistant Quartermaster-General. This will give me eight shillings a day, and will not interfere with my plans here.

The Marquis Wellesley to R. H. Davis, Esq. M.P.

Apsley House, 19th June, 1809.

Lord Wellesley presents his compliments to Mr. Davis, and has the honour to acknowledge the receipt of his two notes under date the 4th and 17th June, together with the papers from Major Whittingham, (this arose from some mistake on his Lordship's part; Samford Whittingham was still only a Captain in the British service, but a Brigadier-General in that of Spain), for whose character and talents Lord Wellesley entertains the highest respect, Lord Wellesley is extremely obliged to Mr. Davis for communicating to him these interesting documents, which he begs leave to return to Mr. Davis with many acknowledgments for his kind attention in permitting Lord Wellesley to peruse them.

Thus, before ever seeing Samford Whittingham, Lord Wellesley, by the mere perusal of his letters and memoranda, had already imbibed a very high opinion of his character. If anyone was ever more ready to acknowledge merit, wherever it appeared, than this truly liberal-minded nobleman, it was the illustrious writer (a few days earlier) of the note which follows:—

His Royal Highness the Duke of Kent to R. H. Davis, Esq. M.P.

Kensington Palace, 12th June, 1809.

The Duke of Kent returns his best acknowledgments to Mr. Davis for his polite note of yesterday, and the obliging attention he has shown in taking the trouble of calling himself at Kensington with the letter from his brother-in-law. Brigadier-General Whittingham, that was sent to his care. The duke conceiving it probable that the general may have instructed Mr. Davis through what channel to forward his letters to him, which he has omitted to do in his communication to the duke, he hopes that Mr. Davis will forgive him for troubling him to take charge of the enclosed for that highly estimable officer, which he is peculiarly desirous should reach him in safety, as he has reason to believe other letters he has written to him before have not found their way to him, as in his last he makes no mention of having received any from the duke.

It appears, indeed, that none of these letters—not even the one which the duke sent to Mr. Davis with the above—ever reached their address. At all events, they have all unfortunately disappeared, and it is, therefore, very satisfactory that another to Mr. Davis, in addition to the above, has reached the editor's hands, which will appear in its proper place.

To his Brother-in-law.

Coria, 5th July, 1809.

I am just returned from Zarza la Maior, where I have been to see Sir Arthur, in consequence of his order. The first division of the British Army marches into this town tomorrow morning! 'General Cuesta is at Almaraz, on the left bank of the Tagus. Victor occupies a position on the left bank of the Alberche River: his headquarters at Ciboya. King Joseph is at Toledo. Sebastiani, reinforced by the greater part of the garrison of Madrid, has advanced against Venegas in La Mancha. Ferrol and Coruña have been evacuated. The Spaniards have taken possession of these towns; and the remains of the divisions of Ney, Soult, and Kellermann (in all 20,000 men), have evacuated Galicia and Asturias, and are directing their march towards this part of the country. It does not appear an easy or safe operation to attack Victor in his present position.

Should the other divisions join him, we shall have occasioned the reunion of the French force, without having increased that of the Spaniards in the same proportion; and the truth of what I have before stated of the good effect to be expected from placing 60,000 men under Sir Arthur will be severely felt. Of course, everything I say to you upon these matters is in perfect confidence. If any military man can save this country, I think it will be Sir Arthur! His great abilities are aided by the most conciliatory manners. He is just the man to please the Spaniards; and, in my humble opinion, if he has the means, he will constantly prove victorious over the French. He is going to wait upon Cuesta in a few days.

★★★★★★

Note:—On the 13th July, Sir A. Wellesley writes to Mr. H.

Frere:—'General Castaños having declined to send a large detachment to the quarter proposed by me, I, of course, have no opportunity of requesting that the Duke of Alburquerque should have the command to which I certainly should have been disposed, as well on account of your recommendation, as from his own character.'

'On the 22nd July, the outposts of the French Army were driven in by the Spanish advanced guard under the command of General Zayas and the Duke of Alburquerque,' writes Sir A. Wellesley to Lord Castlereagh, on the 24th July, 1809.

★★★★★★

The following account of the Battle of Talavera is extracted from the *Recollections:*—

A short time previous to Sir Arthur Wellesley's advance into Spain, I was directed to join his headquarters on the frontiers of Portugal. Cuesta's army had been literally destroyed at Medellin; yet he had collected again a force of 35,000 men, of which 6,000 were cavalry, and had thrown a bridge of boats over the Tagus at Almaraz, of which he was very proud. It was agreed by the two chiefs that their meeting should take place near the bridge; and Sir Arthur advanced to the rendezvous escorted by a squadron of British dragoons. In consequence of this conference. Sir Arthur crossed the Tietar, and the combined armies advanced upon Talavera.

A slight skirmish drove the French from the town, and they took up a commanding position on the left bank of the Alberche.

Sir Arthur reconnoitred the ground carefully and minutely, and proposed to Cuesta that the attack should take place the next morning at break of day, in two columns. The right column, composed of Spaniards, and commanded by Cuesta, was to advance on the high-road leading from Talavera to Madrid; the left column, composed of British troops under Sir Arthur, was to march direct upon the position occupied by the French Army, pass the Alberche, and storm the heights on the left bank. Cuesta's movement by the high-road would thus bring his whole army perpendicular to the left flank of Victor, whilst the front attack would be made by Sir Arthur.

All Sir Arthur's orders were issued; but no decisive answer having been obtained from the Spanish general, I was directed to wait upon him, and to ascertain what his intentions were. My conference with the old general and his staff lasted till eleven o'clock at night; but I could bring him to no final decision, and I was obliged to return to the British headquarters with this unsatisfactory result.

Counter-orders were immediately issued, to suspend the projected attack; and an opportunity was lost of beating the French Army in detail, and of immortalising the opening career of the British General by a suite of brilliant and rapid successes, not surpassed at any period of the Peninsular War.

See my memorandum on the Battle of Talavera. (This memorandum is too long for insertion, and, moreover, is believed to be embodied in Southey's *History of the Peninsular War*).

After much hesitation, Cuesta was at last brought to consent to the attack as first proposed, and a day having been wasted in talk, it was at length determined that the attack should take place next morning. We accordingly crossed the Alberche, and ascended the heights, but it was too late: the bird was flown. Victor had retreated upon Madrid the night before. In spite of the remonstrances of Sir Arthur, Cuesta and all his force set off in the pursuit of the French Army, whilst the British general was occupied in reconnoitring the ground about Talavera, and in choosing the position where he should fight the battle which he foresaw must in a few days take place.

Victor, having been reinforced by the troops of Madrid, was now at the head of 45,000 men, of which 6,000 were cavalry; and Cuesta was forthwith driven back to the entrance of Talavera. It was with the greatest difficulty that Sir Arthur obtained permission to speak to Cuesta (who at five p.m. was asleep in his tent on the left bank of the Alberche), to inform him of the immediate proximity of the enemy, and to request him to occupy, without a moment's loss of time, his position in the general line. In the meantime, the whole of the British cavalry was thrown out to cover his retreat on the Alberche. Colonel Elley, (afterwards General Sir John Elley), and the adjutant-general of the British cavalry, manoeuvred the two lines in a most masterly manner, and so completely checked the rapid advance of the enemy that it was four p.m. before the last of the British squadrons repassed the Alberche.

I had galloped to Talavera to report the result of the cavalry movements to Sir Arthur, when a Staff officer came in from General Mackenzie—whose division occupied a wood on our extreme left—to say that the division had been surprised; that one regiment had given way, and that all was confusion and dismay! In a moment, the general was in his saddle, and in full gallop towards the spot. We advanced into the midst of our skirmishers. The fire was hot, and the enemy rapidly approaching. Sir Arthur leaped off his horse, and scrambled up the wall of an old ruin close at hand. But he was obliged to throw himself down on his hands and knees, and to remount instantly; for the enemy's sharp-shooters had nearly surrounded the building, and a minute's delay would have constituted him a prisoner.

A brigade of infantry was formed, at a short distance in our rear, on the right of which was the 45th Regiment commanded by Colonel Gordon. He was a little fat man, who had commanded the same regiment at Buenos Ayres. Whilst the general was speaking to him, a musket ball went through the blade of his sword, another took off the round knob of his hilt, and a third went through his cap! Sir Arthur then ordered the battalions to retire from the right of companies, in order to pass the wood in their rear. This manoeuvre had scarcely been commenced, when the heads of the French columns showed themselves, and their artillery opened upon us.

Our retreat to the position of Talavera was covered by the Spanish cavalry, and conducted with much order. The left of the Spanish line, in the position, rested upon the right of the British. An English battery of six-pounders, in the centre of the line, was removed to make room for a Spanish battery of eight-pounders; the fire of the six-pounders being found inadequate. I had no particular command in this action; but finding no commander with the Spanish division on the left of their line, I assumed the command, and found a ready obedience in both officers and men.

About ten at night the French threw out parties of light infantry to open a light running fire down the line; probably to ascertain its direction. But our young Spanish soldiers, taking the alarm, commenced a fire so heavy and well kept up that Sir Arthur, who just at that moment came up, said—"Whittingham, if they will but fire as well tomorrow, the day is our own; but as there seems to be nobody to fire at just now, I wish you would try to stop it."—"I have been trying for some time in vain," I replied: and whilst I was speaking three battalions became so frightened at their own noise, that they fairly took to their heels, and fled from the field of battle. "Only look, Whittingham," said the general, "at the ugly hole those fellows have left. I wish you would go to the second line, and try to fill it up."

Nothing could give a more correct idea of the superiority of Sir Arthur's mind than this little incident. He had advanced into the heart of Spain on his own responsibility. He was now in the presence of 45,000 Frenchmen. His whole force consisted of 18,000 British, and 35,000 Spanish troops; the latter hastily assembled since the defeat at Medellin; and, consequently, for the most part a mere rabble. Panic-struck by their own fire, a whole brigade had thrown down their arms and fled. At a moment so awful, when all was at stake. Sir Arthur coolly observed that the hole in the first line was an ugly one, and requested me to bring troops from the second line to fill it up.

During the night a false alarm sent all our servants and baggage to the rear; they carried off our horses also, and I was glad to mount myself on a stray dragoon-horse, which chance threw in my way. We had had nothing to eat for the last forty-eight hours, and I was truly glad to fall in with General Zayas, who gave us an excellent breakfast of *Bacallao con salsa,* (salt fish stewed in tomato sauce). About three p.m., July 28th, the French made a fierce attack upon the left of the Spaniards; but so marvellous is the effect of British courage that, like Falstaff's wit, it is contagious. The same troops who, a few hours previously had run away from their own fire, now fought like lions. The French were received in an echelon of battalions, the left thrown forward, and their attack failed altogether.

A regiment of Spanish cavalry charged the French line with brilliant success. The colonel who led the charge had his arm broken by a musket ball; but the effect was decisive. As I was giving an order to one of the battalions, a musket ball struck me in the mouth, carried away a large portion of my teeth, broke the jaw-bone, and came out behind the ear. I was stunned, but not dismounted, though instantly covered with blood.

The attack on our left having ceased, I proceeded to the left of the line to report to Sir Arthur the result. On my way, I fell in with a party carrying Colonel Gordon to the rear,—he was severely, but not dangerously wounded,—when a shell burst immediately upon him, and killed the colonel and his supporters. On the road to Sir Arthur, I stopped at the Blood Hospital, and had the wound examined, but nothing could be done even to stop the blood.

When I ascended the rising ground on which the general and his staff were standing. Sir Arthur called out to me, "Ah, Whittingham, I wanted you to take a message to the Duke of Alburquerque:" but when he saw the state I was in, he turned on his heel, and said no more. I then sat down on the grass with Lords Fife, (then Lord Macduff, and who succeeded his father on 17th April, 1811, as Earl of Fife), and Burghersh, (afterwards Earl of Westmoreland), drank a tumbler of sherry, and smoked some good cigars with the sound side of my mouth.

About seven in the evening, the French being in full retreat, Lord Fife, Lord Burghersh, and myself bent our course towards Talavera. We had not, however, advanced a hundred yards, when a shell fell just in front of our horses. Lord B. instantly dismounted, and laid himself flat on the ground; whilst Lord Fife, convulsed with laughter, kept calling to me. to look at the extraordinary length of Lord B.'s figure, which he insisted was beyond all mortal bounds. The only wise man of our party was Lord B., for the shell burst and covered us with sand and dust, and our escape was wonderful.

At Talavera my reception at the hospital of the guards was truly kind; but the surgeon wanted experience in gunshot wounds, and so completely mistook my case as to bind up my fractured jaw with a wooden splint, thereby driving all the splinters of the jaw-bone together with the pieces of the ball and teeth into the lacerated flesh. The pain was so exquisite, that before I reached my quarters, I tore off and threw away the whole of the dressing. (It would appear—*vide Preface*—that Lord Macduff took him off the field and tended him at Talavera).

Sir Arthur gave me *carte-blanche* to go home *via* Lisbon, or to go to Seville, where Marquis Wellesley had just arrived as British Ambassador. I should have preferred remaining with Sir Arthur as one of his *aides-de-camp*, but he thought that I should be more useful with the Spanish Army, as *major-general*, to which rank I had been promoted for my services at Talavera by the Supreme Junta.

But we are anticipating, and, leaving the *Recollections* for the present, must return to the correspondence of the period:—

Colonel Roche to R. H. Davis, Esq. M.P.

Talavera, 30th July, 1809.

My dear Sir,—The 28th July will for ever remain memorable for the glory of England and the British arms. The French to the number of 50,000 arrived on the evening of the 27th upon the Alberche, and immediately commenced attacking our outposts, upon which occasion there was some loss on both sides. The following morning the whole line of defence was formed; the British, with their left resting upon a targe of hills, crowned with batteries, and extending across a plain, where it was joined by the left of the Spanish line, which had its right upon the Tagus.

The battle, one of the most bloody and obstinate which was ever fought, commenced at five o'clock on the morning of the 28th. The attack was made with the whole French force upon the British, and lasted until half-past eight at night; and, notwithstanding we had not 17,000 men, the enemy were defeated in all attacks and forced to retreat with immense loss.

We have lost 5,000 men in killed and wounded, and, I am sorry to say, my excellent friend Whittingham is among the latter. His wound is however—I am happy to tell—in the most favourable way, and of no consequence. His escape, however, was miraculous. A musket ball entered his mouth, and came out at his left ear, without injuring or touching a bone or a tooth (?). (The wound would have been more miraculous than the escape, if it had really done no more injury than Colonel Roche at first supposed, deceived by the patient endurance of the wounded man).

He is in the same house with Lord Macduff and myself, and wants for nothing; and, in short, we expect he will be on his horse in a week or ten days. He met with his wound *as he was bringing up a Spanish battalion, in the most gallant manner,* (actually *two* Spanish battalions), and I sincerely congratulate, you and his family *on the distinguished part he has taken in* the most arduous and glorious day England ever saw. Excuse this hasty scrawl, which I could not deny myself the pleasure of writing, as well from my own inclination, as at the desire of my friend about whom you may be perfectly at rest. He is at this moment at my side, in high spirits.

Believe, me, &c.,

K. Roche.

P.S. I forbear all details, as you will see the whole by the dispatches.

★★★★★★

Colonel Roche (afterwards Sir Philip Keating Roche) was a military agent like Whittingham. He was then Major in the British and Colonel in the Spanish service, and the senior officer of the two, and remained so till 1814, when Whittingham was made full Colonel in the British Army.

Colonel Roche alludes to the British numbers only, which was hardly fair to the Spaniards, to whom Sir Arthur Wellesley himself did justice, both in his dispatch home, and also in his letter to Mr. Hookham Frere.

★★★★★★

Extract from Sir A. Wellesley's Dispatch to Viscount Castlereagh, dated Talavera de la Reyna, July 29, 1809.

At the same time he, (the enemy), directed an attack upon Brigadier-General Campbell's position in the centre of the combined armies, and on the right of the British. This attack was most successfully repulsed by Brigadier-General Campbell, supported by the King's regiment of Spanish cavalry, *and two battalions of Spanish infantry*, and Brigadier-General Campbell took the enemy's cannon.

I also received *much assistance* from Colonel O'Lalor, of the Spanish service*, and from Brigadier-General Whittingham, who was wounded in bringing up the two Spanish battalions to the assistance of Brigadier-General Campbell.*

This last sentence was the concluding one of Sir Arthur Wellesley's dispatch, and, therefore, very conspicuous.

On July 29, Sir Arthur writes to Mr. Hookham Frere:—

I was well satisfied with the conduct of the Spanish troops who had an opportunity of assisting us.

And he gives the minister some details in proof. However, as Cuesta still left the British troops without supplies, Sir Arthur was compelled to retreat, though that retreat did not take place immediately.

Lord Wellesley arrived on the 1st of August, but Mr. Hookham Frere continued to transact business for some days longer; and the first official letter addressed by Sir A. Wellesley to his elder brother is dated the 8th of August, 1809. The arrival of the Marquis was an event of some importance to the subject of this *Memoir*, already known to his Lordship by report, and soon destined to make his personal acquaintance, as will be seen in the next chapter.

After considering that extract from the duke's dispatch given above in *italics*, and also reading the letter of Colonel Roche on the gallantry of Whittingham—both the commander-in-chief and the colonel reporting his wound as well as his gallant action— the candid reader will understand how, at a later period, the utter silence of Napier's too partial history excited very natural indignation in the mind of the injured party.

That which was deemed worthy of especial mention in the brief dispatch of the victorious general, was surely entitled, in common fairness, to a place in a voluminous history, going into details far more extended than dispatches can ever admit of when written by victors from the field of battle.

Chapter 5

1809—1810

Brigadier-General Whittingham found his wound a more serious and tedious affair than he had at first anticipated; and he proceeded to Seville for change of air and completeness of cure. We return to his *Recollections:*—

> My journey to Seville was performed on horseback with pain and fatigue, for it was the height of summer, and I lived entirely by suction. At that time, and for six months afterwards, I could take nothing but tea and soaked bread.
>
> On my arrival at Seville, the *marquis* (Wellesley) attached me to his embassy, for the time that I should remain there; and he wrote to the admiral at Cadiz to request that he would send to Seville one of his best surgeons. Kennedy came; and, after examining the jaw, and hearing the account of what had been done, he laughed at the ignorance which had been displayed, and that very evening extracted seven pieces of bone, one of which was upwards of an inch long. Ten years afterwards he extracted, at Madrid, a piece of the ball twisted like a corkscrew, which had remained in the jaw-bone all that time.
>
> During my stay at Seville, I lived as one of Lord Wellesley's family; and there I formed my first acquaintance with that excellent man, Sir William Knighton. Our morning rides were a source of happiness to us both, and our friendship only ended with his life.

In his first official letter, 8th August, 1809, to Marquis Wellesley, as ambassador, Sir Arthur Wellesley writes:

> The plan of operations which I should recommend to the Spanish nation is one generally of defence. They should avoid

general actions, but should take advantage of the strong points in their country to defend themselves and to harass the enemy.

This was good advice; but long before the hero of the Peninsula entered Spain, the subject of this *Memoir* had (as has been shown) repeatedly urged the same advice. Well would it have been for Spain if it had been acted on from the beginning, and mere brainless fighters like Cuesta earlier removed from high command.

However, on the 13th of August, that stupid and infatuated old general sent in his resignation; and General Eguia succeeded to the command. But General Cuesta will, alas! re-appear again; no longer, indeed, to torment the great English chief, but to worry almost beyond endurance, the subject of this *Memoir*.

But the change of commanders not bringing supplies to the English soldiers, Sir A. Wellesley retreated from Spain.

Brigadiers-General Whittingham to his Brother-in-law.
Seville, 22nd August, 1809.
My dear Davis,—-The fracture which has taken place in my jaw-bone will, I fear, protract very considerably the cure of my wound. I have lost all the back teeth on the left side of my face. But I am still gaily disposed, and only anxious to get quickly well, in order to take the field again.

You will have been astonished at our retreat after our glorious victory of the 28th July; all owing to that old fool, Cuesta, who has done everything in his power to ruin his country. I thank God that he is at last removed; and if the command-in-chief be given to Sir Arthur Wellesley, things will yet go well.

Lord Wellesley exceeds even the high idea that I had formed of him! The people here look up to him as their saviour.

Venegas has fallen back upon the Carolina. There will probably be some change in the position of our armies upon the Tagus, of which I shall take care to inform you.

To the Same,
Seville, 2nd September, 1809.
My dear Davis,—You will, I know, be happy to hear that Lord Wellesley has attached me to his service for the present in the most confidential manner; and, as the state of my wound would not allow of my retaking the field for some time, I cannot be more profitably or more agreeably employed. As the first thing Lord Wellesley has encharged to me is the most profound secrecy,

I feel myself called upon to be silent upon everything but simple matter of fact, even with you, the beloved friend of my heart.

It is currently reported that the French are retiring, and even about to abandon Madrid. But I confess that I have strong doubts on this head. The British Army appears to be taking up a strong position on the Portuguese frontier near Yelvas, where it will effectually cover the approaches to Seville, and at the same time refit and recover from its fatigues.

My wound is going on very well. It will be a long time before my cure is completed; but my mind is at ease since his Lordship has been pleased to consider that my services may yet be useful.

At this time there was living at Seville, a Spanish gentleman named Don Pedro de Creus y Ximenes, an Intendant of the Spanish Royal armies. His family, originally from Catalonia, (north-easternmost point of Spain, Cape Creus, gave its name to the family, say the Spanish genealogists), had possessed property in Minorca ever since his ancestor, James de Creus, had, *A.D.* 1285, accompanied King James of Aragon to the conquest of the Balearic Islands, Don Pedro was a widower, with two twin daughters, both remarkable for wit and accomplishments, and the elder distinguished by beauty and grace. (All this is duly certified by the Madrid heralds. Don Pedro's father, Don Francisco Creus, married a lady of the ancient family of Ximenes; thus the formal style of the military intendant was Don Pedro de Creus y Ximenes). Here the English captain, become a Spanish general, lost his heart to the elder, Donna Magdalena; and some years later the younger, Donna Barbara, made a conquest of Mr. Bartlemy Frere, brother of Mr. Hookham Frere, and attached to the Embassy in Spain.

To Lieutenant-Colonel the Hon. Henry Cadogan.

Seville, 12th September, 1809.

My dear Cadogan,—Had I not to plead illness as an excuse for not having sooner answered your truly affectionate letters of the 15th and 22nd July, (see note following), I should be ashamed to address a friend whose good opinion I esteem more, infinitely more, than I can express. I was, as you will have heard, wounded on the evening of the 28th July, at the Battle of Talavera. I did not quit the field for upwards of two hours afterwards; and, as I remained during that time on the hill with Sir Arthur Wellesley and his Staff, I suppose that this led to the conclusion that my wound was slight. It was, however, severe, which I only mention, in order to convince my friend that no trifling cause had prevented my writing to him sooner. The ball entered my mouth, carried off four teeth, broke the jawbone and took its exit behind the ear.

Of the battle, I shall only say that Sir Arthur Wellesley surpassed everything that even my romantic fancy had formed him capable of. In the retreat to the position of the 27th, his timely presence and admirable dispositions saved General Mackenzie's division from utter destruction. Yet Sir Arthur, with a modesty unequalled, attributes the merit of the retreat to that unfortunate general, and from his dispatch, you would not know even that he was present.

Lord Wellesley has displayed in his negotiations with this country such great talents, such a wonderful knowledge of men and things, that whenever his proceedings are made public, his character, high as it now stands, will rise much higher in the opinion of his countrymen. If it be possible to save this unfortunate country, he will save it, (see note following). If he fails, all is lost.

★★★★★★

Note:—None of the letters written by Colonel Cadogan to General Whittingham have reached the editor's hands. It is uncertain whether they were lost in the Peninsula, or returned to his friends after his heroic death on the field of victory at Vittoria in 1813.

The marquis had fully adopted General Whittingham's opinion of Alburquerque, as compared with other Spanish generals. On the 21st August, 1809, his Lordship wrote to Mr. Canning, then Secretary of State for Foreign affairs:— 'The most proper person for the command in Estremadura would be the Duke of Alburquerque, who has been distinguished by several acts of gallantry and spirit in the last campaign. He is, however, an object of jealousy to the *junta*, and if he should be appointed to the command in Estremadura, attempts will be made to reduce the strength of that division of the Spanish Army.'

★★★★★★

Knowing, as you do, how much and how truly I participate in all your joys and all your sorrows, I am not afraid to say that no event of my life has given me more pleasure than your ———'s being placed under your protection. May God grant you both as large a portion of happiness as my heart's best wishes would insure you.

A thousand thanks for your little box. It is a delightful present; and every time I open and shut it—which is very often daily—it brings recollections to my mind, which, I trust, I shall ever cherish as I ought to, and as I now do. Mr. Duff has promised me that your wines shall be of the very best quality that he can procure; the pale sherry, and Paxarete. (The subject of this *Memoir* was always—though a very moderate liver himself—noted for the excellence of his wines). I trust that they have already sailed, but I shall write to him tomorrow on the subject.

As Lord Wellesley's dispatches will probably be very soon laid before Parliament, I shall say nothing upon the unfortunate causes of our retreat after the Battle of Talavera. The whole blame, however, rests with the Spaniards. Would that I could say that they had taken proper steps since that period to remedy the evils which arrested Sir Arthur's steps in his brilliant course of victory. But enough of this subject. You will see it ably, indeed, discussed by the pen of Lord Wellesley. You will, I know, be pleased at hearing that I am honoured by his Lordship's confidence.

I consider this distinction as the finest feather in my cap. Have I not used a French expression? *Adieu*, my dear friend. My wound is getting well fast. Several bones have been extracted. But I cannot open my mouth; and I live like a woodcock—upon suction. In consequence of the Battle of Talavera, the Spanish Government has been pleased to make me a Major-General. (His commission as Mariscal de Campo—as Major-Generals are styled in Spain—was dated 12th August; 1809 see list following). I enclose the Spanish account of the Battle of Talavera.

Believe me, ever yours most truly,

Samford Whittingham.

★★★★★★

Sir Samford Whittingham's Commissions.
In the British Service.

Born	29th January, 1772
Ensign	20th January, 1803
Lieutenant	10th March, 1803
Captain	14th February, 1805
Major	12th March, 1810
Lieutenant-Colonel (back dated to)	30th May, 1811
Colonel	4th June, 1814
Major-General	27th May, 1825
Lieutenant-General	28th June, 1838
Colonel of 71st Highland Light Infantry	28th March, 1838

Colonel	. . . . .	20th July, 1808
Brigadier-General	. . .	2nd March, 1809
Mariscal de Campo	. . .	12th August, 1809
Lieutenant-General	. . .	16th June, 1814

★★★★★★

Mr. Frere had only been minister, but the Marquis of Wellesley had come out as Ambassador Extraordinary. At that period only ambassadors had the title of 'excellency;' and, at all times, an ambassador is the only diplomatist who enjoys full and complete royal honours. But it was not only his superior rank, but also his fame and great abilities, that rendered Lord Wellesley's authority and position in Spain far higher than that of his predecessor, Mr. Hookham Frere. The latter had, however, evidently suited well with Sir Arthur Wellesley; and no candid reader of the dispatches, can fail to perceive that the great general was uneasy at his brother's advent into Spain.

It was indispensable that one Englishman should have the preponderating authority of his country in Spain, and Sir Arthur alone could unite the civil and military power in the same hands. It was necessary, therefore, that the ambassador or minister should play a secondary part; and yet it could hardly be expected that the Marquis of Wellesley in such a situation, would entirely defer to the opinions of his younger brother, and late Indian subordinate.

The British agents attached to Spanish Generals (reporting previously to Mr. Frere) had been placed under the orders of Sir Arthur Wellesley. But Lord Wellesley brought out orders that these important and useful, though subordinate, officers should make their reports to His Excellency the Ambassador; which, as depriving Sir Arthur of the complete control, could not but be displeasing to him. One of the results of this unsatisfactory state of things, which, fortunately, was only temporary, was a series of snubbings to the military agents, both direct and indirect. The following extract, however, is quoted rather as a proof of the magnanimity of Sir Arthur, who could acknowledge an error most gracefully:—

Sir Arthur Wellesley to Marquis Wellesley, K.B.

(Extract.)

Badajos, 17th September, 1809.

My Lord,—I have the honour to enclose the extract of a letter which I have received from Colonel Roche, giving an account of the state of the Spanish army, which, I am sorry to say is, I believe, too well founded. In justice to Colonel Roche, I must

95

add that, before I joined Cuesta's army, he wrote to me an account of its state, to which I was not inclined to pay any attention at that time, but which I afterwards found to be a true account in every respect. (*Wellington Dispatches,* vol. v.).

Thus Colonel Roche, at a later period, had confirmed, in letters to Sir Arthur Wellesley, the accounts which the then Colonel Whittingham had, months before, sent to the minister, Mr. Hookham Frere. Even the greatest of mortals is liable to occasional errors. Sir Arthur had been somewhat too tardy, by his own confession, in appreciating the full demerits of Cuesta's command. Now, Cuesta was the jealous enemy of the gallant Duke of Alburquerque, and may for a time have injured the latter in the British commander's opinion, and caused him to disparage the Spanish duke to the newly arrived British Ambassador. Mr. Hookham Frere and General Whittingham both sympathized with Alburquerque, as against old Cuesta and the Junta of Cadiz; and the subsequent miserable conduct of Cuesta, and the gallant relief of Cadiz by Alburquerque fully justified this preference.

But Cuesta and the *Junta* had then their partisans, and amongst these was evidently Mr. Charles Vaughan, the Secretary of Legation at Cadiz, who appears to have been at that time jealous of the influence which General Whittingham had with Mr. Frere, the minister, as well as with Alburquerque. Mr. Vaughan was, nevertheless, destined, a few years later, when minister himself, officially to record his gratitude to General Whittingham for the aid of his influence. (The strong animosity of Napier to Frere has unmistakeably extended itself to his friend Whittingham; and he eagerly makes use of an expression of the secretary to disparage the judgment of the minister and of the military agent).

On the 21st of September, 1809, Lord Wellington finishes a letter to Marquis Wellesley with this sentence:

Although the Duke of Alburquerque is prone by many, amongst others by Whittingham and Frere, and is feared by the Junta, you will find him out.'

(If the reader refers to the note in the letter to his brother-in-law earlier, Coria, 5th July 1809, he will see that some influence—probably that of General Cuesta—must have been used to change Lord Wellington's former good opinion of Alburquerque).

It is certain that nothing worse was ever found in the gallant Duke of Alburquerque than a too sensitive mind, and that defective education which was then common to the Spanish nobility. His vigour, valour,

and energy, as will be seen hereafter, astonished Lord Wellington himself some months later. How he was persecuted to death by the *Junta* is
touchingly recorded in the pages of the honest and truthful Southey;
one of the rare cases of a man almost literally dying of a broken heart.
Such sensitiveness was not, however, it must be confessed, calculated to
win the confidence of that cold calm hero, who afterwards acquired
the epithet of the *Iron Duke*. The confidence of Marquis Wellesley in
General Whittingham continued, as will be seen, unshaken.

Lord Wellesley wished to assemble the Cortes. Lord Wellington
acknowledged that he had 'a great dislike to a new popular assembly.'
(Lord Wellington's letter to Marquis Wellesley of 22nd September,
1809).

The liberal spirit of the marquis was ready, not only to detect,
but also to patronise merit wherever he found it united to integrity.
Whereas, even a year later, in spite of the continuance of a bloody
war, we find the illustrious, but too aristocratic hero of the age, urging
upon that truly royal 'Soldier's Friend,' the Duke of York, the propriety
of more speedily promoting 'officers of family, fortune, and influence
in the country,' (Vol. vi. of the *Wellington Dispatches*).—As if aristocratic officers were neglected in those days! But these remarks are wholly
of the present age. No such thoughts occurred to the subject of this
Memoir, then almost equally the devoted humble admirer of the two
illustrious brothers; the younger not having as yet entirely eclipsed the
elder, and the elder being decidedly the more amiable as well as the
more liberal of the two.

General Whittingham passed a happy time in the house of the noble and genial ambassador at Seville, and in visiting his future father-
in-law, who then resided in that town. But the stay of Lord Wellesley
in Spain was to be very brief, and ere long he was about to exchange
his not very satisfactory position in the Peninsula for the higher post
of a Cabinet Minister in England. But brief as his sojourn in Spain had
been, it had been long enough to fully appreciate the merits of that
English captain of dragoons, who was now serving as major-general
in the Spanish service.

Major-General Whittingham to his Brother-in-law,
Seville, 4th November, 1809.

I have been so long without writing to you, that I am almost
ashamed to take up my pen. I wish that I could give you a good
account of my wound; but it is very troublesome. Bones are

continually extracting, and matter has repeatedly formed under my skin. There is, however, nothing in it, I believe, dangerous; and patience, the best of all remedies, must be my doctor.

This morning we have accompanied Lord Wellesley to his audience of leave, and to the presentations of Lord Wellington and Mr. Bartlemy Frere. Lord Wellesley goes tomorrow to Cadiz, whither I should accompany him, if my health permitted. He exceeds every idea that I had formed of him. I think that the Marquis as a politician, and Lord Wellington as a general, will save Europe. It will give you great satisfaction to know that Lord Wellesley has treated me with the most marked attention during his residence at Seville, and is, I have reason to believe, well satisfied with me.

Nothing connected with this mission has given me more heartfelt pleasure than the friendship which I have formed with Dr. Knighton, (afterwards Sir William Knighton, well-known private secretary and confidential friend of George IV), .the physician and confidential friend of Marquis Wellesley. I recommend him to you, my dear Davis, in the strongest manner. You will thank me for it hereafter; and I love to hope that I shall have laid the foundation of a lasting and mutually interesting friendship, (and so it, literally, was the case).

I have requested Dr. Knighton, who will deliver to you this letter, to introduce you to Sydenham. He was secretary to Lord Wellesley during his government in India, possesses his confidence most completely, and well, indeed, deserves it. I have known few such men! You will thus become intimately acquainted with Lord Wellesley's character. He is the greatest man I ever knew, in the best sense of the expression. He has a power of attaching men to him that must be felt, for it cannot be described without apparent exaggeration. Notwithstanding, living with Lord Wellesley is more like living with an amiable monarch than with a private person. His good breeding is perfect; and so nice is his sensibility on this point, that the slightest deviation shocks and offends him. In short, you will, I hope, become acquainted with him, and form your own opinion upon this most wonderful man.

I am at present translating our cavalry tactics into Spanish. So soon as my wound is well, I shall apply for the command of a division of Spanish cavalry.

Here follows Lord Wellesley's official acknowledgement of General Whittingham's services; a portion of which is placed in italics by the editor:—

Marquis Wellesley to Major-General Whittingham.

Cadiz, 10th November, 1809.

Sir,—I have the honour to inform you that, having obtained His Majesty's leave of absence from Spain, the charge of the embassy has devolved on Mr. Bartholomew Frere, (thus written in the original, he was so christened; though usually called Bartlemy or Bartle for the sake of brevity), with whom I request you to continue your correspondence, according to the directions which you have received from Lord Castlereagh.

I have great pleasure in availing myself of this opportunity to communicate to you my sincere acknowledgements for the valuable information received from you since my residence in Spain. *On every occasion, your public conduct has been distinguished by the greatest zeal, ability, and integrity; and I discharge a most grateful public duty, in signifying to you my entire approbation of the satisfactory manner in which you have been employed both by the British and Spanish Governments in Spain.* With great respect and esteem, I have the honour to be, Sir,

Your faithful and obedient servant,

Wellesley.

To serve under Marquis Wellesley might certainly be called serving under the shade of the aristocracy; not, indeed, winter's 'cold shade,' but the genial and refreshing shade of summer. Only three months had General Whittingham served under him, and yet how warmly and ungrudgingly had that amiable and all-accomplished nobleman acknowledged his services and his merits.

In a letter to Mr. B. Frere, written a few days after Lord Wellesley's departure, and dated 17th November, 1809, Lord Wellington strongly, though indirectly, acknowledged the military talents of the officer, whose ability in civil matters his brother had so lately recorded. It must be premised that General Alava was already the friend of Lord Wellington, and afterwards served on his personal staff. The hero wrote:

I do not understand the Duque's, (Duke of Alburquerque), retreat from his position. He never apprised me of it. It is very desirable that Alava and Whittingham—as soon as he is able,—should be sent to the Duque de Alburquerque, who, although he does not want spirit, is deficient in other qualifications for a commander, which his confidence in those officers can alone supply. (Vol. v., of the *Wellington Dispatches*).

A sentence of the same letter reminds the editor of one of the most gallant of British nobles, who was a true and staunch friend to General Whittingham, namely. Lord Macduff, afterwards Earl of Fife. Lord Wellington wrote:

I am most anxious about Areyzaga's corps, the fate of which must be decided before this time. If he should fail, the situation of the Duque del Parque will become critical.

Lord Macduff was fighting under the orders of General Areyzaga, whose army of La Mancha was totally defeated at Ocaña on the 19th November, 1809. Lord Macduff exhibited his wonted valour, and exerted himself in vain to retrieve the fortunes of the day. Though without a commission in the British, his Lordship eventually became major-general in the Spanish army. It does not appear, however, though so stated in the Peerage, that he really was wounded at Talavera.

The original of the letter addressed by Lord Wellington to Major-General Whittingham, and dated Badajoz, 22nd December, 1809, is not in the editor's possession; and, from want of space, it is not copied at length from Gurwood's *Dispatches*, (vol. v.) An extract will suffice for this *Memoir*:—

To Major-General Whittingham.

Badajos, 22nd December, 1809.

My dear Sir,—I am concerned to hear that the state of your wound has obliged you to go to Gibraltar; but I wish that while you are in that part of the Peninsula, you would take an opportunity of seeing or writing to General Venegas on the subject of the defence of Cadiz.' (Then his Lordship enters into details of the military preparations required, &c., at great length, and the letter thus terminates): 'These are the points to which, in particular, I would draw the attention of General Venegas if I were likely to see him; but as that is not probable, I beg you either to see or write to him the sentiments which I have above written to you.

Believe me, &c.

Wellington.

Major-General Whittingham.

✶✶✶✶✶✶

In a note to this letter, Gurwood represents Whittingham as then a Lieut.-Colonel in the British Army, whereas he was only a Captain, and gazetted a Major only on the 12th March, 1810. Gurwood was misled, perhaps, by Napier's history. (See list above).

✶✶✶✶✶✶

Thus Lord Wellington, in 1809, recognised Whittingham's rank in Spain as that of a general officer, and never wrote to him nor of him under a lower title till peace was concluded, and he reverted to his humbler position in the British Army. How ignorant of these facts must have been that historian who describes the major-general of 1809 as only a colonel of cavalry in 1811! To be sure, the duke's dispatches generally were not then all available to the historian when he wrote as Colonel Napier, but those announcing victories had at least appeared in the *Gazette*. As early as 1809, in Lord Wellington's dispatch of Talavera, that hero had called Whittingham brigadier-general, the Spanish rank taking full effect in the Peninsular War. But Napier's natural disgust against the Spaniards extended itself, apparently, even to the English who served with them, and his misstatements must be compared (by all lovers of impartiality) with the more correct statements of Southey, and especially with the facts narrated in the *Wellington Dispatches*.

But it is necessary to revert here to General Whittingham's private correspondence:—

To his Brother-in-law.
San Roque, (near Gibraltar), 8th January, 1810.
I love to hope, before I sail for the new world, (there was at that time a plan for sending an expedition to South America, to recover the revolted colonies for Spain), to pass a few months with you and my dear Mrs. D.; and I have now a double interest in this wish, as it will give me an opportunity of introducing my dear Mrs. W., to whom I was married on Friday last at Gibraltar. General Castaños gave her away. We are now at San Roque, and as soon as my wound, which is still very troublesome, will permit, I shall go to Cadiz, where I have some very interesting affairs to canvass with the Governor, General Venegas, by the express desire of Lord Wellington.
I pay the greatest attention to my papers. I keep copies and

originals, as circumstances permit, and when I have the happiness of seeing you, I shall deposit the whole in your hands. (Though much of his correspondence has been lost, yet a great deal has been preserved, which would fill volumes). I have never had so delicate a part to play as at this moment. I am consulted by the leaders of the different parties, and they trust me with their secret views and intentions. I communicate everything to Lord Wellesley, and I am now anxiously waiting his orders. (Lord Wellesley was now Minister for Foreign Affairs).

The Spanish Government will employ me as major-general the moment I return to Seville. I have received a very pressing letter on the subject. But in the present situation of their army, I will not risk the little fame that I may have acquired by taking the command of a division of cavalry. But I will request to be employed as a major-general attached to the staff of the army of the Duke of Alburquerque. This will, in fact, make me second in command, at the same time that I avoid the dreadful responsibility of directly commanding ill-disciplined and disheartened troops.

To the Same.

Gibraltar, 22nd January, 1810.

General Castaños is appointed Captain-General of Andalusia, which gives him, in fact, the supreme command. He takes me with him as one of his generals of division. We leave this place tomorrow. Mrs. W. will remain at Cadiz, and I shall immediately take the field with the general. The French are about to attack the Sierra Morena on three points. I think that their grand attack will be by the road of Almadin de la Plata. I fear that Andalusia will be lost. But the Isla de Leon may be occupied in great force, and will protect the advances to Cadiz, and give time for any combined operations in the rear of the French Army. I pray you don't lose sight of my Majority. (He had applied to be promoted to be major in the British army, being still only a captain).

The *Junta* retire to the Isla de Leon, and the Junta of Seville are entrusted with the defence of the kingdom of Andalusia. My wound is, I hope, well.

On the 2nd February, 1810, after a very rapid march of 260 English miles, Alburquerque entered the Isla de Leon with 8,000 men, and thus saved Cadiz. He was afterwards made Governor of the City and President of the Junta. On the 7th of same month, (*Wellington Dispatches*, vol. v.). Lord Wellington writes from Mafra to the Hon. General Stewart:

> I cannot sufficiently recommend you to endeavour to keep up a good understanding with the Spanish officers. You will find General Castaños, who is at present at the head of the Regency, and General Venegas, who is Governor of Cadiz, highly deserving your confidence; as well as General Whittingham, who is an English officer, and who is, I understand, at present at Cadiz.

★★★★★★

Note:—Two days later, Lord Wellington wrote to Lord Liverpool: 'I have received intelligence, which I believe to be true, that the Duque d'Alburquerque's corps which had been at Carmona on the 24th January, and was supposed to have retired across the Guadalquivir, had retired upon Cadiz, and actually arrived at Xeres on the 1st instant.' Vol. v.

★★★★★★

To his Brother-in-law.

Isla de Leon, 1st March, 1810.

I am occupied from morning till night. The Regency place an unlimited confidence in me. The Duke of Alburquerque consults me upon everything, and has honoured me by the command of the cavalry, with full powers to organise as I may think proper. I have translated Dundas, and formed a corps of carabineers chosen from the different regiments for instruction. The officers assemble every evening at my house, and the practice of the day is rendered familiar and easy by the theory clearly explained at night. The Duke wishes me to take the employment of *Chef de l'Etat Major*. I have no objection to it. It is the next post to the commander-in-chief. (The rest of the letter is filled with military speculations and projects regarding the future campaigns).

General Whittingham, it is plain, commanded all the Spanish cavalry at Isla de Leon, although he there chiefly dedicated himself to the organisation of a select number. He did not thereby (as some have apparently ignorantly imagined) become again a simple colonel of cavalry.

In the beginning of March, the Right Hon. Henry Wellesley arrived at Cadiz, as His Majesty's Minister in Spain, and from this time it was with him that General Whittingham habitually corresponded.

In a letter from Lord Wellington to Mr. Wellesley, dated Viseu, 27th March, 1810, there are two sentences that bear connection with the future proceedings of General Whittingham in Spain, and are, therefore, here inserted.

> Whether the fleet is, or is not sent to Minorca, the security of the Balearic Islands is a consideration of the utmost importance, which must not be lost sight of you and I (I probably more than you) will be considered responsible for everything that occurs, although we have no means in our power, and no power to enforce the execution of what is necessary.
>
> It is desirable that we should advert to everything, and should recommend to the consideration of the Spanish Government those measures which appear to us to be necessary. Accordingly, I suggest to you to pass a note to the Regency, recommending to their serious attention the security of the Balearic Islands, Minorca particularly; they should send there, in the first instance, the Viscomte de Gand's corps which is now in Algarve; they should, besides, endeavour to raise men in Cadiz, where, by proper measures, they could get thousands.

Venegas's politics were considered of a doubtful character, but he was junior to the Duke of Alburquerque, and therefore Lord Wellington writes in February that he considered his opinions immaterial, 'particularly recollecting a letter which I wrote to General Whittingham in December upon this subject, which I know was shown to Venegas, and which was certainly calculated to inspire confidence rather than mistrust of our designs in regard to Cadiz.'

On the 12th March, 1810, Samford Whittingham's name appeared in the *London Gazette,* as promoted from Captain in the 13th Light Dragoons, to be Major of Infantry on half pay. In a letter dated Isla de Leon, 1st April, 1810, he writes, introducing Mr. B. Frere, then about to proceed to England to his brother-in-law, Mr Davis.

To the Same.

Isla de Leon, 8th April, 1810.

I believe that I mentioned to you, that the Duke of Alburquerque has resigned the command of this army, and is going as ambassador to England. The Regency wished me to have accompanied him, and proposed giving me a special commission for the arms and accoutrements of the cavalry; but this plan was objected to by Mr. Wellesley and General Graham, who were pleased to consider my presence here as absolutely necessary!

I have, you know, undertaken to introduce a new system of tactics in the Spanish cavalry. My day is at present thus divided: From eight in the morning till eleven, I exercise three squadrons on foot, which I have selected for the purpose of instruction. From twelve to three, I am occupied in correcting the translation of Dundas on *Cavalry Movements*. From three to five, exercise of a troop on horseback. From seven to nine, academy of all the officers of the three squadrons of instruction at my house, where the principles of cavalry movements are explained to them. Add to all this the visits that I have to make to the commander-in-chief, General Castaños, and the various conferences with Mr, Wellesley and General Graham, and you will, I think, agree with me, that my time is tolerably well taken up.

On Sunday next, the Regency, the Minister of War, Generals Graham and Stuart, General Giron, and all the officers of high rank in the island are to be present at the review of the regiment which I have formed on the new system. The regiment will go through all the principal manoeuvres, and the Government will determine whether the new system is to be adopted or not! Notwithstanding the acknowledged necessity of a system of tactics for the cavalry, and the beauty and goodness of that proposed, I am by no means confident of success. The inspector-general of the cavalry is the declared enemy of my undertaking, and as all recommendations for promotion are made through him, *almost all* the officers of cavalry follow his opinion. Whatever be the result, I have done my duty; and I am perfectly satisfied that, unless a change of system takes place, dishonour and disgrace will ever attend the Spanish cavalry.

In losing the protection of the Duke of Alburquerque, I have, I fear, lost a great support; but be it as it may, nothing would induce me to retain the command of the Spanish cavalry, unless I should be permitted to give it that degree of mobility absolutely necessary for its success in the day of action.

I have entered more into detail than may appear necessary, because if the system of reform be not adopted, I shall request General Castaños to relieve me from this command, and to make me Inspector-General of the troops of the Balearic Islands.

I pray of you to wait upon the Duke of Alburquerque as soon as he comes to town. One of his *aides-de-camp* speaks English very well. I am sure I need not say that anything you can do to serve or to amuse the duke will infinitely oblige me; for no one is better acquainted than yourself with the favours he has conferred on me.

The duke has left the command of this army in consequence of a dispute with the Junta of Cadiz. It was proposed to him by the Regency (when the duke determined to resign his command here) to make him Captain-General of the Balearic Islands! I was to have gone with him as head of his staff. This idea was highly approved of by Mr. Wellesley. The duke was to have full powers to recruit in Spain for the army which he was to form at Majorca and Minorca; and I have no doubt that in less than four months we should have collected 20,000 men. In my humble opinion, this, of all others, was the situation for the duke. At first he thought so himself, but the advice of light and interested men altered his mind, and he determined not to accept it. The embassy was then thought of. It pleased him, and everything was forthwith fixed. The duke has committed a capital error, and of this he will sooner or later be convinced.

(Southey has recorded the sad death of Alburquerque at the Spanish Embassy in London).

To the Same,
Isla de Leon, 26th May, 1810.

As Mr. Wellesley and General Graham have both written to request that I may be made Lieutenant-Colonel in Spain, I am in hopes, notwithstanding the difficulties which at first appear, that the affair may be carried through.' (He was not promoted to a Lieutenant-Colonelcy till the autumn of 1811, but the Lieutenant-Colonelcy was afterwards dated back to 30th May, 1811).

It was settled for me to accompany the duke on his embassy to England; but Mr. Wellesley and General Graham objected to it so strongly, that I was obliged to request General Castaños to state to the duke that it could not be. I still remain in command of the cavalry, and I have every reason to believe that I shall have the honour of introducing a complete new system of tactics for the cavalry of this country. It is incredible the opposition that I have met with, but, thanks to the steady friendship of the duke in the first instance, and subsequently of General Castaños, I am in a fair way of conquering all difficulties. Nothing would enable me to do the Spanish cavalry so much good as clothing, arming, and equipping one corps in the English style.

Mr. Wellesley would send out a complete equipment for 400 hussars, which compose the *corps d'elite* that I have taken from the whole of the cavalry. This corps would serve as a model for clothing, arms, and furniture, and would, I am convinced, induce the Spanish Government to make further contracts in England for the future clothing and arming of their troops.

To the Same.

Isla de Leon, 28th July, 1810.

The enclosed letter for Torrens, I will thank you to seal and forward as soon as you have read it. You will see by its contents my opinion of the present state of affairs. Be assured (but this is entirely *entre nous*) that unless the work at Santi Petri is finished in a proper manner before the French can attack us in force, the island will be lost, and if this unfortunate event should take place, Cadiz must at last fall!

For my own part, as soon as the clothing complete arrives, I shall present the regiment of cavalry that I have formed to the Government; and I may venture to assert that Spain has hitherto possessed no such corps. I have laboured day and night, and I flatter myself that I have succeeded. But as the scale of cavalry in this island is infinitely small, it is my intention to propose to government to raise a corps of two thousand cavalry in Majorca; and I shall endeavour to have the clothing, arms, &c., from Mr. Wellesley.

After using much persuasion to induce Mr. Davis to let his son visit him in the Isla de Leon, he adds:—

He will in me find not only an affectionate uncle, but his father's oldest and best friend. Mrs. W. joins with me in this wish; and I really do think that a few months so employed might be of the greatest utility in his future career, (as a member of Parliament). He might come here with Major Armstrong, who is about to return, and there can be no danger of a warlike nature at present, as it is totally impossible for Buonaparte to attempt anything against this place till he has driven Lord Wellington out of Portugal—an event his Lordship conceives to be far distant.

On the 25th September he writes again to his brother in-law to express his delight at learning that his nephew is coming out, and promises that he shall not enter the service, and also to take good care of him.

To the Same,

Isla. de Leon, 10th November, 1810.

This letter will be delivered to you by Colonel Campbell, who goes to England on the subject of the clothing and appointments of the force to be disciplined, organised, &c. &c. in Majorca by me. I am to have the sole direction of the corps, and to be general, head of the staff, and inspector. It is a great undertaking. Everything is to be created anew; but I trust in God and in my good fortune.

Colonel Campbell is one of my most intimate friends. We have long been in the habit of the greatest intimacy, and I can safely and cordially recommend him to your warmest attentions. I am delighted that Hart is coming. Pray would you choose that he should accompany us to Majorca? I think he might pass a month there pleasantly. He cannot fail to learn Spanish with us. English is hardly ever talked at our house, and Mrs. W. will be happy to give him lessons in her native tongue. He will find an old and intimate friend of his here attached to the Embassy, I mean Mr. Clive.

★★★★★★

Note:—Mr. Hart Davis, junior, General Whittingham's nephew, remained a few years in Parliament, and eventually became Deputy Chairman of the Board of Excise, in which post he established the reputation of great ability and unwearied industry in the public service.

★★★★★★

At the Isla de Leon occurred the first trial of Spanish military organisation on a very small scale. How he laboured at this work, limited as it was to 400 cavalry (officers and men) has been shown in his correspondence with Mr. Davis, his brother-in-law. As to its results, the two subjoined letters will testify:—

Lieut.-General Graham, (afterwards Lord Lynedoch), to Major-
General Whittingham.

Isla de Leon, 10th December, 1810.

My dear General,—Having just heard that you are soon to leave this on an important commission to the Balearic Islands, I am anxious to take this opportunity of testifying my sincere satisfaction at the complete success which has attended your exertions here. I am free to confess that the task appeared to me to be so difficult a one that I much doubted that even your perseverance and skill would have produced the desired effect. For I should have considered it less arduous to have begun with recruits than to instruct on an improved system officers and men who at first probably imagined they required no instruction.

But the readiness and precision with which these squadrons executed every formation, and performed every evolution that can possibly be required of cavalry, convinced me that you had been able to overcome all prejudice, and to bring these squadrons in a very short time into a high state of discipline, that cannot fail to make them a valuable corps. The principle of good instruction and practice is common to both infantry and cavalry; and the advantages resulting from that uniformity must strike forcibly the mind of all military men who give themselves the trouble of thinking on professional points.

But cavalry, above all, requires such a variety of attention that the system of the greatest simplicity must be the best; according to the state of discipline, this arm is formidable to their enemy or dangerous to their friends; and till cavalry has acquired confidence in itself by a thorough knowledge of its powers, by being capable of acting without confusion, one would rather go into action without it.

But I forget myself; for least of all to you can it be necessary to make such reflections.

I am happy to think that you will now have it in your power to exert your talents on a more extensive scale for the benefit of a country and a cause in which our hearts are so warmly engaged. Do not think me vain for thus offering you my tribute of applause. I am merely doing justice to my own feelings.

Believe me ever, my dear General,

Most truly and obediently yours,

Thomas Graham.

★★★★★★

In the British Service, Graham was then a Major-General, and Whittingham only a Major, a fact which renders the tone of deference and respect employed in this letter equally honourable to the modesty of the superior, and to the merits of the subordinate officer.

★★★★★★

The Right Hon. Henry Wellesley to Major-General Whittingham.

Isla de Leon, 16th November, 1810.

Sir,—I cannot avoid expressing to you the satisfaction which I felt at witnessing, this morning, the complete success of your exertions to bring into the field a corps of Spanish cavalry, formed upon the model of a British regiment, and in a perfect state of discipline and efficiency. You may reasonably take to yourself the credit of having introduced into the Spanish cavalry a system of discipline, which, if adopted by the other corps, cannot fail to render them equal, if not superior to the cavalry of the enemy.

The steadiness and temper with which you have resisted all the attempts to defeat this object, and the perseverance and skill which you have manifested in bringing it to perfection, are highly creditable to you, and justify a confident expectation that your efforts will be equally successful in the attainment of a still more important object, which, with a view to the improvement of the Spanish Army, you are now about to undertake.—I have the honour to be, Sir,

Your most obedient, humble servant,

H. Wellesley.

The expectations of Mr. Wellesley were destined to be realised in due time; but in the meantime a great mortification was being prepared by destiny for General Whittingham. But this year closes with a friendly letter from the head of the house of Wellesley:—

Marquis Wellesley to Major-General Whittingham.
(Private.)

Apsley House, 9th December, 1810.

My dear Sir,—I am apprehensive that my silence may have inclined you to suppose that I have not remembered, with sufficient attention, your valuable services at Seville, and my estimation of your talents and character. But I flatter myself that when you reflect on the sudden manner in which I was cast on the turbulent flood of politics in this country, and on the nature of the crisis in which I have been required to act, your indulgence will furnish some excuse for my apparent negligence.

You may be assured that I have used every endeavour to forward every point connected with your most useful plan for raising a corps in Spain, although, from some accident, I have not yet seen Colonel Campbell.

I shall always feel a deep interest in whatever regards your welfare and honour. I hope that you will apprise me at the earliest moment of your wishes on all subjects of importance; and that you will continue to afford me the advantage of your correspondence, and to believe me to be, my dear Sir,

Your faithful friend and obliged humble servant,

Wellesley.

CHAPTER 6

1811

In casting in his lot with the Spanish Army, the great difficulty of General Whittingham had ever been to find good opportunities for distinguishing himself, whilst serving with raw and undisciplined troops under more or less incompetent generals. These premises duly weighed, it may perhaps be considered fortunate that only on one day of his long career has his military conduct been made the subject of hostile criticism, and this not by any official superior—either English or Spanish—but by the pen of an able, eloquent, and gallant, but also prejudiced and partial historian, who himself held a very subordinate position in the Peninsular War, and whose bias against the Spaniards, and against Englishmen who were employed with them, appears to have been indiscriminate and unbounded.

The Battle of Barrosa, fought on March 5, 1811, was certainly an unfortunate day for General Whittingham; but few officers who have seen much service have wholly escaped such days. Even the great hero of the age had had his Seringapatam and his retreat from Burgos. The hero of Barrosa, Graham, also, was not always, though very generally fortunate; but that excellent officer never himself attributed any blame to General Whittingham, much as he found fault with the commander-in-chief, La Pena.

The reader must be reminded, that to this day the Battle of Barrosa is a difficult and complex question to all who take the trouble impartially to study its details in the works of the various historians who have undertaken to describe them. Putting the Spaniards aside, do Frenchmen and Englishmen agree? Is Napier corroborated by Marshal Victor's dispatch, or by Thiers's history of the French empire? But, what is still more important, do the English themselves agree together? Is not the account of the patient and pains-taking civilian,

Southey, diametrically opposed to that of his impetuous military rival? If few persons of judgment will deny that the work of the military historian is a far more brilliant production than that of the civilian; yet on the other hand few will maintain that Napier was as impartial or as desirous to do justice to all parties and to all nations as was the historian Southey.

The latter neither felt personal hatred against the Spaniards, nor could be jealous of those military agents attached to the Spaniards, who obtained higher, but temporary and local rank. This temporary rank they obtained in return for the sacrifice of serving with wretched and undisciplined troops, instead of fighting by the side of those British soldiers who so often, by their valour and stubbornness, more than make up for the ignorance and incompetency of their leaders.

General Graham won the Battle of Barrosa by suddenly taking the command, and setting aside the Spanish commander-in-chief under whom he had himself agreed to serve. The partial success—as to results at all events—that followed the battle, and the prestige of a victory (then much wanted, after the retreat of the army to Portugal), caused the military insubordination of Graham to be converted into a patriotic virtue. But General Whittingham was on that day in a different position from that of Graham, who was only temporarily under La Pena's command, and that by his own desire. Whittingham was under the immediate orders of La Peña as a Spanish general officer, and he was also acting as a British military agent, whose business it was to keep on good terms with the Spanish commander-in-chief. By every principle of duty and policy, and conscience, therefore, he was bound to obey La Peña, as his own commander, as well as the commander of the allied armies. On the other hand, he had every reason to love and respect Graham, who had lately recommended him for promotion, and praised his military talents in a most flattering letter.

General Whittingham ever maintained that he was, and very naturally so, most anxious to be allowed, and had requested in the first instance, to join himself to, Graham's division; but he was refused. But what impartial person could blame La Peña for not consenting to deprive himself of the immediate aid of those 400 Spanish horsemen, who had been trained to unusual excellence of drill and discipline, by the voluntary confession of Graham himself?

Certainly, it was most unfortunate, that the chief command had not originally been invested in General Graham. But La Peña was the senior, and would not waive his rights; for it had been agreed between

Lord Wellington and the Spanish Government that when English and Spanish forces were united, the senior officer of either nation should command the whole army.

From the false statements of the French Marshal Victor (as narrated by Southey) that the English had purposely exposed the Spaniards to the first attack, it does not necessarily follow that the first demonstration of the French was not directed at La Peña's advanced guard. Victor may have been right in his facts, though wrong as to the motives he suggested.

General Graham imputed no blame to 'General Whittingham,' whom he in his dispatch correctly names by his Spanish rank; and who, whilst reserving for La Pena the official report of his proceedings as commander of the Spanish advanced guard, appears to have communicated verbally to Graham after the action the reason why he had been prevented joining him in time with his cavalry. In his dispatch to Lord Wellington, General Graham writes:

> I understand, too, from General Whittingham, that with three squadrons of cavalry, he kept in check a corps of infantry and cavalry that attempted to turn the Barrosa height by the sea. One squadron of the 2nd Hussars, King's German Legion, under Captain Busche, and directed by Lieutenant-Colonel Ponsonby (both had been attached to the Spanish cavalry), joined in time to make a brilliant and most successful charge against a squadron of French dragoons, which were entirely routed.

Unfortunately, General Whittingham, not being under General Graham's orders, did not send him a copy of his dispatch to General La Pena. If he had done so, Graham would have seen that the Spanish advanced guard, which checked the threatened attack of the French on the right, consisted of *infantry as well as cavalry*, and that General Whittingham was not that day a simple commander of cavalry. To explain to General Graham why the Spanish cavalry had not joined him, was of course the only object of General Whittingham 's communication to that officer. It was to his own general, the commander-in-chief, that he had to send the full details of his proceedings. This report he wrote in Spanish with the usual forms employed by Spanish officers.

Of this document he, fortunately (the day after writing it), sent a copy in the original language to his beloved brother-in-law, who was himself a good Spanish scholar. Finally, this document only a few months back (with the rest of Sir Samford Whittingham's long packed-away papers), reached the editor's hands. It had never been seen by Sir Samford since March 8th, 1811, when he dispatched it to his brother-in-law, and consequently, when twenty-two years later he found himself, whilst in India, unexpectedly attacked in Napier's history, he had only his memory to rely on for his defence. That memory, ordinarily good, the inscrutable wisdom of providence permitted on this occasion to be materially, to his own great discomfiture, defective; the sad consequence of which was that the injured veteran was deprived of his invulnerable arms—like Patrocles in his combat with Hector. The box of papers, left at the bottom of a cellar in the public offices of London, was not available to refresh the memory of the veteran wearing away his life in a tropical climate, in the unceasing service of his country!

The following is a translation of Major-General Whittingham's Official Report to the Commander-in-Chief La Pena, of his share in the Battle of Barrosa. (The editor has placed in *italics* those portions of the Report to which he desires to draw the special attention of the reader, see end of chapter for the original Spanish copy of the Report, as sent to Mr. Davis):—

Excellency,—At two o'clock p.m. of the 5th instant I received orders from your Excellency to take post, with three squadrons, and two troops of cavalry, *and* 1,350 *infantry*, commanded by Brigadier Don Antonia Begines de los Rios, at the camp of the Cerro del Puerco. Consequently, I was proceeding to take up my position by joining the infantry, when Colonel Don Louis Michelena informed me that troops were in sight, which appeared to be enemies, by their marching towards us. I hastened the junction (*with the infantry*) and reconnoitred the enemy, who marched in two strong columns; having with them a battalion of light infantry, which formed their vanguard. The one marched directly on my position; the other extending itself to its left for the purpose of outflanking us.

I ordered the infantry to form in squares, and placed the cavalry on the left in echelon, to maintain the position. At this moment I received *your Excellency's order to fall back on the main body of the army*; and I discovered, besides the two hostile columns already mentioned, another stronger one approaching rapidly on my left to occupy the pine wood, between my camp and that of the main army, the only passage by which I could accomplish your Excellency s latest instruction to fall back. The enemy's force was at least quadruple that which I had with me. I determined, *in conformity with the said order*, that the infantry should commence a retreat covered by the cavalry.

The English battalion under the command of Colonel Brown opened the march, followed by the Spanish troops. I took the detachment of Royal carabineers, and one troop of English hussars, (hussars of the German Legion, in the pay of England), with me, to cover the right flank of the line of march in the retreat—interposed between the right flank and the enemy—continuing the retreat up to taking possession of the wood, where I immediately posted Don Juan de la Cruz; ordering him to cover the right flank of the position, which the enemy were already endeavouring to surround.

In compliance with my orders, Major Busche with the English hussars, Lieutenant-Colonels Don Francisco Ramonet, and Don Francisco Serrano with a squadron of grenadiers, and, of the same rank, Don Santiago Wall with two troops under his command, and some guerilla infantry, maintained themselves *till the retreat of the infantry was accomplished, of all the baggage of the army, and of the two pieces of artillery;* which up to the last moment of being sharply attacked, had maintained unflinchingly a very well-directed and vigorous fire upon the enemy.

★★★★★★

Note:—To represent as a mere colonel of a small body of horse a general, who had infantry, artillery, and baggage under his orders *as well as cavalry*, was assuredly a wonderful specimen of ignorance in the popular historian. If, denying him the Spanish rank in which he was then employed, the historian intended to call him by his English rank, he was equally wrong. Whittingham was not even *Lieutenant-Colonel*, but only Major, at the Battle of Barrosa, yet Napier styles him 'Colonel.'

★★★★★★

The cavalry covered the retreat perfectly and in good order, notwithstanding the continued skirmishing, which the enemy's cavalry kept up, throughout the whole of their advance, closing their ranks as they debouched, and stronger by one-third, against ours, separated at that time at several points.''At this moment, I perceived the corps of General Graham issuing out of the wood, and moving towards their former position on the heights now occupied by the enemy. It would be difficult to give a just idea of the impetuosity with which the common enemy was driven back from all the heights by the English bayonets; the same enemy who had charged us with such insolence and confidence as if he had already gained the victory. His force was double that of the English; but the victory, though costly, was complete, and decided by the point of the bayonet.

The fruits of this distinguished day would have been gathered beyond the principal object, if the enemy—who in their precipitate retreat abandoned their wounded of all ranks and descriptions, three guns and two ammunition waggons—*had been charged in flank and threatened in the rear.* (The officer who ever considered obedience as the first and last duty of a soldier, could, nevertheless, not resist on this occasion hinting to the commander-in-chief how, instead of ordering his advanced-guard to retire, he might have advanced himself with the main body and completed the victory).

A squadron of English hussars, which were under my command attacked the guard of Marshal Victor, routed and dispersed it. This squadron of English hussars, jointly with the one already mentioned of the Spanish grenadiers, under the command of Baron Carondelet, and the two troops of Don Santiago Wall, covered the right wing; and supported by the troops of brigadiers Don Antonio Begines, and Don Juan de la Cruz, prevented the enemy, by their gallant conduct and manoeuvres, from surrounding us along the shore, as they had twice attempted to do. These two troops behaved with gallantry; retiring from and advancing upon the enemy, at the right moment, as equally did the detachment of the Royal carabineers. All the cavalry in short brilliantly fulfilled their duty.

The enemy, after finding himself repulsed from the heights, commenced his retreat in an orderly manner, covered by his cavalry. This was the moment in which I proposed to myself to collect together and act on the offensive with my 400 horse, which I had under my orders.

★★★★★★

Note:—This corps, which he had himself trained and organised, to the admiration of General Graham and Mr. Wellesley, was under his *special orders;* though as General (as his dispatch clearly proves) he on that day commanded, under La Pena, the whole Spanish advanced-guard—amounting, apparently, to about 2,500 of all ranks—a small force against such an enemy; but still no *Colonel's* command.

★★★★★★

With this view I had desired Ramonet and Serrano, in union with Wall, to observe and to co-operate with the movements of the English hussars and the Royal carabineers, which I kept with me; when, upon the right of the whole line, there appeared a column of infantry of about 500 men, preceded by a party of horse, and moving as if to turn our flank. It was indispensable to manoeuvre so as to keep them under observation, whilst a sergeant and six men of the squadron of carabineers reconnoitred them; *and the opportunity thus escaped me of charging*, with the whole of my disposable cavalry, the enemy who was retiring rapidly.

At the head of the English hussars I followed them, resolving to attack a body of cavalry, posted at the side of a lake, which covered their left flank. But on my advance, I discovered that the whole of the enemy's infantry were collected on their right, supported by the artillery, and covered by the pine wood; a situation which did not allow of a partial or isolated movement against the above mentioned force, so well protected.

In this situation, two pieces of artillery were placed in position by General Graham which by a well-directed fire obliged the enemy to continue his retreat between the lake and the pine wood in the direction of Chiclava. I cannot do less than entreat your Excellency to make known to their Serene Highnesses, (the Regency of Spain), the particular merit evinced in all circumstances, by the commanders, officers, and troops in this action, without being able to select or individualise any to your Excellency, where all have emulously and honourably fulfilled their duty, on this happy occasion thus offered to them, of showing themselves to the nation as its defenders.

God preserve your Excellency.

His Excellency Major-General
Señor Don Santiago Whittingham,
to his Excellency Lieutenant-General
Señor Don Manuel de la Pena, General-in-Chief.
Camp of Cerro del Puerco, 7th March, 1811.

This dispatch demonstrates that notwithstanding La Pena's orders to retire, it was simply an accident over which he had no control, that delayed the advance of General Whittingham, after the successful charge of the British under General Graham.

That some of these details, as well as those regarding his rank and position, should have escaped his recollection after about a quarter of a century had elapsed—a period passed in nearly ceaseless laborious duties and occupations—is less extraordinary than that an historian sitting at home at ease should have made so many mistakes, and egregiously misrepresented the proceedings of that small part of La Peña's army which took part in the Battle of Barrosa.

As usual, so on this occasion, General Whittingham was with the advanced guard of the Spanish army. The fatiguing marches which the Spaniards had undergone, may have palliated the tardiness of La Pena, who had also perhaps a just right to complain of the disobedience of his subordinate General Graham. But certainly La Pena was not in sight of the action that day, and interfered only to order the retreat of his advanced guard, on to the main body.

It may be that Southey is too severe on Graham, under the circumstances; but at least he appears to have discussed the question with studied calmness and impartiality, as well as with a fullness of details, which may have exhausted the patience of some of his readers. But most assuredly if truth and accuracy are the most important points in a history, in that respect Southey has borne the palm from his military rival, even though it is probable that some errors also exist in his painstaking accounts of Barrosa.

The painful uncertainty of history, of which many examples have been furnished in the present century, was never more patent than in the conflicting testimonies, regarding that battle, in acting in which, General Whittingham appears to have done his duty under most trying circumstances. That he was indignant with the Spanish commander-in-chief, and that all his sympathies were with General Graham, is proved by the following private letter written three days after the action, more plainly than etiquette would admit of in the official dispatch:—

Major-General Whittingham to his Brother-in-law.
Isla de Leon, 8th March, 1811.
My dear Davis,—The time is so short, that I have scarcely time to send you a copy of my report, (he means, scarcely time to

do more than send a copy of his report), to the Commander-in-Chief La Peña of the part I had in the action of the 5th. If the English had been supported by an advance movement of the Spaniards in the wood, the siege of Cadiz must have been raised, and the whole business would have been most glorious. As it is, the British Army gained a most complete victory against double the number of French, and covered themselves with immortal honour.

The loss of the English exceeds 1,200 men, and after such a specimen of Spanish generalship, it is not to be believed that General Graham will again engage in offensive operations, unless he has the command-in-chief. The Spaniards still keep the bridge of boats upon the river, and talk of undertaking offensive operations alone. As everything relative to my expedition to Majorca is settled, I shall give up my command here, as soon as they may choose to take away the bridge of Santi Petri. Colonel Macdonald will do me the favour to deliver this letter. He is Adjutant-General of the British forces here, and I beg to recommend him to your particular attentions. My best love to Mrs. Davis and all the family, as well as to James Whittingham and his family, and believe me,

Ever yours most affectionately,

Samford Whittingham.

If Napier had delayed his history till after the publication of the *Wellington Dispatches* (since the duke refused him access to them), he would probably have done more justice to General Whittingham, of whom so much honourable mention is therein made. Above all he would have read the duke's all-comprehensive testimony to the merits and services of Sir Samford Whittingham, from the commencement to the close of the Peninsular War. Three years after Barrosa the duke wrote in favour of the subject of this *Memoir* that he had 'served most *zealously* and *gallantly*, from the commencement of the war in the Peninsula, and I have had *every* reason to be satisfied with his conduct, in *every* situation in which he has been placed.'

Let the reader mark the two *everys* employed by one who weighed his words; and was not Barrosa one of the situations in which the subject of this *Memoir* had been placed?

A month later the Premier, Mr. Perceval, thanked Mr. Davis for a copy of General Whittingham's translation of Dundas's *Cavalry Tactics*, and expressed the 'most sanguine hopes of the benefit the Spanish cause will derive from his being entrusted with the formation of a considerable body of their army.'

But the following letter must have given General Whittingham greater pleasure than all the other acknowledgements he received of the copies of his military Spanish publication:—

H.R.H. the Duke of Kent to R. H. Davis, Esq. M.P.

Kensington Palace, 16th April, 1811.

The Duke of Kent does himself the honour of acknowledging Mr. Hart Davis's polite note of yesterday, enclosing a copy of General Whittingham's translation of Dundas's *Cavalry Tactics* into Spanish; and the duke begs to assure Mr. Davis that he values most highly the general's attention, as well as the very handsome manner in which Mr. Davis has become the instrument of imparting it.

The duke cannot resist, upon this opportunity, paying what he considers a just tribute to the merits of General Whittingham, by observing that he views him as a high ornament to the British service, and a most efficient aid in the prosecution of the Spanish cause. (The editor deems such spontaneous praise from the excellent father of Her Gracious Majesty, worthy of being placed in italics).

Hart Davis, Esq.

At this time, as the *Wellington Dispatches* testify, General Castaños, who had been appointed a member of the Regency, as well as commander-in-chief, was fast gaining the confidence and friendship of Lord Wellington, to the great delight of his former *aide-de-camp*, who was now starting to undertake the very difficult task of raising and organising a large Spanish division, with at first one only other British officer to assist him, and to the very last obtaining little aid from any but Spanish officers trained by himself.

'Exmo. Señor,—Como á las dos de la tarde del dia 5 del corriente recibí órden de V. E. para quedarme con tres escuadrones y dos compañias de Caballeria, y mil trecientos cincuenta hombres de la Infanteria que mandaba el Brigadier Don Antonio Begines de los Rios en el campo del Cerro del Puerco, en consecuencia iba á tomar posicion, uniendome á la Infanteria, cuando me avisó el Coronel Don Luis Michelena que se veian tropas que parecian enemigas por su marcha acia nosotros. Aceleré la reunion, y reconocí al enemigo que marchaba en dos fuertes columnas, llevando un batallon de tropas ligeras á su vanguardia; la una marchaba directamente á mi posicion, y la otra se prolongaba por su izquierda para envolverme. Mandé formar la Infanteria en cuadros, y la Caballeria al flanco izquierdo en escalones para sostener el punto. Á este tiempo recibí la órden de V. E. para replegarme sobre el grueso del exercito, y descubrí ademas de las dos columnas enemigas ya dichas, otra mas fuerte que venia acceleradamente sobre mi izquierda para interponerse al Pinar que mediaba entre mi campo y el del exercito, unico paso que me quedaba para cumplir, replegandome, la última resolucion de V. E. Las fuerzas enemigas eran quadruplas cuando menos á las que yo tenia.

'Determiné, en virtud de dicha órden, que la Infanteria emprendiese su retirada cubierta por la Caballeria. El batallon Ingles, á las órdenes del Coronel Bran, rompió la marcha, y en seguida las tropas Españolas. Llevé conmigo el destacamento de Carabineros Reales, y una compañia de Husares Ingleses para cubrir el flanco derecho de la linea de marcha retrograda, y interponiendome entre esta y el enemigo, continuando la retirada hasta tomar posesion del bosque, donde inmediatamente coloqué al Brigadier Don Juan de la Cruz, encargandole cubriese el flanco derecho de la posicion que el enemigo ya intentaba envolver. En cumplimiento á mis instrucciones, el Mayor Bush, con los Husares Ingleses, los Tenientes Coroneles Don Francisco Ramonet y Don Francisco Serrano con un escuadron de Granaderos, y él de la misma clase Don Santiago Wall con dos compañias del de su mando, se sostuvieron con algunas guerillas de Infanteria, hasta que se retiró la Infanteria, todo el bagage del exercito, y las dos piezas de artilleria, que hasta el momento de ser atacadas vivamente, hicieron firmes un muy acertado y vigoroso fuego sobre los enemigos.

'La Caballeria cubrió perfectamente la retirada, y en buen órden, no obstante las continuadas escaramuzas que hizo la enemiga en todo su avance, reunida desde que se avistó, y mas fuerte en una tercera parte contra la nuestra, repartida entónces en varios puntos.

'En este momento divisé el cuerpo del General Graham, que salia del bosque, dirigiendose sobre su antigua posicion de las alturas ya ocupadas por el enemigo. Dificil seria dar una justa idea del impetu con que fué arrojado de todas ellas por las bayonetas Inglesas el enemigo comun que venia cargandonos con tanto orgullo y confianza, como si tuviera ya la victoria conseguida. Su fuerza era doble de la Inglesa, pero la victoria, aunque costosa, fué completa, y decidida por el acero de las bayonetas. Se hubiera recogido el fruto de esta señalada jornada, aun mas allá del objeto principal, si los enemigos en su precipitada retirada—pues abandonaron allí sus heridos de todas clases y caracter, tres piezas, y dos carros de municiones—hubieran sido cargados de flanco, ó amenazados por la retaguardia.

'Un escuadron de Husares Ingleses que estaba á mi mando atacó al de Guardia del Mariscal Victor, lo destrozo, y dispersó completamente. Dicho escuadron de Husares Ingleses, juntamente con el ya indicado de Granaderos Españoles al mando del Baron de Carondelet, y las dos compañias de Don Santiago Wall, cubrían el ala derecha, y sostenidos por las tropas de los Brigadieres Don Antonio Begines y Don Juan de la Cruz, evitaron por su bizarra conducta, y maniobras, que el enemigo nos envolviese por la playa como lo intentó por dos veces. Aquellas dos compañias se portaron con bizarria, retirandose y avanzando oportunamente sobre el enemigo, como igualmente el destacamento de Carabineros Reales. Toda la Caballeria en fin cumplió brillantemente con su deber.

'El exercito enemigo, despues de verse rechazado de las alturas, emprendió su retirada en órden, cubierto por su Caballeria. Este fué el instante en que me prometí reunir y obrar ofensivamente con los cuatrocientos caballos que tenia á mi disposicion, para lo que avisé á Ramonet, y Serrano, que en union con Wall observasen y cooperasen á los movimientos de los Husares Ingleses y Carabineros Reales que yo llevaba conmigo, cuando se dejó ver sobre la derecha de toda la linea una columna de Infanteria como de quinientos hombres, precedida de una partida de Caballeria, y moviendose como para ganar nuestra espalda. Fué indispensable maniobrar en su observacion mientras la reconocia un sargento y seis hombres del escuadron de Granaderos, y se me escapó la ocasion de cargar al enemigo, que se retiraba de priesa, con toda mi Caballeria disponible. Á la cabeza de los Husares Ingleses seguí sobre el, y resolví atacar un trozo de Caballeria situado al lado de una laguna, que cubria su flanco izquierdo; mas en mi marcha descubrí que toda la Infanteria enemiga se habia colocado á su derecha, y sostenido por su Artilleria, apoyandose en el Pinar, situacion que no permitia un movimiento aislado ó parcial contra dicho trozo protegido tan inmediatamente. En esta situacion se colocaron en posicion por el General Graham dos piezas de artilleria, que tirando con acierto, obligaron al enemigo á continuar su retirada entre la laguna y el Pinar con direccion á Chiclana.

'No puedo menos de suplicar á V. E. haga presente á S. A. S. el particular merito á toda prueba que han contrahido todos los gefes, oficiales, y tropa que en esta accion se hallaron á mis órdenes, sin resolverme á individualizar ante V. E. á ninguno, pues todos á porfía llenaron cumplido, y honrosamente, con su deber, al paso que les llegaba la ocasion feliz de mostrar á la nacion que son sus defensores.

'Dios guarde á V. E. muchos años.

'Campo del Cerro de los Martires, 7 de Marzo de 1811.

'Exmo. Señor Don Santiago Whittingham.

'Exmo. Señor Don Manuel de la Peña,
    General en Gefe.'

Chapter 7

1811—Continued

The arduous task undertaken by General Whittingham—to raise, organise, pay, clothe, feed, drill, and instruct a large division of Spanish troops in Majorca, is now partly represented by a large manuscript folio volume, containing the written copies of the correspondence which such a Herculean task necessarily occasioned. The word partly is used advisedly, as much of his personal active military exertions were never represented on paper. His financial duties especially weighed on his mind; no English paymaster having been appointed to assist him, whilst in the Spanish paymasters he could not feel complete confidence. Colonel Patrick Campbell, indeed, of the Majorca division, acted voluntarily as his deputy paymaster; but the entire responsibility rested with himself, and became the greatest, as it was the most unjustifiable, of the burdens he had to bear in the island.

The chief advantage of having a deputy arose from the fact that the actual money did not pass through the general's hands, though disbursed by his orders; and this arrangement, without lessening the legal, of course diminished his moral responsibility; which rested chiefly with Colonel Campbell, who had charge of the monies.

It is of course but a small fraction of his voluminous Majorcan correspondence, that will now be laid before the reader; but sufficient to show the nature and extent of his task.

The Right Hon. Henry Wellesley to Major-General
Whittingham.

Cadiz, 8th June, 1811.

Sir,—Upon your arrival at Gibraltar, you are to consider this letter as sufficient authority for you to draw from that place, on His Majesty's Treasury in London, for one hundred and fifty thousand dollars.

I am, with much respect. Sir, your most obedient and humble servant,

Henry Wellesley.

On June 13th, 1811, General Whittingham landed at Gibraltar. When three years earlier he had first landed on the rock, as Captain Whittingham, kind and courteously had he been received by Sir Hew Dalrymple. This time it was different. The pompous Governor was difficult of access, and the new arrival was anxious to arrange without loss of time, the cashing of his Treasury order, and to proceed on his mission to Majorca.

He, therefore, armed with the above-mentioned authority, proceeded to negotiate with the merchants of Gibraltar; Mr. Wellesley not having authorised him to consult anyone whatever, and having limited his powers as to rate of exchange, so that the utmost secrecy was necessary, in order to raise the money on the required terms.

But the governor discovering the negotiations, and more mindful of his own dignity than of the efficiency of the public service, flew into a violent passion, and commencing a most harsh correspondence with the unintentional offender, ended by ordering him to proceed 'on his mission with the least possible delay.' The matter was reported on both sides to their respective superiors, and entailed plenty of correspondence; but apparently the various departments concerned never came to any positive understanding on the matter. At all events it does not appear that it was ever satisfactorily settled. General Whittingham, however, effected his business in a few days.

Before leaving Gibraltar he wrote to Mr. Wellesley and to Marquis Wellesley; to the former, a justification of his conduct, as his official superior, to the latter an account of the affair as to his friend and protector, and to his brother-in-law he of course explained everything. Assuredly this dispute was forced upon him, without any fault of his own; as he was denied all opportunity for amicable explanation. The details of his financial proceedings at Gibraltar are recorded with the accuracy of a counting-house. He succeeded so well that government made a better bargain than could have been made at Cadiz, all which he explained to Mr. Wellesley for the information of the Treasury.

On the 28th June, he landed at Palma in Majorca, where he immediately hired a house for his stores, and commenced disembarking the clothing and arms which had arrived for the use of the army of reserve about to be raised in the island; of all which proceedings

Mr. Wellesley and Admiral Sir Charles Cotton were duly informed in clear and ample details. Long letters follow on the statistical state of the island and of its intricate politics, and regarding the French leanings of some of the inhabitants.

A serious danger was the number of French prisoners in the Balearic Islands, whom, especially the officers, it was difficult to keep from intriguing with the inhabitants, on whose loyalty the retreat of Lord Wellington to Portugal had had a bad effect. Many of the first families in Majorca were more than suspected of conspiring with the French officers on parole with a view to a revolution in the interest of Napoleon.

In communicating these and other facts to Admiral Sir Edward Pellew, Bart., (afterwards the celebrated Viscount Exmouth), on the 14th July, 1811, General Whittingham adds, amongst his postscripts, this curious sentence:

I should think it would be highly advisable to remove the French officers, at least, from this place to Mahon for the present, and that without losing a moment's time. My information comes from the Church, *through means which they alone possess*, and therefore cannot be doubted.

Amongst the prisoners were some Germans, who had only reluctantly served with the French, and these after some correspondence, General Whittingham was allowed to enlist into his Majorca division; and they were found to be a valuable acquisition.

On the 13th July he reported his arrival and proceedings to Marquis Wellesley, who it appears had used his influence with Ministers in England to cause the adoption of General Whittingham's plans of raising troops in Majorca. With the Spanish authorities he corresponded in their own language, as his Majorca letter-book testifies.

But of all his worries and misfortunes in Majorca (and their name was legion) the greatest was undoubtedly the fact that Don Gregorio Cuesta (the man whose stupid obstinacy, dislike of the English, and utter incompetency. General Whittingham had exposed and denounced to Mr. Hookham Frere, before the arrival in Spain of Sir Arthur Wellesley) was at this time, Captain-General of the Balearic Islands, with full and unlimited powers! Now that he could no longer worry the hero of the age he vented his malice on the British officer now serving as a Major-General in the province he commanded as Captain-General. It is very probable, also, that he was not wholly unaware of how the friend of Alburquerque had formerly thought, spoken, and written of Cuesta's jealousies and incapacity, and that he was glad of an opportunity of revenging himself. But of Cuesta more hereafter.

Major-General Whittingham to Colonel Torrens. (Military Secretary to H.R.H. the Duke of York, afterwards Sir Henry Torrens, who died as Adjutant-General at the Horse-Guards in 1828).

Palm 5th July, 1811.

My dear Torrens,—I hasten to inform you of my arrival here, and to assure you that I shall lose no opportunity of giving you an exact account of everything that occurs, and particularly relative to this army of reserve. In the meantime, I must inform you that your friend. Captain Clarke, having gone as a volunteer with General Blake to Estremadura, it was not in my power to take him with me when I left Cadiz; but I sent him a message by Lord William Russell, (elder brother of Earl Russell, afterwards Major-General, and in 1836 Envoy at Berlin), desiring him to join me as soon as possible, and offering him a troop of Hussars. . . .

The unfortunate loss of Tarragona has deprived me of 200 Catalans, who were upon the point of being sent here; but the number will be easily made up in Valencia and Murcia. I am extremely anxious to organise a few battalions, as the force at present on the island is so very small that we cannot by any means be considered in a state of security. We have in the island of Cabrera, 4,000 prisoners; a considerable part of them Germans from Westphalia and Hesse Cassel, and consequently good soldiers, and not attached to French principles. If I had the power of selecting, I could get some excellent recruits. There are also eighty officers prisoners, belonging to these men in this island, and it certainly would be very much for the good of the service that they should be removed elsewhere without loss of time, as they are daily forming to themselves an interest with the inhabitants.

I remain, &c.,

Samford Whittingham.

Major-General Whittingham to the Right Hon. Henry

Wellesley.
(Extract.)

Palma, 1st August, 1811.

I have the honour to enclose a copy of my letter of this day's date to Mr. Bardaxi, (member of the *Junta*, well-disposed to the English, the enclosures are all in Spanish, in which language he carried on his correspondence with all the Spanish authorities since his arrival in the country, as he wrote and spoke it as fluently as English), being also a copy of that which I have written to the Minister of War, relative to certain points of service, which if they are not finally and satisfactorily settled, must lead to the most unpleasant disputes between myself and General Cuesta.

You will have the goodness to observe that I rest my argument upon the Spanish *ordenanza*, which provide, that whenever a reunion of troops be ordered in any province of the monarchy, and a general appointed to command them, all military command of these troops is vested in him, and the captain-general of the province has only to direct with regard to the civil jurisdiction, destination of quarters, &c.

I have already experienced a sufficient degree of opposition from General Cuesta to alarm me at least for the future; and I am, therefore, extremely anxious, that by a complete and total separation of command, every possible disagreement should be avoided. . .

The conscription and war contribution may meet with those obstacles which originate in intrigue; but I am satisfied that they may, as far as concerns the people, be carried into effect without difficulty or danger.

I beg to call your attention in the most earnest manner to the settling of the points of service mentioned in the enclosed letter; as I am convinced that there can be no other way of avoiding disputes which must inevitably in the end ruin the plan altogether.

To prove what difficulties General Whittingham had to contend with in his dealings with General Cuesta, Lord Wellington's remark to Mr. Wellesley in his dispatch of the 29th August, 1811, is worthy of record; *viz.* 'I am quite convinced that the majority of the officers of the Spanish army would prefer submitting to the French, to allowing us to have anything to say to their troops.' (*Wellington Dispatches*, vol. viii.).

On the 23rd August, 1811, General Whittingham dispatched a letter, containing four foolscap pages, to Mr. Wellesley; sending on the same day a similar letter to Marquis Wellesley in London, and a copy besides to his brother-in-law. It was a brief treatise on the Island of Majorca, under three distinct points of view. First, as to its intrinsic value. Secondly, as to the security it affords Port Mahon. Thirdly, as to the best means of deriving from it every advantage, with the least possible expense. At that time, as we have seen, Lord Wellington attached great importance to the possession of the Balearic Islands. But the interest of this subject having wholly passed away, it is unnecessary to make any extracts from this document.

On the 20th September, in a friendly letter to the naval officer then at Palma, the Honourable Captain Blackwood, he rejoices at the departure of the French prisoners, whose presence and machinations had given him so much trouble; adding:

The friends of the good cause hold up their heads and begin to fancy themselves out of danger; and, on the other hand, the French party are become circumspect and silent.

After alluding to some consular intrigues, he adds:

I am sorry to inform you that the Captain-General Cuesta has taken possession, for his own riding, of the horse which I intended for you. I am not surprised, though the enemy was, at your having taken up an anchorage at Hare's Bay. Sir Edward Pellew's character is too well known to allow of a supposition that he would leave anything undone which could be done. . . .

On the 20th September he writes to Admiral Sir Edward Pellew, amongst other matters, as follows:

I cannot help expressing how much service it would be rendering the division, if you could possibly allow the *Guadalope*, or any other small vessel, to go to Oran, to take the money for the purchase of the barley, and to bring the vessel loaded with that grain. (Thus he acted as the commissary, as well as the paymaster of the division which he had to *raise, organise, discipline, instruct, and command*). The *Junta* superior of this island has positively refused to provide me either with barley or straw. And, although I conceive that their conduct will not be sanctioned by the Regency, yet, as it is impossible to wait in these cases for distant decision, I have directed a person of confidence at Oran to buy, for the use of this army, 7,000 *fanegas* of barley. But I am totally without the means of bringing barley here, or of sending him the money which he must have advanced for the purpose. I enclose a fresh return of the force under my command, which you will see is gradually increasing.

It is quite impossible to give in this work an adequate idea of the labours and difficulties which General Whittingham had to contend with in Majorca. Their contemplation fills the editor's mind with astonishment, that such a burden of responsibility, care, labour, and ceaseless annoyance, should have been not only endured with temper and patience, but carried out to a triumphant conclusion, by an almost solitary Englishman in the midst of half-civilised Spaniards.

Colonel Torrens, Military Secretary, to Mr. Davis.
(Extract.)

Horse-Guards, 22nd September, 1811.

My dear Davis,—I return you the interesting papers enclosed to me in your letter of the 20th instant; and I am most thankful to you for the perusal of them.

After alluding to the interesting command now held by Whittingham, he adds:

He will have many difficulties to encounter; but I know no person so well calculated to overcome them. (This letter is written on the back of the docket enclosing the returned papers).

On the 1st October, General Whittingham wrote a long letter to Lieutenant-Colonel Torrens, detailing his proceedings in the raising and organisation of his division; a few extracts from which may be interesting:—

I expect, in a short time, 300 horses from the coast of Africa. The requisition in this island will give me at least 200 more; and the officer employed on that service in Sardinia, informs me that he can purchase for me on this island from 600 to 700 more, as soon as I furnish him with the pecuniary means. So that, as to mounting my two regiments of cavalry, I am under no alarm, and you may be assured that they shall not be wanting as to discipline. Still, however, there is always a shade of doubt upon my mind; inasmuch as they will be wholly composed of new levies, and, consequently, at first they must be incapable of comprehending the full extent of their own powers. Even the oldest and best of the Spanish troops never fight by themselves as they do in the presence of the British. How much stronger, therefore, must this necessity be, when the troops in question have never been under fire! (The concluding sentence of this letter refers to a most gallant Irishman, doomed to an early but glorious death). If it be possible, I should much wish that Captain O'Reilly, of the 13th Foot, should be sent to me with leave to serve in the Spanish Army, I knew him well at High Wycombe, and he would be particularly useful to me in the Quartermaster-General's Department.

On the same day (the 1st October) General Whittingham describes to his brother-in-law, his joy at the news of his promotion to Lieutenant-Colonel, which had evidently taken place only in August; but was afterwards backdated to 30th May, 1811.

On the 7th October, General Whittingham writes to Mr. Davis a long letter regarding the struggles carried on in Majorca, between the patriotic party, anxious in order to further the organisation of the division of troops, to increase General Whittingham's powers, by causing him to be made Governor of Majorca; and the opposite faction, which from jealousy of the Englishman, and from love of intrigue, violently opposed the project. To his brother-in-law the general writes:—

In respect to the Government of Majorca, it is to me a matter of perfect indifference, although the person actually holding that employment is certainly a very improper man [to hold it], from his too well-known attachment to French principles. But I should wish to be acquainted with the sentiments of His Majesty's Ministers on that head, in case General Valdes, who is now appointed Captain-General of the Balearic Islands, (either this was a false report, or the appointment was afterwards cancelled), instead of Cuesta, should press the employment upon me.

Enclosed in this letter to Mr. Davis was a copy of the Report of a certain very intelligent Captain of the Spanish Royal Navy, who had been sent by General Whittingham, on a special mission, to Cadiz, to defend his interest and the good of the cause, with Mr. Wellesley and the Spanish Junta. As a graphic description of some of the difficulties in the way of carrying out the Majorca scheme, and also as a picture of

Spanish intrigue, it may amuse some readers, and is therefore inserted here:—

Remarks and Occurrences in a Voyage from Majorca to Cadiz and back, by A. Briarly, Captain Spanish Navy, 1811.
(Extract.)

General Whittingham observed to me on the 22nd July, that a foul plot or conspiracy has been entered into by a French party in this island, for the purpose of giving it up to the French; and that they were in communication with the French officers, who were prisoners in the Castle of Belver. He at the same time urged the necessity of my going to Cadiz with the dispatches; as the Junta had applied to him for an officer of confidence. He also observed that there were many things of great consequence, necessary for the use of his division, which I could at the same time apply for.

I consented to go; but there was no vessel of any kind except a schooner of eight guns, which had been taken whilst smuggling a cargo of tobacco. This vessel lay empty at the quay; and was offered to me, provided that I would man and victual her; as they were not able. This I consented to do; and on the morning of the 27th July I sailed from Palma with thirty-six seamen on board.

I arrived at Cadiz, on the 7th August, and immediately waited upon the Regency with my dispatches; next upon the Secretary of War, Heredia; and, finally upon the British Minister, Mr. Wellesley, who promised me that he would do everything in his power to have me dispatched as soon as possible; and that he would see about having the prisoners removed from Cabrera, and, at all events, the officers from the island of Majorca immediately.

The Secretary of State for War assured me that he would do everything in his power for the safety of the island; and that all General Whittingham's wants should be paid attention to immediately. At the end of the first week, however, I found that the only thing done to forward me was the taking the schooner from me, in consequence of a requisition made by the British Admiral and the British Minister.

I found that the promises, which I had obtained from every part of the Government, were nothing more than words of course. For at the end of August, although I had not missed a single day without paying a visit to every one of the Ministers upon the subject of my dispatches, I was just where I started. The Bishop of Majorca, Llaneres, and the two deputies in the Cortes for the island, exerted themselves as much as possible also, and were it not for their interference nothing would have been accomplished.

Mr. Wellesley observed to me, that General Whittingham must not purchase provisions of any kind with the money given to him; as when that should be expended he would not give him any more. He also desired me to tell General Whittingham, that he was not to interfere, in any way whatever, with the government of the island, nor in any of their political discussions; that he was solely to organise his division; and not to have anything, directly or indirectly, to do with anything that did not concern it.

This last observation was stated, no doubt, in consequence of the dispatches of the Cortes for the island having insisted on both the Captain-General of the Balearic Islands, and the Governor of Palma being removed; and the Bishop of Majorca and the others, (the two deputies from Majorca), wishing to put in Admiral Valdes as Captain-General; and I am sure that it was, and is their intention still, to have General Whittingham appointed Governor of Palma, (he means of Majorca, of which Palma is the capital). And there can be little doubt of their succeeding in their wishes, when they have got Valdes appointed Captain-General, (see note following).

★★★★★★

Note:—Valdes never was appointed Captain-General, and so the well-meant scheme of the good bishop and of the patriotic island deputies to increase the powers of the English general, and thereby facilitate the formation of the division, was frustrated.

★★★★★★

On the 2nd September I called upon the British Vice Consul, Mr. Archdeacon, to inquire if any of the transports loaded with clothing for General Whittingham had arrived, or were likely to arrive. On looking over his books he told me, that there was a transport the *Wellington,* loaded with clothing for the general, which had arrived and been in Cadiz for two months: and that

Mr. Wellesley had been informed of it on that vessel's arrival. I went and told Mr. Wellesley, and he observed that I might take her up to Majorca if I would get a convoy for her. I applied to the agent of transports, who wrote to the Admiral, he being out cruising off the Gulf of Gibraltar; and finally on the 10th September a convoy was appointed.

Captain Briarly arrived in Palma with his supplies on the 28th September, to the great joy of his general, as may be well supposed.

General Whittingham was often applied to by half-pay British officers, and even by civilians, who wanted commissions in some regiment of his division. Some of them came out strongly recommended. But as he had only a few posts reserved for Englishmen (for fear of giving great and impolitic offence to the Spaniards), so he was generally compelled to decline such applications; and thus unintentionally to multiply his enemies, and to augment the feelings of jealousy to which his high position in the Spanish Army often exposed him. But he kept his temper, and continued with patient perseverance to fulfil his onerous duties to the best of his power and judgment.

On the 29th of October, 1811, General Whittingham pointed out to Mr. Wellesley in a long dispatch the breach of faith on the part of the Junta, and especially of the war minister, in regard to the stipulations originally made as to the recruiting and organisation of the Majorca division; one sentence in which is interesting, from certain circumstances which eventually caused the interference of Lord Wellington himself.

By the enclosed copy of a letter from General Valcarcel of the 24th September, you will see an attempt made to take the inspection, and consequently the proposal of officers out of my hands. For if all my *propuestas*, (proposals or recommendations for promotions and appointments), are to be submitted to the opinion of the Inspectors in Cadiz, it is a perfect joke to decorate me with the title of Inspector-General of this division.

The jealousy of General Whittingham imbibed by some of the Spanish ministers, vented itself in various annoying ways, on which there is no space to dwell.

No wonder that at last, the patience which Mr. Wellesley had admired, when displayed in the lighter work at Isla de Leon, was nearly exhausted by the heavy burden at Majorca, and that to his brother-in-law he began to display his half-formed wish to retire from the

Spanish service.

On the 2nd November, after passing nearly five months on the island, he pours out all his feelings on the conduct of those...

...whose dearest interest it should be to protect the formation of a division, which might lay the foundation of the salvation of the Spanish monarchy; but which, at all events must ensure the safety of the Balearic Islands. The Minister of War is at the head of the whole intrigue; (the man who scrupled not officially to worry and insult Lord Wellington himself), and not a day passes without orders being given directly contrary to the basis of the agreement between Mr. Wellesley and the Spanish Government; and tending only to a repetition of insults to induce me to throw up the command, and leave the island.

Had I only to do with the Spanish Government, I should not have hesitated a moment; but I am now held by other ties to me ten thousand times more strong. I am compromised with the British Government, and therefore whatever may happen, I shall not take a single step without its being first sanctioned by its approbation.

On the 10th, 11th, and 12th November, three more letters, long and full, are dispatched to Mr. Wellesley, exposing the conduct of the Spanish authorities and the defenceless state in which they had left Majorca and the injurious treatment which he had met at their hands. The letter of the 12th commences thus:

Every day brings fresh proofs of the decided enmity borne by General Cuesta to everything English, and of his particular hostility to me.

The letter continues:

Conceiving it of importance to forward my dispatches to you of the 11th and 10th of this month, by a safe conveyance, I sent an officer of my staff to General Cuesta's secretary's office to ask for a passport to Cadiz, for Lieutenant Niel Macdoudel of His Majesty's 75th Regiment of infantry. The reception which this officer met with is too scandalous to be related. The captain-general made use of language to him, which ought only to be used by porters;—asked him who had constituted him the defender of Englishmen, and threatened him with punishment if he again interfered in such like commissions.

Aware that this behaviour, on the part of the captain-general could only proceed from a desire to irritate me, and, by throwing me off my guard, induce me to commit myself by some act of violence, I abstained from seeing him on the subject, and contented myself with sending him an official letter requesting a passport for a British officer to go to Gibraltar.

The passport, which Lieutenant Macdoudel, who is nephew to Colonel Campbell, will have the honour to show you, was the answer. I beg leave once more to state, that my stay here cannot but lead to the worst consequences, unless the captain-general be removed, and unless the independence of my command be fully and decidedly established.

On the 13th and 25th November he again impresses on the Minister the state of his relations with the Spanish officials, and the difficulties he has to encounter in obtaining necessary supplies for men and horses. In that of the 25th, he reports on the enlisting of some Germans into his division:

Baron Halberg, an Austrian officer in the service, was sent by me to Cabrera to choose out the Germans only, and not even to take Italians or Poles. He in consequence brought with him 133 men, all Germans, and who have since conducted themselves with the greatest propriety.

In a letter dated 7th September, 1811, Mr. Wellesley writes:

I am informed by M. de Bardaxi that the *Junta* has consented that your troops should be supplied with rations from the island; that the necessary buildings will be allotted for their accommodation, and that you are to be allowed to recruit from the German prisoners at Cabrera to the extent of 600 men.

On the 20th December General Whittingham congratulates Mr. Wellesley upon his appointment, from simple minister and envoy, to the post of ambassador extraordinary, but accidentally omits entirely the title 'excellency' which was now Mr. Wellesley's due. One sentence in this letter, *without comment of any kind*, records a fact, which must nevertheless, have afforded unspeakable relief to the writer:

CHAPTER 8

1812

One of the great disadvantages under which General Whittingham laboured was that the unpopularity of the Spaniards with the English army abroad, and with Englishmen at home, extended itself to the English officers employed in the Spanish service. The extra army rank of these agents, though for the most part only local and temporary yet, perhaps not unnaturally, excited the jealousy of the regimental officers. Lord Wellington, however, very early in the war, recorded his opinion that no officers more deserved their promotion than the British agents with the Spanish Army; whose duties, indeed, were arduous and hazardous, and required much exertion and intelligence to perform them efficiently.

Lord Wellington was not always satisfied with all of them, but all the readers of his dispatches knew that he recorded his complete satisfaction at the close of the war, with the conduct of General Whittingham, who, whilst only a captain in the British Army, had been addressed by his Lordship as a Spanish Major-General. Nevertheless, the year 1811 had not on the whole been a fortunate one to the major-general. But 1812 opened more cheerfully; the death of General Cuesta having removed one great enemy to the raising of the Majorca division under the command of an Englishman.

Major-General Whittingham to the Right Hon,
Henry Wellesley.
(Extract.)

Palma, 6th January, 1812.

Enclosed I have the honour to send you a return of the force under my command, by which you will see its gradual increase. The state of discipline of this small corps is so far advanced, that they manoeuvre in line without difficulty, and the interior of regiments will bear the minutest inspection.

I beg leave to submit to your better judgment the good effect that would be produced by the naming Brigadier Marquis de Vivot my second in command. He was wounded in Catalonia, but he is now well enough to mount on horseback. The *marquis* is the head of the nobility of this island, has very considerable estates here, and is particularly attached to the English. It is at his express desire that I take the liberty of soliciting this favour. (Mr. Wellesley's answer is not extant, but there can be little doubt that the request here made was complied with).

About the 24th of January General Whittingham embarked for Minorca on some military business, returning to Palma in fifteen days. The following is the translation of an official letter written to him by his chief of the staff during his absence. (It appears that the letter was written only two days before the return of the General from Minorca, and was probably delivered to him on landing). It proves how necessary to the peace and security of Majorca was the presence of the energetic English commander:—

Colonel Francisco Serrano to Major-General Whittingham,
Palma, 6th February, 1812.

General,—From circumstances, which have occurred here during the thirteen days of your absence, I am very anxious for your return; and have determined to dispatch Captain Dominguez to you with this letter, giving a detail of the events most deserving your attention.

Shortly after your departure reports were circulated of a rising and assembling of the people; and some attempts were made to seduce the soldiers of the division, who immediately communicated the fact to their officers; and from other circumstances that occurred, I conceived it prudent to assemble the commanding officers. I issued out ammunition; secretly reinforced the guards; and pointed out their alarm-posts to the different corps, in such a manner that, at the least commotion, they should assemble and occupy the most important posts, to support the public authorities, and to quell any tumult which might arise.

I conceived it prudent to take these necessary measures of precaution, as the alarm had been very general, and had extended itself to all the constituted authorities. The commanding officers of corps have behaved as you could wish, and may be fully depended upon in case of need.

I have, &c.,

Francisco Serrano.'

The following letter speaks for itself:—

To Vice-Admiral Sir Edward Pellew, Bart.

Palma, 14th February, 1812.

Sir,—I have the honour to enclose the prospectus and regulations of a college for the officers and cadets of the division under my command, which I have established in this town.

From the entire neglect of education in Spain, during the last twenty years, and more particularly since the Revolution, most of the young men commencing their military careers as cadets scarcely know how to read and write. The expense of the establishment at the present moment would have been a serious objection, had it not been done away with by the zeal and patriotism of various individuals.

The Bishop of Majorca, (Llaneres)—independently of a donation of 20,000 *reals vellon*, (£200, so generous and liberal-minded a bishop in Spain was truly a wonderful phenomenon).—has given up a house for the academy. The masters have all undertaken their employments gratis; and as the officers and cadets all belong to the division, I have the satisfaction of seeing my ideas realised, without the smallest expense, either to the British or Spanish Government.

I have, &c.,

Samford Whittingham.

Major-General Whittingham to the Right Hon. H. Wellesley.
(Extract.)

Palma, 18th February, 1812.

Sir,—I have the honour to inform you of the arrival of Colonel Campbell on the 8th instant, and beg leave to offer you my warmest thanks for your very zealous interference and support in obviating the many difficulties under which I have hitherto laboured; the result of which will, I feel assured, prove highly beneficial to this division.

I beg leave to enclose for your information the following papers:—

No. 1. The translation of my exposition to the *Junta*; which I felt myself imperiously called upon to make, from the critical position this island is placed in, owing to the late success of the enemy on the opposite coast.

No. 2. My letter to the admiral.

No. 3. Copy of a letter to me from the chief of my staff during my absence.

No. 4. General return of the strength of the division. (No copy of this return has reached the editor's hands).

No. 5. Translation of my observations on Puerto Pi, a small port in the Bay of Palma; and the advantages which might be derived from employing the French prisoners in its enlargement.

I found it necessary to go to Minorca, for the purpose of personal communication with the admiral, relative to the prisoners here, and other important points, and my absence was prolonged by contrary winds to fifteen days.

The admiral was pleased to express his unqualified approbation and concurrence in the proposed system of pontoons; and offered to fit them out, and equip them completely, and to send a frigate and brig to guard them. He also expressed his earnest desire that I should establish the telegraphs as soon as possible.

The excellent disposition and the zealous support which I have experienced from the (*acting*) Captain General Gregory will make me regret the loss of one so every way qualified for this important command; as he combines discernment and judgment with energy, and decision, and has given me his most decided support in everything relative to the division, and, as you will see, by No. 3, we require here one of his firm and determined character.

A levy of all the idle strangers takes place tomorrow; and the *Alistamento Generate* immediately follows. The volunteers of Colonel Campbell's battalion, not having presented themselves within the period allotted, the privilege of limited service is done away with, and no exceptions are to be permitted in the conscription.

On referring to No. 3, you will perceive that the disaffected party here were in movement during my absence; tampering with the troops, posting placards, &c. But their attempts were rendered abortive by the excellent disposition of the officers, whose conduct it is impossible to praise more forcibly, than by stating that they obeyed the orders of the chief of my staff, (although there were several of superior rank) with the same zeal and promptitude as though I had been present. The same excellent dispositions were manifested by the soldiers of the division. I must beg leave to call to your attention our financial necessities, and to submit to your better judgment the importance of the Balearic Islands, whose safety, at this critical moment, may be confidently said to depend on the existence of this division, the resources of which must entirely depend on your countenance and support.

Convinced that nothing is so much wanting among Spanish officers as the means of the acquiring military information—and satisfied of the necessity of giving to the cadets a military education,—I have established a college here on the basis of the enclosed prospectus. It was opened yesterday, in the presence of the captain general, several bishops, and all the principal officers and people of rank in the island.

It is not a trifling consideration, at the present moment, to be able to say that the establishment will be of no expense. The generosity of the bishop has furnished us with a house, and 20,000 *rs. vn.* to purchase books, &c., and as all the masters attend *gratis*, and the officers and cadets belong to the division, no disbursement of any kind will be necessary.

The safety of the Balearic Islands was considered of great importance at that time by Lord Wellington; and General Whittingham was in constant correspondence with the admiral and ambassador, upon the defence of the islands, and upon plans for future aggressions against the enemy on the main-land. These letters display a consummate military knowledge both in theory and in detail; but the extracts must here be limited to a few of the most interesting particulars.

To the Right Hon. H. Wellesley.
(Extract.)
Palma, 21st February, 1812.

The force at present under my command is only 2,200 men, (see note following); but if I may judge from the firm measures adopted by General Gregory, this number will be more than doubled in less than two months: and nothing would give me so much pleasure as to be employed in any plan of attack which might merit Sir Edward Pellew's approbation.

✶✶✶✶✶✶

Note:—Hitherto the comparatively slow growth of the division had been caused mainly by the hostilities of old General Cuesta, and by the jealousy of the Minister of War, and the neglect of provincial *Juntas* to fulfil their engagements.

✶✶✶✶✶✶

As the difficulties we have hitherto met with will probably cease now that a Regency is appointed, so every way deserving of the national confidence, and which appears so completely to merit your approbation, I have not the smallest doubt that a few months will enable me to repay the confidence with which you have honoured me, by efficient co-operation on my part, with the admiral in his plans of attack; at the same time that I may be able to answer for the safety of these valuable islands.

However, the finances of Majorca are in such confusion, as to make it wholly out of its power to meet the expense of paying the troops; and indeed, to such a state are they reduced that the officers of the 2nd and 3rd battalions of Cordova and Burgos are *literally begging charity; and a few days ago, one of them fainted away in the coffee-room from absolute want.* (In the original the words—judging by the book into which the letter was copied—do not appear to have been underlined; but the editor deems them worthy of *italics*).

Foreseeing, as I must of necessity do, the situation in which I shall see myself, with the troops under my command, should my pecuniary resources entirely fail, I take the liberty of earnestly entreating you—not only as British Ambassador, but as a friend, to whose kindness I have been indebted for many favours,—that, should the British Government consider the existence of a division of 4,000 or 5,000 men in the Island of Majorca, as not necessary either for co-operation in the plans of attack of Admiral Sir Edward Pellew, or for the defence and security of the Balearic Islands,—and should therefore determine to lend it no further assistance—you will have the goodness to obtain an order to have all these troops sent immediately to any part of the continent that may be judged proper; and, at the same time to give in my resignation to the Spanish Government, in order that I may proceed without loss of time to join the British Army in Portugal. It will be the last time, my dear sir, that I shall be troublesome to you; but I do most earnestly beg and entreat, that you will add this favour to the very long list, and enable me to avoid the wretchedness of witnessing the misery of those we esteem, without having the power of applying any remedy.

In a letter from Lord Wellington to Sir Henry Wellesley, K.B., dated, Badajoz, 11th April, 1812, there occurs this sentence:

Fourthly; that 3,000 men of General Roche's division at Alicante, and 3,000 men of General Whittingham's division at Majorca, should be prepared to be embarked early in June, in order to join and co-operate on the eastern coast, with the troops under Lord William Bentinck, which will come from Sicily.

In another letter from the same to the same, dated 17th May, Lord Wellington appears to have rightly estimated the future strength of the Majorca division, which (after the death of General Cuesta and the change of Regency in Spain) had already considerably augmented in numbers.

There are other points for consideration: First; how many men is it expedient to leave in Majorca for the defence of the Island, of the 7,000 of which it is supposed General Whittingham's division will consist? Secondly, General Whittingham's division will have been newly raised, excepting 3,000 men. How many of the 7,000 men would it be expedient to leave behind, as being recruits and unfit for service?

On that same date (and the day following) General Whittingham was corresponding with the admiral and the ambassador, on the details of the expedition, embarkation, &c.

He had also to correspond semi-officially with his father-in-law, who was military intendant of Majorca in the service of the King of Spain:—

Major-General Whittingham to Don Pedro Creus.

Palma, 18th May, 1812.

My dear Sir,—The extreme distress in which I have found this island at my return from Cadiz, in spite of every effort of the Marquis of Compigny, (later Captain-General of the Balearic Islands), to provide against the growing difficulties, makes me particularly anxious to call your attention to this important point, in the hopes that you will use your best endeavours with Sir Edward Pellew, to induce him to aid and assist us in our manifold wants.

The *marquis* is ready to give me 2,000 conscripts immediately, which will complete the division to 5,000 men. But as even for the existing force it is almost impossible to find bread, he will, I much fear, be induced to delay the levies of men till after the harvest, which would be too late to be of any service to the division. If it were possible for Sir Edward Pellew to furnish me with a sufficient quantity of flour to supply the rations of 5,000 men at one and a half pound of bread per day for one month, the harvest would be got in, and our difficulties would be at an end. But without this assistance I am too well convinced that I shall not be able to effect the organisation of the proposed division as speedily as I would wish, and as the service I know will require.

Should it be in Sir Edward's power to furnish us with the proposed supply, the 4,000 conscripts will be given me immediately; and the *marquis* will give bills on the Spanish Government for the supply. Have the goodness to state the extreme necessity of our case to Sir Edward; and believe me to be, &c.,

Samford Whittingham.

He wrote also direct to Sir Edward, on the same subject, and estimated the force he proposed to embark, including some expected troops from Alicante, at upwards of 4,200 men.

The following letter is worthy of record, for it contains a prophecy which was destined to be no idle or sanguine boast, but a fact established on undeniable testimonies:—

To Vice-Admiral Sir Edward Pellew, Bart.

Palma, 24th May, 1812.

My dear Sir,—The extreme anxiety which I feel to get the division in a perfect state to meet yours and Lord William Bentinck's wishes by the end of next month, makes me, I fear, very troublesome. But your well-known zeal for the service will plead my best excuse.

For God's sake press Compigny not to lose a moment's time; and you may rest assured *that the troops of this small and gallant division will prove themselves worthy of fighting by the side of Englishmen.*

I have, &c.,

Samford Whittingham.

On the 28th May he sends to Sir Henry Wellesley his accounts of expenditure and receipts, and trusts that by the end of June his division will amount to 4,000 effective muskets, exclusive of cavalry and artillery; and he repeats the promise of their future effectiveness in the field in nearly the same words as he had lately addressed to the admiral.

To the Right Hon. Sir H. Wellesley, K.B,

Palma, 20th June, 1812.

Sir,—The division being now paid by the British Government, according to the existing agreement between the allied courts, I beg to submit to your Excellency's consideration the necessity of appointing a British paymaster general, or other officer, who will be responsible for, and charged with the accounts of the division.

Hitherto those accounts have been kept by persons appointed by the Spanish Government for that purpose; and I have taken the precaution to have them regularly examined, and made out in triplicates. But it is utterly impossible that in the midst of active duties, I can remain charged with such a weight of responsibility, and with accounts of so complicated a nature.

I trust that you will perceive the necessity of calling the attention of His Majesty's Government to this important object; and that until a person so authorized can come from England, you will be pleased to send an officer of the paymaster's department to take charge of the accounts of this division, which will be more satisfactory to your Excellency. Besides, should any accident happen to me, the presence of such a person would obviate every difficulty, which would otherwise arise. And I trust that your Excellency will pardon my pressing this subject, and urging the speedy departure of the person you may appoint, when you consider the very great responsibility attached to the families of persons entrusted with public monies.

I have, &c.,

Samford Whittingham.

On the 24th July, 1812, the Majorca division embarked at Palma: the infantry portion of which consisted of 159 officers, 3 chaplains, 8 surgeons and 4,180 non-commissioned officers and men. (of the cavalry and artillery that embarked, no returns are extant).

From, 'on board the *Romulus* at sea off Alicant' on the '8th August,'

General Whittingham, amongst other matters, again urges the affair of the pay mastership on Sir Henry Wellesley. What led him the day following to send in his resignation of his Spanish command can only be surmised, as Sir Henry's letter which induced the resignation is not forthcoming.

Major-General Whittingham to his Brother-in-law.

Muchamiel, 2nd September, 1812.

By the enclosed letter for Colonel Gordon, you will see the state of the force which I brought with me; of that which I left at Palma, and Mahon; and the total strength of the division. The detail of our military operations is also enclosed.

The troops under my command have conducted themselves with so much order and discipline, and have made their marches in so military a manner, that they have merited the approbation of everybody; and I have not the smallest doubt, that whenever we come into action, they will do themselves much honour. But unless things are put upon another footing, it is impossible for me to continue in this command.

He then repeats his paymastership grievances and adds:

I have repeatedly written to Sir Henry Wellesley requesting to have a paymaster of the division appointed, but without effect. And I have finally written to him to say that as soon as a general action will allow me to retire with credit, I shall give up the command of the division and return to England. I am sure that you will see the extreme necessity for taking a speedy determination.

However, Sir Henry Wellesley was in no hurry to accept of the resignation of such an officer:—

Sir Henry Wellesley, KB. to Major-General Whittingham.

(Extract.)

Cadiz, 6th September, 1812.

I have the honour to acknowledge the receipt of your letter of the 9th August, which only reached me last night.

I can hardly bring myself to believe that the contents of my letter of the 25th July can have given rise to the resolution which you have announced to me of resigning your present command. There was nothing in that letter which was intended to hurt your feelings, and if you will recollect that I am personally responsible for every shilling of public money placed at my disposal in the service of Spain, you cannot be surprised that I should have adverted to the expenses of your corps, and the necessity of confining these expenses within certain limits.

If your resolution to resign was occasioned by the contents of my letter of the 27th July, I hope that this explanation will satisfy you that it was written in the mere performance of my duty, and that it was not intended in any way to reflect on you personally.

I believe that I might venture to add, that from the moment of my arrival in Spain, I have given you all the assistance and support in my power, and I am sincerely disposed to continue them to you, as long as the means of doing so shall be entrusted to me. I cannot therefore but hope that you will be induced to relinquish your intention of resigning.

No doubt the fact of his being still left without the assistance of a paymaster had, in the confinement of a ship, preyed with additional force upon the mind of General Whittingham, and caused him to feel acutely those criticisms as to his official expenditure, to which all officers in command are liable. Perhaps also his anxious desire to provide for the comfort of his officers and men inclined him to greater liberality than governments are usually prepared to sanction.

On the 21st September General Whittingham writes a long and grateful letter to Captain General O'Donnell the hero of Catalonia, who had written to him a very complimentary epistle on the state of the Majorca division.

Major-General Whittingham to Sir Henry Wellesley.
(Extract.)
Muchamiel, 3rd October, 1812.

Dear Sir,—I have the honour to acknowledge the receipt of your letter of the 6th September; and I beg leave to return you my most grateful thanks for this fresh proof of your kindness and attention. I should be the most ungrateful man alive were I even for a moment to forget the many and great favours which I have received at your hands; and it will ever be the first wish of my heart to acknowledge publicly and privately my sentiments of gratitude and respect towards you. It is quite sufficient for me to know that you wish me to continue in the command of this division, to do away with every idea of giving it up. But at the same time I wish with all respect to call to your mind the delicacy of my situation. The only thing that I ever had a dread of was to become a public accountant! As long, however, as the troops were in garrison I conceived, that by the greatest care and attention, and with the assistance of Colonel Campbell, I might have every account, with all the requisite receipts, arranged monthly, and thus be always in a state to meet examination.

But now that the troops are in campaign, and that I am unavoidably exposed to lose my papers by any of the very many accidents that so often occur in war, I tremble at a responsibility that may not only ruin my own private fortune, but, what is infinitely worse, compromise my good name and place my honour in doubt in the public opinion. Allow me to say, my dear sir, with the freedom which your friendship entitles me to use, that you are not in the same situation. It is true that you are answerable for the public monies entrusted to your charge: but there can be no difficulty in showing the sums that you have entrusted to me; and for the expenditure I alone am answerable. I have ever been of opinion that it is not sufficient for a man to be most honourable in all the transactions of life, but that it is indispensable that he should never be stained by even the shadow of a doubt. Having said thus much, I shall forbear in future to return to this unpleasant subject.

To his Brother-in-law,

Muchamiel, 20th October, 1812.

The Majorca division has the honour of occupying all the outposts of the army. I am just returned from them, and avail myself of the opportunity of a vessel going to Cadiz to let you know what is going on. We have had since our arrival a great number of affairs of posts, in all of which my troops have been successful; and have in consequence begun to form a character which I hope and trust will soon be established. My force at present is rather more than 6,000 men; but I expect another battalion from Minorca in a few days, which will complete my force to 7,000 men. (He was only a lieutenant-colonel in the British service then, and in that capacity could not have expected a command of more than six or eight hundred men). I have besides two strong battalions in Majorca clothed and formed by me, which the captain-general, Marquis de Compigny, has refused to send to me. But I have written to Sir Henry Wellesley and the Spanish Government on the subject, and daily expect their positive order to bring them here.

On the 18th, the French of the army of Suchet fell back from Sax, Villena, and Biar, upon Fuente la Higuera; and from Alcoy upon Concentayna, Albayda, and San Felipe. In consequence of this movement, my advanced posts are now at Sax, Biar, and Alcoy.

If you should be able to procure me a good strong hunter, and send him out to me at Cadiz, or at Alicante, you would do me the greatest favour. I have several good horses, but not one of right good confidence for a long day's action. Hart would, I dare say, undertake the commission. I wish you both joy of your success. I have read Hart's maiden speech with delight.

Mr. R. H. Davis had just been returned for the first time as member for Bristol, and been succeeded at Colchester by his eldest son, whose very great abilities gave promise of a brilliant parliamentary career, which was too soon frustrated, by the state of his health compelling him to retire from parliament.

General Whittingham soon afterwards cancelled the commission for another horse, as finding the expenses of a general of division were already beyond his means, both public and private.

To the Same.
Muchamiel, 18th December, 1812.

I advanced a few days since with the whole of my division on Alcoy, to make a diversion in favour of General Elio, who was to have attacked Requena. His movement did not take place; and, after occupying Alcoy some days, I received orders to break up, and to reoccupy my former cantonments. My troops have in charge the whole of the outposts of the army.

To the Same.
Muchamiel, 29th December, 1812.

As Sir Henry Wellesley has not engaged to supply me for the present with more than 35,000 dollars monthly—which I understand he gives me out of the money at his disposal for the service of Spain—I much fear that nothing will be done in regard to the paymaster, unless the British Government should agree to take a certain number of battalions and regiments of cavalry into their pay; and this, I should suppose, they would not do without consulting Lord Wellington. I am not aware that Sir Henry has ever officially desired that a paymaster should be appointed to this division. I should think that he had not. But as far as I am concerned, I should prefer very much giving up the command altogether to the continuing a responsibility which sooner or later will in all probability reduce me to beggary! You well know the money I have spent in Spain, (see note following). . . . Thus, whilst others have been making fortunes, I have been spending more than I could afford, without any security that, at the winding-up of the peace, the complication of long and difficult accounts may not ruin my character and my fortune.

★★★★★★

Note:—Out of his private fortune he means, having got into debt, besides spending all his private income, in the country. He had afterwards to sell out some of his original capital.

★★★★★★

On the 30th December, he states that he had forwarded to Mr. Wellesley an application for the paymastership of the division from Captain Foley, and a prospect of relief from an unjust and intolerable burden closed the year 1812.

CHAPTER 9

1813

In the 10th volume of the *Wellington Dispatches* there is a long letter from Lord Wellington to Major-General Whittingham, dated Cadiz, 8th January, 1813. Amongst Sir Samford Whittingham's papers there was found a kind of condensed extract from this letter (probably made with the view of translating it for the benefit of the officers of his now considerable division) comprising all that he thought necessary to publish, and which will doubtless also be sufficient for the reader. Lord Wellington was a Spanish *grandee*, (Duke of Ciudad Rodrigo), and Commander-in-Chief at this time, of the Spanish, as well as of the British, army:—

Copy of the Order of His Excellency the Duke of Ciudad Rodrigo to General Whittingham,
dated Cadiz, 8th January, 1813.

The corps of troops under your command in the Peninsula is one of those which I am desirous should be paid out of the funds set apart by Great Britain for the support of the Spanish cause. The clothing, arms, and furniture of the corps under your orders being for the account of Great Britain, the said funds must by no means be applied to the liquidation of those charges. Nor must they be expended in provisions, hospitals, or means of transport, as these branches are to be provided for by the Spanish Government, in the same manner as for the other Spanish troops. The pay of absent officers and privates must likewise be for the account of the Spanish Government; for it is my intention that nothing be paid out of the said funds to any officer or private not appearing on the monthly returns to be in the actual discharge of his duty. The pay of the general and other officers and privates of your division present, and in the actual exercise of their duty, is all that should be supplied put of those funds.

You will send on the 20th of every month to His Excellency Sir Henry Wellesley, an estimate of the money wanted for the payment of the officers and privates under your command for that month, on the principles before expressed; and on the receipt of the month's pay, whether the produce of bills or otherwise, you will distribute it in the proper proportions to the individuals entitled thereto, taking their receipts, which will be your discharge for the amount received. You will, however, adopt all necessary means to ensure the just application of these allowances to officers and privates, according to the regulations of the Spanish service.

You will appoint Patrick Foley, Esq., to be Paymaster-General of your division. (It would appear that Captain Foley was no longer in the regular army, when he obtained his new appointment). He will take the detail of this service under his direction and responsibility; and as all payments are to be made one month in arrear, you will take care that the money be distributed as soon as received, as beforesaid.

I do not wish the division under your orders to exceed 6,000 effective men in the field. In order to keep up this, you must establish a depot at Alicante; and I will take care that you shall receive the pay of 7,000 men, inclusively of such as are in hospital; for whom, as I said before, the Spanish Government must provide.

The appointment of Captain Foley was a truly great relief, for which General Whittingham felt grateful. But a few days later he received a letter from Lord Wellington which caused him much vexation, as threatening to nullify that independence of subordinate Spanish authorities, which from the incompetency of the latter, he considered to be indispensable to the efficiency of his division;—

The Marquis of Wellington to Major-General Whittingham,
Freneda, 19th February, 1813.

Sir,—Sir Henry Wellesley has transmitted to me your letter of the 3rd January, in regard to your holding the office of inspector of the division of Spanish troops under your command, and to the abuses and inconveniences to which your troops would be liable in case your expectations in this respect were disappointed; and having conversed with the chief of the staff, and with the Inspectors-General of cavalry and infantry on this subject, I have been informed by each of those officers that it was particularly settled with you, that when the troops under your command should serve in the Peninsula, they were to come under the control of the Inspector's office, and were to have Deputy Inspectors attached to them in the same manner as other Spanish troops. (In Majorca he had had the full powers and offices of Inspector, both of cavalry and infantry, according to previous agreement).

This being the case, it remains to be considered whether, adverting to the inconveniences to which you refer, it is proper I should now exempt the troops under your command from this control. Upon this point I have to observe, first, that I hope to be able to prevent the abuses of which you complain, as well as of others; secondly, that even if I should not succeed entirely, it is not worthwhile to enter into the disputes and complaints which a partial departure from a system long established in the Spanish army would occasion.

I have therefore desired the Inspectors-General of infantry and cavalry to appoint Deputy-Inspectors for your division, and I beg you to submit to their control. (These orders were given by Lord Wellington, as Commander-in-Chief of the Spanish armies).

I have the honour to be, &c.,

Wellington.

Major-General Whittingham.'

This letter was a truly discouraging one to General Whittingham, but, as will be seen, it was soon rescinded.

To his Brother-in-law.

San Juan, 22nd February, 1813.

Your truly amiable and excellent friend General Clinton remained only a very short time in command here. Major-General Campbell, Adjutant-General to the army in Sicily, arrived soon after him and being his senior, the command, of course, devolved upon him.

In respect to the operations of the ensuing campaigns, in my humble opinion, Lord Wellington himself must open it before this army can do anything of consequence. I beg leave to call your attention to the judicious position taken up by Soult at Toledo, where he has his headquarters. He is in the centre of Lord Wellington's two lines of operations; and as his force is extended over La Mancha, he would, in case of our moving forward upon Valencia, be upon our left flank and rear before any assistance could be received from Lord Wellington! It is therefore my opinion that his Lordship must open the campaign himself, and, by drawing towards him the mass of the French force enable us to make a brilliant and decisive attack upon what remains.

The French attempted a few nights since to surprise Xigona, which is one of our outposts. One of the Italian regiments raised by Lord William Bentinck in Sicily, and composed from deserters from all parts of the world, formed part of the garrison of Xigona. In the course of forty-eight hours upwards of 86 men from this regiment had passed over to the French; and Colonel Grant assured me that it was his opinion, and that of all his officers, that none of the men could be depended on; and that it was his and their opinion that if they were ordered to march to Alicante, the greater part of them would desert on the road. The last party of deserters had taken their officer with them; and had spared his life only in consequence of the intercession of one of the corporals.

All circumstances considered, I determined to send off an orderly dragoon to General Campbell, requesting his instructions how to proceed. The general came in the course of the morning to Xigona, and directed me to disarm the regiment, and to send them as prisoners to Alicante. The garrison of Xigona consisted of my battalion of grenadiers and of this Italian regiment. On the first alarm I had directed the battalion of Murcia to march to Xigona; and General Campbell had ordered the 1st battalion 27th Regiment to follow them, together with a squadron of the 20th Dragoons. About half-past five p.m. the British troops came up. The Italian regiment was marched into an open space, and disarmed without the smallest difficulty, and immediately afterwards marched off to Alicante, escorted by the 27th Regiment, the squadron of dragoons, and my battalion of Murcia. On their arrival at Alicante they were all sent on board ship.

I remained at Xigona with my battalion of grenadiers; and about eight p.m. the 1st battalion of the 58th British Regiment marched in by Palomos, by General Campbell's orders, to strengthen the post. The French (who were undoubtedly in concert with the Italians, but who knew nothing of what had passed) determined upon attacking Xigona that night; and at seven p.m. Generals Hubert and Gudin marched from Alcoy with 1,500 infantry and 150 cavalry.

At half-past two a.m. the firing of the outposts began. The troops, both Spanish and English, were under arms with admirable celerity; and every disposition was taken to make it impossible for the enemy to force the post. Our outposts were after some time driven in, and the French descended to the ravine; which they could not, however, pass from the briskness of our fire. They then extended themselves by their left to endeavour to open a communication with the Italian barracks'([which they still believed to be occupied by their friends).

Upon the first glimpse of day we crossed the ravine with the light companies; and, upon ascending the hill on the other side, we discovered the French columns more than halfway up the mountain, and their light troops covering their rear. They had probably discovered the change which had taken place in the troops, and in consequence had begun their retreat an hour before daylight, leaving only a few light troops on the borders of the ravine, being well assured that we should not quit the strong position we occupied to attack them till daylight should enable us to examine their force, and make our dispositions in consequence. I had the satisfaction of being told by Lieut.-Colonel David Walker and the officers of the 58th Regiment that he and they should be at all times most happy to serve under my orders, and that they were all satisfied and delighted with the dispositions that I had made that night. (What enhances this compliment is the fact that Col. Walker was considerably the senior in rank in the British service, and so continued).

We took six prisoners, and thus ended an affair which I should not have thought worth relating to you, but for the providential escape we all had, in consequence of having removed the battalion of Italians that day. (see note following). For, had the French been aided, as they expected, by these people, the battalion of grenadiers and I myself must have been sacrificed without the possibility of avoiding it. The worst of all would have been the moral effect which it would have produced in the country; where it would have been generally believed that a British battalion (for, being dressed in scarlet, they would have been supposed to be British) had fired upon the Spaniards and joined the French. To do away such an impression would have been a work of time and difficulty.

★★★★★★

Note:—In the *Recollections*, it is said that 'Major Bourke, an Irish Austrian officer of twenty-five years' service,' commanded the first battalion of Italians in General Whittingham's division, and that 'his *tact and judgment* made him the glory and pride of his men.' The main cause on the other hand, of the infamous behaviour—as recorded in the text—of the 2nd battalion of Italians, was attributed to 'Grant's want of those qualities,' which 'induced him to adopt all the minute worry of the old British school, and made him cordially detested by all the men of his regiment.' Unfortunately, the second regiment and not the first had garrisoned Xigona, on this occasion.

★★★★★★

How admirably the details of the Majorca division were carried on in active service is shown by eight documents in the Editor's possession. Of these Spanish returns, six are dated Concentayna, 31st August, and the other two dated 12th August, 1813. All appear to be monthly returns, and are made out with a neatness and precision that could not be exceeded by the orderly room of the smartest British regiment at the present day.

Colonel Serrano, General Whittingham's able and trusted chief of the staff, was dispatched to Freneda, with a packet of letters, to undertake the by no means easy task of persuading the victorious chief of the British and Spanish armies to rescind the order which he had given that the Majorca division was to submit to Spanish deputy-inspectors; and thus to transfer to these officers from the hands of General Whittingham not only the power of rewarding and censuring officers and men, but also of recommending them for promotion in, or appointments to, regiments both of cavalry and infantry.

The copy of the 'duplicate' original of Lord Wellington's reply is now before the editor. It is written in a fair clerk's hand; and though an important letter (reversing a previous decision), is merely signed by Lord Wellington, though doubtless he either wrote out the original draft, or at least dictated every word of it:—

(Some readers will consider this explanation unnecessary. But the writer has met with civilians of intelligence who have believed that all the correspondence Lord Wellington signed was sent in his own handwriting; a task which would have put to shame all the labours of Hercules!)

The Marquis of Wellington to Major-General Whittingham,
(Wellington Dispatches, vol. x.)
(Duplicate.)

Frenada, 1st March, 1813.

Sir,—I have had the honour of receiving your several letters to the 1st February, by the chief of the staff of your division, who arrived here yesterday.

In answer to your letter of the 26th January, I have to inform you that Captain Grey being employed on the eastern coast of Spain, on the service of the regiment to which he belongs, I cannot allow him to serve in the Spanish army.

I have settled with the inspectors–general of cavalry and infantry, *that you shall be appointed the inspector of both arms in the division of troops under your command*; and you will carry out that duty according to the orders and regulations of the Spanish Government.

I have settled with the inspectors of the cavalry to draft the Hussars of Aragon and the regiment of Cuença into the regiment of Almanza and Olivenza. This draft will make those regiments over complete in men; but you will dispose of the horses as you may think proper among the trained men of the regiment as already formed; and the others you will have trained either in Spain or Majorca, until I shall send orders for the disposal of them.—I have the honour to be, Sir,

Your most obedient servant,

Wellington.

Major-General Whittingham.

Lord Wellington, who, as their commander–in–chief, naturally studied to please the Spaniards, gave the above consent most reluctantly, and afterwards refused permission to act on it as a precedent in the case of others, to Lord William Bentinck, on his Lordship's application for that purpose. Could Lord Wellington have given a greater proof of the confidence and esteem which he entertained for General

Whittingham?

The manner in which Lord Wellington yielded on this occasion, was the more remarkable from the impatience with which he received the suggestions and remonstrances of another British Agent, who was senior in rank to General Whittingham. To the officer in question he wrote a few days later as follows:—

> If you dislike your situation, or make any further difficulties about obeying the orders you receive, or fail to carry on the service, you must either resign your command, or in the latter case, I shall recommend to the Government that another officer may be appointed to it. (*Wellington Dispatches*, Vol. X.).

Sir Samford Whittingham's *Recollections* contain a dramatic account of the surprise which the French attempted at Xigona. But there were some (though trifling) inaccuracies, chiefly of names of persons, which occasioned the preference which has been here given to the matter-of-fact letter, written at the period to his brother-in-law, over the more picturesque account written for the amusement of the general's nieces. But the gallant action of one of his own trained Spanish officers is now given from the *Recollections*, in which alone it is recorded:—

> My headquarters were at a place called Muchamiel, about three miles from Alicante. At Xigona I had a strong detachment: but the commander of the forces directed me to occupy Tibi, a village on the farther side of the mountain, and about ten miles in advance of Xigona. I obeyed much against my will. For Tibi was an insulated post, totally unconnected with my chain, and exposed to be attacked by two battalions of French infantry at Onteniente on the right, and by 300 cavalry under the Baron de Lort on the left. (Although on military grounds he considered the order unwise, yet he obeyed it without any expostulation. He always taught that the *first*, *second* and *third* duty of a soldier was obedience!)
>
> I selected for the command of this dangerous post, Captain Ruti, a young *aide-de-camp* of mine of great promise, to whom I was much attached; and I placed under his orders 200 infantry, and 50 hussars of his own regiment of Almanza. I went over the whole ground with Ruti; and pointed out to him the danger of his position, and the line of retreat that I wished him to follow, and the manner in which it should be conducted.

Many nights had not elapsed when the infantry outposts were driven in by a very superior force. But the retreat was conducted with great order and regularity to the *plaza* of Tibi, where Ruti waited to receive them at the head of the troop of the Almanza Hussars. As had been previously arranged, the infantry then retired to the entrance of the pass in the mountains, which led to Xigona, where they halted and formed to cover the retreat of the cavalry through the defile.

In the meantime Ruti had detached a subaltern and ten hussars on the road by which de Lort and his cavalry must come, with orders, on falling in with the enemy, to take ground to his left, to open a desultory fire to detain the movement, and to dispatch a trusty soldier to him (Ruti) at Tibi. The order was perfect: not so, the execution! The young subaltern in command of the party fell in with the enemy as expected, remembered to take ground to his left, but forgot everything else—for he sent no report to Ruti, and he never halted till he arrived at Tibi, several miles distant. Ruti, with the rest of his cavalry, forty hussars, remained formed in the *plaza* till daylight; when despairing of receiving any report from his detachment, he determined upon commencing his retreat upon his infantry. Scarcely, however, had he cleared the village when he saw, drawn up across the only road he could take, four lines of the 24th French dragoons, to intercept his retreat upon Xigona.

Ruti was a second *Chevalier Bayard*. (That is, '*sans peur et sans reproche*,' the very words applied to Sir Samford Whittingham himself by an able reviewer). He saw the extent of his danger, but he felt how greatly his honour would be compromised by suffering his post to be surprised, when he had been especially selected by the general, as peculiarly trustworthy. He did not hesitate, but, briefly addressing his men, told them of his determination to charge, and asked them whether they would dare to follow him. They all shouted *Santiago, y à ellos!* (the Spanish war cry, "St. James, and have at them") and Ruti, at the head of his forty hussars, charged and broke through the first line of French dragoons with little or no loss. The second line was broken through in a similar manner, but with considerable loss; and in the charge against the third line, Ruti fell covered with wounds. His head was dreadfully cut up; and a sabre had passed through his body. Still the charge was continued; and ultimately eleven out of the party joined me at Xigona!

The French were so enchanted at the daring bravery displayed by Ruti, that they carried him on a litter to Onteniente, the headquarters of their commandant; procured for him the best medical aid; and when miraculously cured of his wounds they sent him to my headquarters. I returned the compliment by restoring to liberty two of their (the French's) comrades, who were in my power. For this action Ruti was made a knight of the military order of San Fernando, and shortly afterwards promoted to the rank of Brigadier of cavalry. (This order consisted of Knights; Knights-Commanders; and Knights-Grand-Cross.)

The affair of Concentayna will next be given from the *Recollections*:—

Not long after this splendid skirmish, a general advance took place; and my headquarters were stationed at Alcoy. Sir John Murray had now taken the command of the army at Alicante; and a general reconnaissance to our front was determined on. I had with me at Alcoy five battalions of infantry, a squadron of cavalry, and some mountain guns carried by mules; and on the morning of the reconnaissance I assembled the five battalions, the squadron of cavalry (Cazadores de Olivencia) and two guns, in contiguous close columns, near to Alcoy: and gave verbally the necessary orders for the advance.

My advanced guard consisted of the whole of Colonel Campbell's regiment of light infantry 1,500 strong, a troop of cavalry, and two guns; and was supported by three battalions of infantry, a troop of cavalry, and two mountain guns.

Before the day had well broken we fell in with the French advanced posts, which occupied a wood in front of Onteniente. They were immediately driven back, but rallied on their reserves. As I wished to ascertain the strength of the French force before me, I determined to appear to give way, and sounded the retreat. This brought the French on, hand over hand—and as the whole of Campbell's battalion was at the time in extended order supported by the three battalion columns, the length of the line was immense; and the left being too much thrown forward was in some danger of being cut off, on the rapid and sudden advance of the French.

To provide against this evil I directed the troop of *chasseurs* under Lieutenant Fernandez to charge the centre of the French line, whilst my bugles sounded: *Change front on the centre the left thrown back.* This movement was executed as beautifully and correctly as it could have been done on parade, whilst the sabre of Fernandez almost divided in two a soldier who ventured to oppose him. Every little error being rectified we continued our retreat to where the attack had commenced.

Having thus led the French to show what their force really was, I determined to drive them from their present position and beyond the pass of Albayda. Accordingly, we again advanced with the whole of the light infantry in extended order, supported as before stated; and we drove the enemy at double quick time, from tree to tree, till he was clear of the wood, at the extremity of which his line was formed.

A momentary halt, which I unavoidably made, to give orders as to the occupying a road on our right, which led to the headquarters of General Abert, enabled one of the French sharpshooters to take good aim at my head and to hit me on the right side of my mouth. My former wound was on the left side. This last, however, was only a flesh wound, and I had no time to attend to it. Our advance through the wood was most brilliant and as soon as we had cleared it, our guns were instantly in position; and the two first shots directed by Captain Arabin plunged into the centre of the French line, and created considerable confusion. I forthwith ordered a general advance of all the troops under my command; nor was there any further check till we had conducted the French through the pass of Albayda. General Abert's force and mine were nearly equal, each consisting of about 4,000 bayonets.

★★★★★★

Captain Arabin died as Colonel Arabin, in command of the Royal Artillery at Bermuda, on the 17th August, 1843. On the 8th April, 1847, the eldest son of Sir Samford Whittingham, married Eliza, the eldest daughter of Colonel Arabin.

★★★★★★

Here at last Spanish troops, unaided by British soldiers (except their English chief, and the Scotch colonel), had under skilful guidance, proved more than a match for veteran French warriors. The disgusts and the labours experienced at Majorca were here at last repaid by undeniable fruits on the two occasions narrated; and which were to be officially acknowledged without delay:—

General Order.
Headquarters, Alcoy 8th March, 1813.
In the attack which took place yesterday, Lieutenant-General Sir John Murray received particular satisfaction from observing the brilliant conduct of the Spanish troops engaged; and he begs General Whittingham will make known his approbation in the strongest terms to the officers, and desire them to communicate his sentiments to the troops.

Thomas Molloy,
Assistant Adjutant-General.

The above referred to the Xigona affair. That of Concentayna, or the Puente de Albayda, deserved and received warmer acknowledgment:—

General Order.
Headquarters, Alicante, 17th March, 1813.
No. 2.—Lieutenant-General Sir John Murray has again to draw the attention of the army to the spirit and gallantry with which the Spanish division of Major-General Whittingham conducted itself on the 15th instant.
The attack on that side was much more serious; but by the able dispositions of Major-General Whittingham, and the bravery with which he was supported, the enemy was driven from his positions, and pursued with great loss as far as the Major-General thought expedient.
Lieutenant-General Sir John Murray requests Major-General Whittingham to acquaint the corps engaged, how much their steadiness and general good conduct is approved.

G. A. Harzenbuhler,
Assistant Adjutant-General.

The Marquis of Wellington to Earl Bathurst
(*Wellington Dispatches*, vol. x.)
(Extract.)
Freneda, 7th April, 1813.
Since the movement made by Lieutenant-General Sir John Murray, of which I enclosed the report in my last dispatch, it appears that Marshal Suchet has collected his troops on the right of the Jucar, and has established his headquarters at San

Felipe de Xativa. General Whittingham's division of Spanish troops had driven the enemy's advanced guard beyond the Puente de Albayda.

★★★★★★

Except an allusion to General Donkin's successful reconnaissance this little dispatch of the duke's is all in honour of General Whittingham's two successful affairs previously to the Battle of Castalla.

★★★★★★

As military agent General Whittingham wrote an official account of the action of Concentayna to the ambassador:—

His Excellency the Right Hon. Sir Henry Wellesley, K.B.

Alcoy, 16th March, 1813.

Sir,—I have the honour to inform your Excellency that, in consequence of orders from Lieutenant-General Sir John Murray directing me to make a strong reconnaissance on the enemy's force near Concentayna, I advanced from this at 3 o'clock yesterday morning, with the greater part of the division of Majorca. I also directed Lieutenant-Colonel Bourke commanding the 1st Italian Regiment, which was in La Sarga, to occupy Alcoy with his battalion at daylight; and having situated the regiments of Murcia and Cordova with two four-pounders, and a howitzer in a position previously marked out, about half a, league beyond Alcoy on the Concentayna road, in front of a ravine (on which we had constructed some rough breastworks, and cut the bridge across it so as only to allow one man at a time to pass); I marched out with the remainder in the following order:—

ADVANCED GUARD.

3 companies of Cazadores de Mallorca Light company of Murcia Light company of Cordova 1 Subaltern and 10 Dragoons of Olivencia	*Commanding Officer,* Lieut.-Colonel Mouet, of Cazadores de Mallorca.

COLUMN.

5 companies of Cazadores de Mallorca 2 English mountain four-pounders 5th battalion of Grenadiers 1 Cap. 1 Subⁿ. and 25 Dragoons of Olivencia	*Commanding Officer,* Colonel Campbell.†

On arriving near Concentayna, I posted the grenadier battalion on a rising ground commanding the entrance to the town; the advanced guard entered it; and Colonel Campbell formed the rest of his regiment in close column in the road leading into Concentayna.

Lieutenant-Colonel Mouet passed through the town, and proceeded on by the high road to Albayda; and, a few minutes before sunrise, fell in with an advanced post of the enemy at the Cruz de Valencia, about half a mile from Concentayna. This advanced French party fell back on the next post, followed by Lieutenant-Colonel Mouet's skirmishers; and the enemy, having sent forward reinforcements, there was a very warm fire kept up on both sides, during which Mouet drove the enemy before him for more than a mile; when the French having considerably reinforced their skirmishers, and having drawn up, in position, a battalion of about 600 infantry and 150 dragoons, I directed Lieutenant-Colonel Mouet to retire slowly towards Concentayna, in the hope of drawing the enemy from his position.

Colonel Campbell at the same time moved forward with the five companies of his regiment in close column and with one of the mountain four-pounders under the command of Captain Arabin of the British artillery. The dragoons of Olivencia, with some light infantry moved by the right flank along the road to Muro, and occupied Alcudieta; where the commanding officer was informed that, as soon as the firing began, the French troops which were in Muro and the neighbourhood, had posted themselves at the bottom of the hill near the Puerto de Albayda. (Puente de Albayda it is called in the *Wellington Dispatches*; that is, *bridge* instead of *gate*, Gurwood took such trouble and pains in fixing the proper spelling, and general correctness of the Spanish words, that probably Puente is right). The column having come up near the rear of the advance, Lieutenant-Colonel Mouet again drove the enemy before him, followed by the column, which, with the four-pounders, having arrived within five or six hundred yards of the enemy, halted; when Captain Arabin opened a well-directed fire on the enemy's battalion, which, after a few rounds, retired towards the Puerto de Albayda. Having thus fulfilled Sir John Murray's instructions, I directed Colonel Campbell and Lieutenant-Colonel Mouet to fall back on their former position, which was done without the least molestation on the part of the enemy. The firing began about six in the morning, and lasted till half-past ten in the forenoon.

The enemy's loss, as I understand from different deserters who have since come in, is about sixty men, and two horses killed and wounded. We have counted fourteen dead bodies and two horses. On my part not a man killed, but one captain and five privates of the Cazadores de Mallorca, and two privates of the light company of Murcia are wounded; and I have received a musketshot in the right cheek. (No doubt the rapidity of the attack and pursuit—leaving the enemy little of the leisure and coolness necessary for good firing—was the cause that the victors suffered so little, but of the few wounded the general was one).

I have every reason to be highly satisfied with the gallantry and coolness of the officers and soldiers of the division under my command; who, on this as on every other occasion, have most completely acted up to my expectations, and fulfilled the duty which they owe to their country.

I have the honour to be, your Excellency's most
    obedient and humble servant,

Samford Whittingham.

★★★★★★

Official military letters are apt to scorn full stops, and to prolong sentences into pages, that they may be both written and read with rapidity.

★★★★★★

To conclude the Concentayna affair, the ambassador's reply is here inserted at once:—

Sir Henry Wellesley to Major-General Whittingham.

Cadiz, 1st April, 1813.

Sir,—I have the honour to acknowledge the receipt of your letters of the 16th and 19th *ultimo*, which reached me this morning; and it is with the most sincere satisfaction that I now congratulate you upon the signal proofs afforded by the conduct of your corps in the several affairs in which it has been engaged, of the efficacy of your exertions to bring it to perfection. I shall not fail to transmit to Lord Wellington a copy of your letter to me, and another copy for information of the Government of His Royal Highness the Prince Regent.

I am very happy to learn that the wound which you have received is not of a nature to deprive the country of your services in the field for any considerable time.

I will endeavour to obtain an order to the Marquis of Compigny to the effect mentioned in your letter of the 19th March. (See note following). I will also use my utmost endeavours to procure the confirmation of Colonel O'Reilly in the command of the 5th battalion of Grenadiers.

I have, &c.,

H. Wellesley.

★★★★★★

Note: The letter of the 19th is one of many letters too numerous for insertion in this work. It complained that the Marquis, then Captain-General of the Balearic Islands, kept back in Majorca troops of General Whittingham's division that should have been sent to join the latter.

★★★★★★

In vol. x., of the *Wellington Dispatches*, there is a long memorandum written by his Lordship, (dated 14th April, 1813), regarding the coming operations on the eastern coast, which frequently refers to the Majorca division: but of which only one sentence will here be quoted, namely—the last paragraph:—

If General Sir John Murray's allied British and Sicilian corps, and the whole or part of General Whittingham's division should embark, General the Duque del Parque will direct the operations ordered in this memorandum to be carried on in the kingdom of Valencia; but, in either case, the general officers commanding the first, second, and third armies, and General Whittingham, must command each their separate corps.

This was putting a general of division on the footing of a general commanding an army, as subordinate only to the actual Commander of the Forces—a strong mark of confidence. This was written a fortnight before Lord Wellington received Sir John Murray's report of the Battle of Castalla, which established yet higher the reputation of the Majorca division.

To his Brother-in-law.

Division, Majorca Headquarters,
Alcoy, 19th March, 1813.

My dear Davis,—I enclose an account of an affair which took place on the 15th. You will see with pleasure that the division has been twice thanked in General Orders.

As my wound is painful, though not in the least dangerous, pray send a copy of the enclosed to Colonel Torrens, and beg him to excuse my writing.

The French have fifteen battalions in my front, at Albayda and San Felipe. Our army is concentrating itself, and a few days will, I hope, bring on a general action, at which, I thank God, I shall still be able to play my part.

Best love to all, and believe me, ever yours,

Samford Whittingham.

The Battle of Castalla was fought and won on the 13th April, 1813, by the allied English and Spanish troops; but mainly by two corps of that army; namely, one of Englishmen under Colonel Adam, (see note following), which gained the chief honours of the day; and the other of Spaniards under Major-General Whittingham, who proved themselves worthy of fighting with British soldiers, and contributed largely to the successful result.

★★★★★★

Colonel Adam, of the 21st Foot, (afterwards Sir Frederick Adam, K.C.B., G.C.M.G.,) was far senior *in the British Army* to Lieutenant-Colonel Whittingham; for on the same 4th of June, 1814, on which the latter was made a Colonel, the former was gazetted a Major-General. It was not till 1825, that Whittingham became a Major-General in the British service. Sir F. Adam was the second Lord High Commissioner of the Ionian Islands.

★★★★★★

But let the commander-in-chief on that day have, as is right, the first word:—

General Order.

Headquarters, Castalla, 14th April, 1813.

Lieutenant-General Sir John Murray congratulates the army he has the honour to command, on the result of the action which took place yesterday. Marshal Suchet collected his whole force, for the express purpose of destroying this army; trusting to the good fortune which had hitherto attended his arms. He has been defeated, and forced to retreat, by a small portion of it.

The lieutenant-general requests the officers and soldiers of the corps engaged to accept his best thanks for their gallantry; and assures them, that he will not fail to draw the attention of His Royal Highness the Prince Regent, and of the Spanish Government, to the bravery, spirit, and discipline displayed.

As the reports from the officers commanding divisions, of what immediately passed under their direction, have not yet reached the lieutenant-general, he is obliged to defer the just tribute of applause to those corps and individuals who have been fortunate enough to find an opportunity of distinguishing themselves. But, from Sir John Murray's own observation, he is fully authorised to hold up to every army in Europe the conduct of Colonel Adam and his brave corps, on the 12th and 13th instant, as an example worthy of applause and imitation; and he has the satisfaction of expressing a no less degree of approbation of the conduct of Major-General Whittingham and his gallant troops in the action of the 13th. (Thus three times in five weeks was the Majorca division praised in General Orders).

The lieutenant-general has much satisfaction in conveying his approbation of the spirit displayed by every other part of the army on the 12th and 13th instant. They had not the fortunate lot of the advance, and of General Whittingham; but it was evident that had the enemy waited the attack on the 13th, in the plains of Castalla, that he would have found the same spirit to have existed throughout the whole allied army.

'The lieutenant-general has experienced, ever since he has held this honourable command, every support and assistance from the general officers and brigadiers, (see note following), of the army; and he is happy that an opportunity has been afforded him of expressing that gratitude which he deeply feels. Nor is he less indebted to the general staff of the army, for their cordial support, and the cheerful alacrity with which every part of the service is performed. In mentioning the general staff of the army Sir John Murray feels that he would be wanting in justice if he omitted the name of Major-General Donkin, to whom he is more particularly indebted.

The lieutenant-general has now only pointedly to express his approbation of the artillery corps engaged in every part, and to assure Captain Arabin that, so far from finding the slightest grounds of censure for the loss of the two mountain guns, he highly approved the spirit and motive which induced him to keep them in their position, till it became impossible, in their crippled state to remove them.

Deeply as every soldier feels the loss of a brave comrade who may fall, it is a consolation to think that the allied army has, in comparison with that of the enemy, suffered, in numbers at least, a trifling loss.

Thomas Kenagh,
Assistant Adjutant-General.

★★★★★★

Note:—Colonel Adam appears to have been one of these brigadiers, as he is described as commanding a body of troops. He was Lieut.-Colonel of the 21st Regiment of Foot, the North British Fusiliers.

★★★★★★

General Whittingham's official report was as follows:—

To His Excellency the General-in-Chief of the Allied Army.
Camp of Guerra, 14th April, 1813.
Sir,—Yesterday the 13th, in consequence of your Excellency's orders communicated to me by Lieutenant-Colonel Catinelli, I marched at mid-day by my left, from my position on the heights of Guerra, with the 5th battalion of Grenadiers, the 2nd of Murcia, and that of the Cazadores of Majorca, by the road of the Montana, which joins that of Sax; prolonging the left of the line, and leaving in my position the 1st battalion of Cordova and the 2nd of Burgos, under Colonel Juan Romero.

After marching about half an hour I received a message from Major Guerra (whom I had left with two companies covering the heights of Nadal) informing me that three columns of the enemy were forming at the foot of his position, and were preparing to attack him. I immediately ordered Colonel Serrano, chief of my staff, to march rapidly and place the 2nd Regiment of Murcia so as to support Major Guerra; giving positive orders to Colonel Casans that the post should be defended at whatever cost, and that he should proceed to the heights of Guerra, and acquaint me with the state of that point.

The fire was already general along the line; and observing that the enemy was possessing himself of the last height on the left—from whence he might flank those on the Nadal, I ordered Colonel Campbell, of the Majorca Cazadores, to obtain possession of that height with two companies; which he accomplished most promptly at the point of the bayonet. Leaving the remainder of this corps on this part of the line, I hastened

170

with the 5th Regiment of Grenadiers back to the position on the heights of Guerra, which was now vigorously attacked. On my march I received a verbal communication from Colonel Serrano, informing me that it was absolutely necessary to strengthen that point with more troops, as Colonel Romero, with the Cordova and Burgos Regiments, was sorely pressed, and required support.

The moment I arrived, I formed the grenadiers into two columns on the flat on the top of the heights of Guerra, fronting the two most accessible points, and against which the attacks were principally directed. A strong column of French grenadiers had taken the height of Sarratella, with another still stronger column of fusiliers on their right. I ordered the reserves to advance, Romero maintained himself on the first line with great firmness. After a very obstinate fight on both sides, the enemy determined to attack with the bayonet; his first column advancing by the crest of the mountain; the second, lower, down, by the opening of Palliser.

I immediately directed Lieutenant-Colonel Ochoa to advance with our reserve, and sustain the first point; and Colonel Serrano took the other (commanded by Major Ontiveros) by his left to cover the opening of Palliser. The enemy advanced boldly to the edge of the position; but the reserves immediately deployed, and advanced to the charge with so much spirit (supported by the troops of the first line) that the enemy was overthrown and put into the greatest confusion; nor could he again form until he had returned to his position on the summit of the hill of Doncel.

Colonel Casans of the 2nd Regiment of Murcia, to whom, as already mentioned, I had trusted the command of the left, was attacked by upwards of 800 men in strong skirmishing parties, supported by a column of grenadiers and *chasseurs*, and a numerous reserve. But this officer ordered his grenadiers and *cazadores* to advance and support the Majorca Regiment, which was warmly attacked; and with that of Murcia, in the post of Olla Redonda, the *cazadores* of the 5th Grenadiers, and the 1st of Guadalaxara kept up a steady fire; which the enemy notwithstanding disregarded, being resolved to break the line.

But Colonel Casans having brought out his reserves, and given the command of his right to Major Bascon, of his left to Lieutenant-Colonel M. Sas, and of his centre to Major Guerra, they kept up the fire till half-past four in the afternoon; when, annoyed by the obstinacy of the enemy, Colonel Casans ordered the before mentioned troops, with four companies of the *cazadores* of Majorca, to charge with the bayonet; which they did immediately with such a countenance that the French dared not await them, but fled shamefully, and with too much expedition to allow our men, who were much fatigued, to make many prisoners.

I can assure. your Excellency that the force with which the enemy attacked us was greatly superior to mine; and that, after a most obstinate conflict of three hours and a half, he was repulsed at the same time on the whole line, leaving the field covered with his dead.

I subsequently received your Excellency's orders to move my line forward, in proportion as the other troops of the army should advance. As soon as I perceived the general movement, I left Colonel Casteras with the battalion of Burgos in the position, and advanced with the 5th Grenadiers and the 1st of Cordova, covering my front with two companies of Majorca as skirmishers.

I marched in this order to the summit of Doncel, following the first line of the English troops, on which my right leaned. (It is meant that he *dressed* his line by that of the English in its advance). At the same time, I sent by my left, by the Montana del Aquila, Colonel Casans with the regiments of Murcia and Majorca, strengthened by his Britannic Majesty's 1st Italian battalion, with the view of flanking the enemy's right; which they accomplished by descending into the plain, and taking the direction of Monte de los Zerres. The skirmishers were charged at the foot of that hill by a detachment of the enemy's cavalry, which they succeeded in repulsing with loss, when the whole column halted, on the approach of night, and returned to its position, by your Excellency's orders.

To your Excellency I particularly recommend, in the strongest terms, Colonel Serrano, chief of my staff, to whose exertions, valour, and knowledge, is owing much of the success of this day. I also particularly recommend Lieutenant-Colonel Catanelli, who was in the whole of the action and gave much assistance. The second adjutant of the general staff, and the assistants, Don

Joseph Serrano and Don Samuel Alvares, Colonel Gelabert, quartermaster-general. Captain Montenegro, of the engineers, and my *aide-de-camp*, Don Antonio Ruti, and the Baron de Halberg, completely fulfilled their duties and carried my orders with the greatest dispatch and precision.

The spirit and correctness of the officers of my division have been so distinguished, that I must in justice call your Excellency's attention to the conduct of Colonels Casans, Romero, Campbell, Casteras, and Lieutenant-Colonel Ochoa, and all the other commanders and officers. In one word, both men and officers have completely done their duty; and having been all equally engaged, they are equally entitled to the gratitude of their country; particularly the memory of those brave men, Lieutenant-Colonel Sudrez of the 5th Grenadiers, Lieutenant-Colonel Pizarro of the regiment of Burgos, and Lieutenant-Colonel Puerto of the Majorca, who fell in the action. Major Bascon received a contusion. Lieutenant Morales of the Cordova, Lieutenant Castaneda of the Guadalaxara, and the sublieutenant of the Majorca, Serrano, were wounded; with 66 rank and file killed, and 163 wounded; which with the 29 men that the battalion there engaged lost on the 12th on the pass of Biar, make a total of 258 men.

I have, &c.,

Samford Whittingham.

It is proved by two dispatches of Lord Wellington, dated 5th May and 9th August, 1813, that the Spanish division of General Roche was at Castalla very weak in the field, nearly all the men being at the depot. Moreover, that division being on the right, was not actively engaged. The state and conduct of the Majorca division appear to have been achievements *with Spanish troops* quite unrivalled in the Peninsula.

The following extracts from Sir John Murray's dispatch of the Battle of Castalla to the Marquis of Wellington, refer to General Whittingham and his division;—

The position of the allied army was extensive. The left wag posted on a strong range of hills, occupied by Major-General Whittingham's division of Spanish troops, and the advance of the allied army under Colonel Adam.

The skill, judgment, and gallantry displayed by Major-General Whittingham and his division of the Spanish Army, rivals, though it cannot surpass, the conduct of Colonel Adam and the advance.

That the British general-in-chief, should thus acknowledge that Spaniards had rivalled Britons in the battle was assuredly a sufficient proof that the labours of the zealous organiser in Majorca had not been thrown away. General Murray also forwarded and endorsed the recommendations made by General Whittingham of his gallant subordinates. (Though *thrice* honourably mentioned in General Orders, and again in the dispatch, no one would suppose from Napier's accounts of the Eastern Campaign, that either Whittingham or his Spanish division had done anything particular. *The duke* knew better).

On the 9th May, 1813, the great hero deigned to indite a paper of 'Observations on General Whittingham's memorandum of the 24th April, 1812, in regard to the draft of supplies from the country' (Vol. x); and though he declared it to be 'impracticable to execute what is proposed,' he yet discussed it with respect and condemned the project solely on the ground of the inferiority to the French on certain points both of English and Spanish troops. Such measures experience indeed proved, owing to Lord Wellington's marvellous successes, to be unnecessary.

But it might have been otherwise, but for the invasion of Russia; and if Napoleon, abandoning that mad project, had reinforced his Peninsular army by 100,000 more soldiers. In that case forced requisitions, or an abandonment of Spain would have been the only alternatives to keep the army from starving. The retreat after Talavera was mainly caused by the absence of such requisitions, and by the indolence and ill-will of the Spanish authorities, who scrupled not themselves to take what was wanted for their own troops, though they took no trouble to supply the British.

After the praise given to the Majorca division by Sir John Murray on so many occasions, it will surprise no one that the Spaniards were rendered almost wild with enthusiasm by the accounts of the prowess of their countrymen against the detested invaders. In the *Redactor General* (a Spanish journal) of April 1813, there is a long and glowing article on the *Te Deums* and rejoicings on account of the victory of Castalla, in the usual inflated style of warm southern imaginations. The translation of one of its paragraphs is sufficient on the present occasion:—

General Whittingham, that chief so zealous in inspiring all warlike virtues into his beloved soldiers, must be superabundantly satisfied and recompensed in seeing his labours in the organising of these never-sufficiently-to-be-praised Spaniards thus crowned with success.

The following incident of the Battle of Castalla is taken from the *Recollections*:—

I was directed to march upon Castalla with the whole of the force under my command, except two battalions which were to remain at Alcoy. On my arrival at Castalla, I occupied a range of heights on the left of the town. The British left and my right were contiguous. Suchet had advanced from Valencia with about 12,000 men; and had attacked some posts of General Elio, and taken a thousand prisoners. Our advanced guard under Brigadier Adam was driven through the pass of Biar upon our main body at Castalla. But the retreat was a beautiful field-day, by alternate battalions.

The volleys were admirable, and the successive passage of several ravines conducted with perfect order and steadiness. From the heights occupied by my troops it was one of the most delightful panoramas that I ever beheld!

About ten o'clock on the next morning, I received orders from Sir John Murray, through Lieutenant-Colonel Catanelli (an Italian officer on the staff of Lord William Bentinck) to take ground to my left till 1 should reach the head of a ravine in that direction, then to bring my left shoulder forwards, descending the valley, and form perpendicularly to the right of Suchet's line.

In the meantime Sir John was to advance with his whole force from Castalla, and attack Suchet in front. I told Catanelli that I should of course obey but that I did not believe in the correctness of his communication; and Sir John Murray afterwards assured me that he had never given any order to Catanelli. Luckily, foreseeing that the heights which I occupied would probably be attacked as soon as my movement to the left should be perceived, I left all the advanced posts and their supports standing; and passing by their rear in columns of companies left in front, I had hardly begun to descend the valley in single file, when a report was brought to me that the French were advancing to the attack of the heights of Castalla, and that the outposts

175

were already warmly engaged. I instantly countermarched, and formed columns of companies at double quick, as the troops successively cleared the defile; and I re-occupied my former position just in time to repel the final attack of the French. (See note following).Our loss did not exceed 300 men; the French suffered severely, not having fewer than 3,000 men *hors de combat.*

★★★★★★

Note:—This account of the mistake of Catanelli is confirmed by Southey. Indeed, he probably received the particulars from General Whittingham, or found them at the Horse-Guards, in the letters of that officer.

★★★★★★

Our advantage was not followed up, and Suchet was permitted to retire without further molestation, through the pass of Biar, by which he had advanced.

CHAPTER 10

1813—Continued

General Whittingham to his Brother-in-law.

Alcoy, 13th May, 1813.

Suchet's force has been reinforced since the action [of Castalla] by the junction of the division that he had in Aragon (about 5,000 men), and by the arrival of about 2,000 conscripts. Ours had been lessened by 3,000 men lost by General Elio at Gerla and Biar, and by the detachment of three regiments sent to Sicily. We received yesterday the news that General Hill had entered Toledo, and that the Duke del Parque was at Almaraz.

The Spaniards are not in a state to act alone even a subordinate part; and one of two things must result from sending Sir John Murray's army away. Either the army acts alone, entirely composed of Spanish troops, and under the command of the Duke del Parque, in which case it will be entirely destroyed in the first action in which it may be engaged; or Lord Wellington will be obliged to detach General Hill with his *corps d'armée* to take the supreme command here; and by so doing weaken considerably the effect of his great mass of troops; had he been able to keep them concentrated in one sole line of operation.

As to this unfortunate country I see it in a more deplorable point of view every day. Nine months have nearly passed away since the Battle of Salamanca, two-thirds of Spain have been free during that period; and yet the only increase to our army is about 12,000 men under O'Donnel, and the troops are neither better paid nor better fed than when Spain was reduced to Cadiz.

My little division has established a certain reputation in the country, which is highly advantageous to the *esprit de corps* that

I have always endeavoured to keep up. (More than he was then aware of, since its commander had gained—as will be seen hereafter—the high esteem of the able Marshal Suchet, Duke of Albufera). But as I have no means of recruiting my losses, a few months of active campaign will lead us fairly and softly to a natural death. I live in hopes, however, that in consequence of the Battle of Castalla, I may receive some augmentations to my force.

The death of his dear friend the Honourable Henry Cadogan at Vittoria on the 21st June, 1813, must have been a grievous blow to the subject of this *Memoir* and deserves a passing allusion. Cadogan had been gazetted on the 4th June to the rank of Colonel, but he died before his promotion was known in the Peninsula. (Had Colonel Cadogan survived, he would have succeeded to the earldom of Cadogan in 1832, instead of his younger brother George).

Lord Wellington on the 22nd of June, in his dispatch to Earl Bathurst, writes:

I am concerned to have to report that Lieutenant-Colonel the Hon. H. Cadogan has died of a wound which he received. In him His Majesty has lost an officer of great merit and tried gallantry, who had already acquired the respect and regard of the whole profession, and of whom it might have been expected that, if he had lived, he would have rendered the most important services to his country.

On the 24th, Lord Wellington writes to his brother Sir Henry Wellesley:

I know how much you will feel for the loss of poor Cadogan, which has distressed me exceedingly. He was so anxious respecting what was going on, that after he was wounded and knew that he was dying, he had himself carried to a place whence he could see all the operations.

Thus heroically died the beloved and loving friend of Samford Whittingham.

On the 28th of May, Sir John Murray's army embarked for Catalonia, and sailed on the 31st; disembarked on the 3rd June, and immediately invested Tarragona. The abandonment of that enterprise, owing to the advance, with a large force, of Marshal Suchet to the relief of the town, was effected in such haste as to cause a considerable loss of guns and military stores, and also eventually to bring before a court-martial the British Commander of the Forces. On the 17th June, Lord William Bentinck relieved Sir John Murray of his command, and then was renewed the acquaintance between that distinguished nobleman and General Whittingham, which quickly ripened into mutual esteem, and ended in durable friendship. We resume the *Recollections*:—

At the siege of Tarragona, my division of infantry occupied the left of the investment. Suchet had advanced to the relief with 10,000 men, but without artillery. I submitted to the consideration of Sir John Murray that General Copons, and the Spanish corps under his command, should be left before Tarragona, and that he himself should move upon Suchet with all his force. My opinion was not approved; and a few days afterwards the siege was ordered to be raised, and with such precipitation that several guns were abandoned, and our honour unnecessarily compromised. Before our re-embarkation for Alicante Lord William Bentinck had arrived, and taken the command of the army. His Lordship forthwith advanced a second time upon Tarragona, but by land. Suchet, determined to save the place if possible, brought up all the disposable force under his command, to the amount of 30,000 men.

Lord William's army consisted of the divisions of Sarsfield and Whittingham, about 6,000 men each, and of the force under the Duke del Parque of 12,000 men. The three generals were directed to meet at Lord William's headquarters, and a council of war was held on the expediency of risking a general action with Suchet. It was determined in the negative; and a general retreat being ordered, I was left to cover it with my division.

The country which we then occupied was intersected by stone walls enclosing fields of a moderate size, and every road formed a small defile. Between my advanced post and the enemy there was a deep but very accessible ravine, at the head of which stood a village occupied by my troops. In rear of the village there was a large open space; and beyond that a long wall of about four feet high, pierced through its centre by the common road. Besides the infantry, I had with me two eight-pounders, horse artillery, and nearly 2,000 cavalry. Having ascertained the proximate approach of the enemy, I sent the artillery and cavalry to the rear, excepting only fifty hussars, which, with two companies of grenadiers, I pushed across the ravine, as a check upon the too rapid advance of the French. I then lined the wall on the farther side of the common with Campbell's light infantry, and sent a staff-officer with all the battalions of the line, to form them on either side of the road at convenient distances successively, in order the better to secure our retreat.

I had scarcely made all these arrangements, when the troops on the farther side of the ravine were driven in at double quick; and they had just commenced filing to the rear through the opening in the wall, when the French hussars came through the village at a gallop—formed to the front—and charged the troops entering the defile.

It was now my turn. The whole battalion of light infantry, which had been concealed behind the wall, stood up; and commenced, from that rest, (on the wall for their muskets; ensuring steadiness of aim a most destructive fire), which brought down a great number, and sent the remainder to the right-about as speedily as their horses' legs could carry them. A general of division should always be *the first to advance and the last to retreat*. That is invariably his post. I consequently retired with Campbell's battalion, and gradually and successively sent on the different battalions, as they came up in their echelons to more distant points in our rear.

The pursuit was warmly followed up till nightfall; when having crossed a ravine at ——, (name was left blank, having slipped from the memory of the writer), we ascended the height on the opposite side, and took up our position for the night. In the village we found five thousand rations of bread, which had been prepared for the French. I ordered them to be distributed to our men, in spite of the reclamations of the civil authorities. I then proceeded to open communications through the walls in my rear for the passage of the troops, on their retreat in the morning; and having detached on our right a subaltern and twenty hussars, to ascertain the security of that flank, I threw myself down on a bundle of straw, and in a moment was fast asleep; for I do not recollect ever, in my whole life, to have been half so tired.

At one o'clock a.m., my servant awoke me to say that a dish of stewed partridge was ready; and I certainly did eat, as most starved people are wont to do—like a hunter. (The critical reader must remember that these *Recollections*—as explained in the *Preface*—were written for a beloved niece, and were never intended for publication).

I waited the next morning till near daylight, in the hope that my hussar patrol would make its appearance. But I was disappointed; for it turned out that the young officer had disobeyed my orders not to dismount, much less to enter any house, and had in consequence been surprised and taken prisoner with the whole of his party. Our further retreat to Lord William's headquarters was effected without loss. The distance was ten miles, and we marched it in two hours and a half.

Lord Wellington did not approve of the Spanish system of divisional inspectors, but as commander-in-chief of the Spanish armies he did not venture to abolish them generally:—

The Marquis of Wellington to Lieutenant-General Lord
William Bentinck.
(Vol. X. *Wellington Dispatches*).
(Extract.)

Irurita, 8th July, 1813.

You will have seen that by the Constitution, all military regulation is in the hands of the Cortes, and they have a board of officers now sitting to consider of a military constitution for the army, which it is intended to republicanize. Any proposal for an alteration, therefore, is laid aside till the new military constitution shall be fixed. One of the defects in the constitution of the Spanish army, as now existing, is in the office and power of the inspectors of cavalry and infantry, in whose hands is the nomination of all officers to commission, and for promotion.

This cannot *be altered. Whittingham, contrary to all rule, is both Commander and Inspector of his own division. I have not the power to make the same arrangement in favour of anybody else.*

I have no objection to your allowing the Duque del Parque cavalry to act under the command of Whittingham for the moment; but I beg you not to make any alteration in the existing organisation of any of the Spanish armies. If you do, you will bring me into difficulties.

★★★★★★

The editor ventures to place in italics a sentence so honourable to the subject of this *Memoir*. Not only the confidence of the illustrious chief is here displayed, but the great popularity of General Whittingham in Spain is strikingly manifested.

★★★★★★

With Lord William Bentinck, as with every commander he successively served under, confidence in General Whittingham seems to have been the invariable rule: but indeed it appears to have been equally so in the case of civilians, whether statesmen or diplomatists, with whom he came in contact; always excepting that brief episode with the Governor of Gibraltar, where he had not the opportunity by personal intercourse of gaining the esteem of that over-punctilious functionary.

The formation of the rival division of General Roche appears to have been, comparatively speaking, a failure; as on the 9th August, 1813, we find Lord Wellington writing to Lord William Bentinck: 'I shall not allow any pay in future for a division under General Roche, as he has no such division serving in the field.' This clearly proves (and it is therefore quoted) the immense difficulty of the task which General Whittingham succeeded in accomplishing at Majorca.

To his Brother-in-law.

Torrente, 11th July, 1813.

At the request of Lord William Bentinck, of the Duke del Parque, and of General Elio, I have taken the command of the cavalry of the 2nd and 3rd army, which, added to that of my division, makes about 2,500 horse. I have accepted this command because I have been ordered to do so; but I have declared to them all that I cannot be answerable for the consequences. If I had them for some months, they might be formed into good soldiers. But at present there is no time for instruction; and in the present condition of the Spanish cavalry, there is not a single regiment in a state to fight the French, with the most distant chance of success.

In the year which has elapsed since the Battle of Salamanca, the Spanish Army has not been increased by 20,000 men; nor do I see the least hope of a change of system. Lord Wellington has been doing wonders; but England, as I have repeated again and again, can never save Spain if Spain will do nothing for herself. 'In short, my dear Davis, I am tired of a scene where my mind is continually harassed, and where it is not in my power to do the least good; and I entreat you to obtain an order for me to

182

return home, and get my accounts with Government passed. They are long and voluminous, and, if not settled during my life, they will probably be the cause of infinite vexation and loss to my family.

No man has considered the Spanish Revolution with greater impartiality than myself. When we were reduced to Cadiz and the Balearic Islands, my spirits were high, and I trusted that a day of reaction would arrive which would place the Spaniards in the situation of the French in the year '94. That day has arrived. Lord. Wellington's memorable Battle of Salamanca put the Spaniards in possession of the best part of their country, and gave them the means of forming great and powerful armies!

Have they taken advantage of these circumstances? Have they done anything for their own salvation? Their whole time has been occupied in the forming of a cursed Constitution, and their army has been forgotten and neglected! We have not, I again repeat, increased our army 20,000 men in the last year, nor is there in my opinion any hopes of amendment.

About four months ago General Freyre, with 3,500 cavalry, was sent to Seville by order of Lord Wellington, to clothe, arm, equip, and instruct the corps. I saw a letter from General Freyre, about a fortnight since, in which he states that he had received nothing; and that he was not able to exercise his cavalry *for want of money to pay for the horses' shoes!*

You must be satisfied that a year's reflection is sufficient. That time has elapsed since I first wrote to you on the subject. Get me recalled, and allow me to pass some years at least of happiness with you and yours.

In a letter marked *private*, and dated Torrente, 17th July, 1813, he gives to his brother-in-law a detail of the advice he had given to Sir John Murray at the camp of Tarragona, which, as it is embodied in Southey's history, need not be here detailed.

To Colonel Torrens, Military Secretary.

Torrente, 17th July, 1813.

My dear Friend,—I beg leave to recommend to your attentions and civilities, my *aide-de-camp,* Baron Halberg, who passes through London on his way to Germany. He is a gentleman I much esteem as an officer, and a friend; and as he has been with me for two years, he can give you a good account of the state of the troops which I have the honour to command.

I remain, my dear Friend,

Yours most truly,

Samford Whittingham.

Although General Whittingham was exceedingly popular with the Spaniards with whom he came in contact, or rather, perhaps, on that very account, high-placed Spanish officials were often very jealous of the Englishman, who by his zeal and energy appeared to put to shame their own lack of such qualities. These officials gratified their malice by all kinds of slights and insults, and amongst the worst of them were the Ministers of War and Finance. At last matters were carried to such a length, that patience was exhausted. On the 5th August, 1813, General Whittingham sent in his resignation to the Regency; and on the day following he sent it also to Lord Wellington, who was not only the Commander-in-Chief of the Spanish Army, but to whom the ambassador, Sir Henry Wellesley, had yielded the chief control over the British military agents.

Thus, in the course of a year, the two brothers had successively received letters of resignation from the same subordinate. Sir Henry Wellesley had condescended to request the withdrawal of the resignation in 1812. The Majorca division and its commander had since greatly distinguished themselves; but Lord Wellington was different from, and sterner than, his brother. Would he condescend in a similar manner? General Whittingham, at all events, expected no such result:—

Major-General Whittingham to the Marquis of Wellington.

Camp before Tarragona, 6th August, 1813.

My Lord,—I have the honour to enclose translations of various official letters which have passed relative to the subsistence of the troops under my command. I have endeavoured to the best of my power to act up to your Lordship's instructions considering that if a smaller sum than had at first appeared necessary, should be found sufficient, the difference ought necessarily to result in diminishing the sum appropriated by the British Government; inasmuch as your Lordship's order is positive that no part of the money destined for the division of Majorca should be employed in the purchase of provisions. The Duke del Parque, and General Elio, both perfectly agreed with me in the interpretation of your Lordship's instructions; but the official communication which I have just received upon this subject from the Minister of Finance is couched in such terms that I cannot in justice to my own feelings avoid sending in my resignation, which I have directed to General Wimpffen, to be forwarded, with your Lordship's permission, to the Spanish Government.

I cannot take my leave of this country without availing myself of the opportunity of returning my most grateful thanks to your Lordship for the many favours which I have received at your hands. The obligations, indeed, which I am under to your Lordship, to Marquis Wellesley, and to Sir Henry, will never be effaced from my memory; and nothing will afford me through life so much satisfaction, as to have an opportunity in my limited sphere, of proving the sentiments of respect and gratitude which animate my mind towards everything bearing the name of Wellesley.

If your Lordship will be pleased to grant me permission, I wish to return immediately to England, and I should take it as a particular favour if Captain Foley might be permitted to accompany me; as I am extremely desirous of getting my account with the British Government settled as soon as possible.

I have the honour to be, with the highest respect,

 Your Lordship's most obedient humble servant,

         Samford Whittinham.

On the 22nd August, he gives to his brother-in-law the reasons in detail which had induced him to resign. The minister, had begun to stop indirectly his acknowledged right to promote the officers of his division; in one case going so far as to separate the regiment of Burgos, which he had formed, from his command. They took in fact every opportunity of slighting him, and letting it be understood that his favour was no recommendation in their eyes. Carrying insult to the extreme limits of falsehood, the *intendant* of the 2nd army—eager, no doubt, to please the ministers—told some of General Whittingham's officers, 'that the division of Majorca was more prejudicial than useful to the nation, and the Minister of Finance ventures to tell me that I am ignorant of the duties of a Spanish general.' The letter continues as follows:—

The measure, my dear Davis, is at last *full*, I have borne with patience insults and persecutions, because I conceived that my efforts would do good, in our great and glorious cause. In the present case, the opposite impression is strong upon my mind. I am satisfied that, not having it in my power to forward the interests of the war—inasmuch as I am become the innocent cause of ruining the career of all who serve under my orders—it is my duty not to hold a command which could only serve to flatter my vanity at the expense of interests that I have always held dearer than my own. I have, as Buonaparte says of his politics, a morality of my own; and I can never for a moment consent that for my personal advantage, the interests of those whom I am bound to protect and cherish should suffer the least detriment.

On, the point of quitting the military career, I have had the satisfaction of executing two operations well.

When Lord William retired from before Tarragona, on the approach of Soult, my corps which was the most advanced, was attacked by a French column of 5,000 infantry, and 300 cavalry. I had with me 1,300 infantry, and 40 dragoons. This little force retired with admirable order upwards of ten miles—checked and repulsed the enemy whenever he pressed upon us, and about seven in the evening effected a junction with the remainder of the division, which by my orders occupied a commanding position in Biar. At one in the morning we again began our retreat, and joined the main body of the army at Cambrils. Our retreat was from the Coll de St. Christina to Brassin-Valls—Reus, and Cambrils—a distance of thirty-three miles.

On the 17th, Lord William Bentinck ordered me to leave the division of infantry of my command at Coll de Balaguer; and with the whole of the Spanish cavalry to continue my retreat to the Ebro, and to cross the river as quickly as possible. The whole of the baggage of the 3rd army, and one division of 2,000 men under the command of the Duke del Parque had taken the same route the evening before.

At ten at night I arrived on the banks of the Ebro, and found the only means of passage to be a raft, capable of carrying over four carts; and one small boat. Tortosa was distant two leagues; its garrison 6,500 men; and reinforcements immediately expected from Suchet.

The division of infantry of the duke's army took up a position on our right. The baggage of the duke's army began to pass, and by dint of the greatest efforts, I collected by the morning eight small boats; each boat held two men with their saddles, &c.; and two horses swam the river, *each man leading his horse*. (This was a slight error, corrected in his *Recollections*, as will be seen hereafter. With these miserable means, I passed over in the day and night of the 18th August the whole of the cavalry and artillery, excepting six pieces and two squadrons.

On the morning of the 19th, the French attacked General Berenger (who commanded the covering division) with six pieces of cannon, 4,000 infantry, and ninety dragoons. Things looked very ill; when the rapid advance of three of my guns on the right, and three on the left, and their truly well-directed fire, checked the progress of the enemy, and induced him to order a retreat. A battalion of grenadiers, sent by the duke from the other side of the river, ably supported by the guns on the left, and the arrival of the head of the duke's staff, remedied the errors and follies of the general commanding,—*who, I am grieved to say, was literally as drunk as a beast*

My artillery had never been in fire before; but they did wonders. The French General Robert's *aide-de-camp* dined with me yesterday, and informed me that they thought the whole of our cavalry and artillery had crossed the river; and that General Robert determined upon retreating as soon as he found out his mistake. We had two other guns, which could not be used for want of men and horses, these being on the other side of the river. I drew them up, however, in the plain, and formed on their right an immense squadron of all the servants and mounted followers of the army; who made a great show, and served to impose not a little.

We have lost about 400 men in killed and wounded, and the French about double that number. Suchet has blown up the works of Tarragona, and our troops have entered the town.

I hope to be with you in the month October: and I trust in God that we shall pass many happy days together in the renewal of those first and beloved impressions which in good minds are never to be effaced.

In his *Recollections*, Sir Samford has given a very graphic account of his passage of the Ebro, which, though more picturesque, differs from the letter written at the period in only one very trifling fact, and, strange to say, in that, the *Recollections* appear the more accurate and probable. Perhaps the letter written on active service was hurried. What was written in 1840, is as follows:—

> On arriving at the Ebro we found ourselves without boats to effect our passage. We tried to swim the horses over without dismounting the men. But invariably as soon as the horse felt a little tired he dropped his hind quarters, and his rider floated out of the saddle. I linked a division of horses together, but they had not half crossed the river, when they began to fight, and they were all drowned. I finally adopted the plan of putting two men in a small boat, *one to row and one to lead the horses.*

That portion of the *Recollections* on this subject which only repeats what has been already given in quotations from the letter of 22nd August is omitted, but what comes next is here subjoined, beginning after the repulse of the garrison of Tortosa:—

> Having failed in their surprise, the French continued their re-treat closely followed by our troops. Like old and experienced soldiers, they took advantage of every obstacle to impede our advance, and to cover their retreat. In this affair I lost a dear and much esteemed friend, O'Reilly. He was nephew to the famous Count O'Reilly, and as gallant a soldier as ever drew sword. We had studied together at High Wycombe: and on his joining me in Spain, I made him colonel of a regiment of grenadiers;—for all power of promotion, of organisation, of distribution, and of employment of the troops under my command had been placed by the Spanish Government, with the approbation of the Duke of Wellington, exclusively in my hands.
>
> In following up the French too eagerly, at the head of a single detachment of cavalry, his (O'Reilly's) horse was shot under him, and he fell. His cavalry fled, and the French soldiers who had fired from behind a wall, leaped over and murdered him in cold blood. I was not two hundred yards from the spot when he fell; but in a moment he was stripped, and on his bleeding body were discovered no less than seven bayonet wounds, one of which was quite through the throat. Severely, however, did the enemy pay for this act of barbarity. Several hundreds of their wounded men remained on the field of battle, every one of

whom fell a sacrifice to the manes of O'Reilly, for our infuriated soldiers gave no quarter after his death.

The exact time when the following circumstance occurred, the editor has not been able to discover. The account is taken from the *Recollections*, and is worthy of being recorded:—

My instructions during my stay in Aragon were to take care of the condition of the horses, and to form the largest possible depot of grain, and of the means of transport for our future advance into Catalonia. I had no other means of feeding my troops but by requisitions, which, however, the commissary-general alone was allowed to make, countersigned by me. But the distribution of the quantity to be furnished by each town was made by the municipality of the principal town in the district, upon the returns furnished by the chief Commissary, which returns were countersigned by me. All arbitrary proceedings were thus checked; and the receipts of the commissary were invariably received by the Spanish Government in payment of taxes and dues of all kinds.

I adopted the same system in Aragon; but the result had not been satisfactory, and the horses were starving for want of food. Had this abomination been suffered to continue for a fortnight longer, so far from being in every respect ready for the field, my 3,000 cavalry and 36 pieces of horse-artillery (the whole of my force in Aragon) would have been totally inefficient, and good for nothing. Sancho has an apt saying for such desperate cases, *A males graves remedios fuertes*; (great evils require strong remedies.) So I directed my favourite Ruti to take fifty hussars, and to collect and bring to my quarters every *alcalde* (mayor) who had failed to obey my orders. He brought thirteen!

"Gentlemen," said I to them, "it grieves me more than I have words to express, to be forced, by your want of patriotism, to have recourse to measures of severity, at all times repugnant to my feelings, but peculiarly so in a war entered into in defence of your religion, your country, and your king! Coolly and deliberately you appear to have made up your minds to aid and assist the French, by every indirect means in your power; and as I cannot tolerate so pernicious a system, I am desirous that you should experience personally how very disagreeable it is to be reduced in point of diet to the lowest possible expression; and how little can be expected of men or animals so treated.

"Ruti," I continued, "escort these gentlemen to the castle. Let each be lodged in a separate cell, and be furnished *daily* with a loaf of bread and a pitcher of water. Furnish them also with pen, ink, and paper for their correspondence; and let them know, that no change will take place in their position till all my requisitions have been attended to."

In less than a week my magazines were full, and I never had any further cause of complaint.

We now return to the correspondence of the period, at an interesting moment to General Whittingham.

On the 9th August, 1812, he had sent in his resignation to the English Ambassador of his Spanish command; but had withdrawn it at the request of that amiable and distinguished functionary, under whom he was serving as a military agent. Since then the division had established an honourable reputation. Yet on the 5th August, 1813, he once more resigned his Spanish command in disgust at the treatment he had received from Spanish Ministers. On that day he sent his resignation to the Regency; and the day following to Lord Wellington.

On the 28th and 31st August, and on the 4th September small parties of the Majorca division greatly distinguished themselves in skirmishes; the details of which are carefully preserved in Reports numbered 1, 2, and 3. There is only space to record that on the 28th August, Captain Francisco Fernandez, of the regiment of Light Dragoons of Olivencia, by repeated and successful charges against a superior body of French horse and foot, covered himself with glory and put the enemy to flight.

The following letter signed by the illustrious commander-in chief of the allied armies, after being carefully written by one of his Staff, (evidently meant to be secret and confidential, though not so marked) instead of as usually in a clerk's hand, speaks for itself:—

The Marquis of Wellington to Major-General Whittingham.
(The editor does not know why Colonel Gurwood left blanks in this letter, which was so flattering a testimony to the value of General Whittingham's services).

Lesaca, 20th September, 1813,
(see note following).

Sir,—I have received your letter of the 6th August, by the chief of the staff of the division of troops under your command, who now returns with this answer.

I feel the utmost concern that you should think it necessary to retire from the Spanish service in consequence of the use of an expression in the correspondence between two ministers, which would never have reached you if the arrangement made with me by the Spanish Govt. had been adhered to—that all reports and applications from the army to the Govt., and their answer, should pass through my hands.

I must also observe, that you have mistaken my intentions in my letter of the 8th of January, 1813. I stated that the funds placed in your hands by His Majesty's Ambassador, were not to be employed in provisions, hospitals, or means of transport, but in the pay of the General and other officers and soldiers present with the division.

What I meant by ordering that the money should not be employed in provisions, was that it should not be employed in the purchase of bread, to which every Spanish soldier has a right, besides his daily full pay, which article was to be found by the Spanish Govt.; but I understood then, as I now understand, that when a Spanish soldier receives his full pay, he is not entitled to what is called *étape*, or any other support from Govt., excepting bread; and I could not, therefore, mean that the money should not be laid out to supply the soldier with food necessary for him besides bread, according to the Ordenanzas of the Spanish Govt.

I think this is sufficiently clear in my letter of the 8th January; but if that letter should leave any doubt on that subject, the enclosed extract of a letter to General Sir John Murray, which I have reason to believe was communicated to you, and to General Roche, will have shown in positive words what my opinions were.

The practice upon this subject has, I believe, differed from the regulation, and this may have fallen into disuse; and at all events, it may be difficult to subsist the soldier upon his pay. But that is a matter for representation and further regulation, but not for your resignation.

Under these circumstances, I have thought it best to withhold your papers till I shall hear further from you in answer to this letter.

I am afraid that it is not in my power to prevail on the Govt. to promote Colonel Serrano.

In regard to the other objects referred to in your letter of the 22nd August, as it is possible that you may alter your determination of retiring from the Spanish service in consequence of this letter, it is not necessary that I should consider them at present.

I have the honour to be, Sir,

Your most obedient servant,

Wellington.

M.-General Whittingham, &c., &c., &c.'

★★★★★★

Note:—In the punctuation of the above letter, Gurwood is followed; but the rest of it accurately copies the original now lying before the editor, which differs from the letters given by Gurwood—1st, in the order of dating; 2nd, in the number of the word 'arrangement'; 3rd, in abbreviations of the word 'Government.'

★★★★★★

As for the mistake referred to in this letter, (a mistake equally made by General Elio, and General the Duke del Parque,) that was a circumstance of comparative indifference to General Whittingham. That Lord Wellington felt *the utmost concern* at his leaving the Spanish service, was inducement enough to make him brave any amount of mortifications which continuance in that service might entail.

On the 9th August Lord Wellington informed Sir John Murray that the English Government had determined, on Admiral Hallowel's letter, to bring him to a court-martial. Later in the year, in a letter dated Reus, 25th November, 1813, General Whittingham writes to Colonel Torrens the military secretary at the Horse-Guards:

I hope Sir John Murray will not call on me as an evidence. It was my opinion and still is—and Sir John knew it all the time,—that we ought to have marched on the 9th against Decaen,—have driven him across the Llobregat, blown up the bridge, and returned instantly to meet Suchet, who could not have been at Montoblanco before the 16th. It is, and was my opinion, that Sir John might on a small scale have equalled the glory of Buonaparte at Mantua. The evening before we broke up, Sir John came to my camp, and told me that he had determined to march against Decaen, and that I should move at daylight with three of my battalions. I have hitherto not mentioned my opinions, or what passed between Sir John and me to anyone. He is unfortunate, and God forbid that I should appear against him in the light of a public accuser.

To his Brother-in-law.
(In this letter he announces the birth of his eldest surviving—son)

Calanda, 7th October, 1813.

I have received so kind a letter from Lord Wellington, in which his Lordship is pleased to say that he feels the utmost concern at my idea of leaving the Spanish service, that I have determined to remain and take my chance to the end of the war. His Lordship has appointed me to a very large command of cavalry; not less than 5,000 horse.

I have with me, at this place, fifteen squadrons. Our daily exercises have already rendered them very dexterous, and I do think that another month will make them everything I could wish. This is the first time you have heard me speak with enthusiasm of the Spanish cavalry. I cannot, however, help feeling a considerable degree of pleasure at the idea of succeeding in the regeneration of the Spanish cavalry, when everybody else has failed! 5,000 horse, with fifteen pieces of horse artillery, is certainly a fine command; and if I can make the rest of the cavalry as good as that which I have now with me, I do not doubt that the exit will be as favourable as we could wish.

If you see General Donkin in town, I pray you be attentive to him. He is a real friend of mine, and a good officer and worthy man. In my opinion, he has been very unfairly coupled with Sir John Murray, in the unfortunate affair of Tarragona!

'I should be obliged to you if you would order from Whippy a hussar saddle complete, such as he has always made for me, and a hussar bridle; the bit of which to be large and heavy like those used by the soldiers of the 1st regiment of German hussars.

I am grieved most deeply to be again deprived of the pleasure of seeing you and yours this winter. But I am sure that you will agree with me, that when such a man as Lord Wellington condescends to express a wish, it must be the glory, as well as the duty, of any soldier to obey him.

Yours ever,

Samford Whittingham.

General Whittingham was not present at the action, in the pass of

Ordel, in which Lord William Bentinck's advance guard under Colonel Adam (who had so distinguished himself at Castalla) was attacked and forced to retire with the loss of four pieces of artillery. In his dispatch to Field-Marshal the Marquis of Wellington dated Tarragona, 15th September, 1813, Lord William states:

> I had not numbers equal to those which the French could bring against me; I had been obliged to leave the division of General Whittingham at Reus and Vals, from the want of provisions and means of transport.

General Whittingham must have been greatly mortified at his enforced absence on this occasion, though he must have derived some consolation from learning that such of the Spanish troops as were present at that unfortunate affair, equally, with the English, distinguished themselves by their steadiness and gallantry.

To his Brother-in-law.
Calanda, 10th October, 1813.

The state of politics in this country is woeful. The government are doing everything in their power to incommode Lord Wellington. But great changes are soon expected.

The Spanish cavalry has done nothing during the war. It is in a state of complete disorganisation: immoveable from want of discipline and instruction; sunk and depressed from misery and want; accustomed to defeat, and almost deprived of the hope of success! Under these circumstances, you will readily conceive that I have not a moment to lose in commencing a system of organisation, and I may say of regeneration; which must either, on the trial of the effects produced, lead them and me to immortal glory, or plunge us one and all into the abyss of disgrace and dishonour!

I have been for the last month at work with twelve squadrons. Their daily progress has exceeded my warmest expectations, and I trust in God and our good cause that "*every man will do his duty.*"

If, in speaking to you in the confidence of the truest friendship, any expression should escape me which may look like self-praise, do not attribute it to vanity. I certainly believe and hope that it could not proceed from so poor a source.

The great advantage that I have hitherto had in the different commands which I have held in the Spanish service, has arisen from the study I have always made it to cultivate the greatest harmony and goodwill amongst the corps, officers and soldiers, of the troops under my orders.

I have laid it down as a system—to behave kindly to all,—to cultivate by every means in my power the happiness and comfort of officers and men; to forgive and forget the errors and wanderings of youth and inexperience, and to punish with a severity even beyond the law everything which could throw the slightest blemish upon that honour and exaltation of sentiment, without which no soldier can deserve the name. (This sentiment has long been carefully fostered in the Prussian Army, and greatly contributes to its excellence).

The result, my dear Davis, has been the heartfelt satisfaction of being idolised both by soldiers and officers; and of seeing officers and soldiers of these different armies, all now united under my command, living together as one family, and without a single instance having occurred of the slightest dispute or disagreement.

On this basis I build my principal hopes of success. The morale of the Spanish cavalry has been destroyed by neglect, and I hope to raise it by being their friend and protector; by participating in all their hardships and sufferings, by providing, by every means in my power, for their wants and necessities, and above all by showing them on the day of battle, that example, without which all the tactics in the world are of no avail.

If the reader will recollect that the writer was a British lieutenant-colonel of only little more than two years' standing, he will not be surprised that the being entrusted by Lord Wellington and the Spanish Government with the prospective command of 5,000 cavalry, should have raised his hopes of being serviceable to his country and its allies, to the highest pitch of enthusiasm. Had the Peninsular war been prolonged for a couple of years, the example of the Majorca division might have been repeated on a larger scale, by the cavalry of Spain, under the orders of an Englishman who had gained the confidence of the Duke of Wellington and of the Spanish nation.

> To his Brother-in-law.
> Reus, (see note following),
> 18th November, 1813.

I have this moment received your affectionate letter of the

2nd October, and am grieved beyond measure that my silence should have occasioned so much uneasiness to you. It was occasioned by my waiting for Lord Wellington's decision upon my resignation. With his lordship's flattering answer you are already acquainted. I have for the last two months been hard at work with the cavalry. The twelve squadrons, which I have sent to Saragossa, manoeuvre well at a gallop, and charge in a very fine style. In Calanda I have as many more to form; and the whole is shortly to be increased to 5,000—if any attention can be paid to rumours; my future destiny is still, however, undecided. One report says that I am to command all the cavalry of the right; another, that I am to command a separate *corps d'armée* in upper Aragon; a third, that Copons goes to the Ministry of War, and that I am to command in chief the army of Catalonia.

★★★★★★

Note:—Here he had been left, as already explained, by Lord William Bentinck; and was thus saved from sharing a repulse: which, however, it is by no means improbable his division might have changed into a victory, as it was by superior numbers that the French gained their advantage.

★★★★★★

Colonel Torrens to R. H, Davis, Esq. M.P,
(Extract.)
Horse-Guards, 19th November, 1813.

I now return the interesting papers which you enclosed me in your letter of the 31st *ultimo*; and I assure you that in those which so strongly mark the military energy and talents of my friend Whittingham, I have derived a satisfaction equally decided with the disgust and indignation naturally excited by a perusal of his correspondence with the Spanish Government. It is no wonder that such treatment and base insinuation should induce him to give in his resignation; though, at the same time, one could not help regretting that he should have given way to the evident aim which they had in view. Now that danger is removed from the immediate door of the Spanish nation, their little jealousies will lead them to disgust, and dismiss if they can, every foreign officer.

But I rejoice to find that Lord Wellington's interference has induced Whittingham to disappoint them for this time. The command which his Lordship has given W. is most desirable and flattering; and I have no doubt but that he will derive great credit from it. I have also had a letter from him, acquainting me with this change in his destination.

Major-General Whittingham to his Brother-in-law.

Reus, 25th November, 1813.

Lord Wellington has proposed that I shall have the command of about 6,000 cavalry. Nine regiments are already under my orders. I am ordered to reorganise them completely. I have already sent four regiments to Saragossa in a very good state of manoeuvre. Having now this very large command of cavalry, I have been obliged to mount myself with a couple of good English hunters; and, I am sorry to say, they have cost me so much money that I fear that my affairs will be a little deranged by it. They have each cost me 550 dollars.

Torrens, in a *private letter* of the 21st October, concludes his truly kind and affectionate epistle by saying: "Should you quit the Spanish service, you *must* be placed at the head of a regiment of cavalry: I have already mentioned this to the duke, (of York— the commander-in-chief), who has received it most graciously." What a magnificent thing this would be for me!

This was a bitter subject to him afterwards. Though his only real English regimental service had been in the cavalry, yet, unfortunately, his promotions successively to Major and Lieutenant-Colonel had been to infantry half-pay. At the period in question he might have been transferred to the cavalry. But in later years, when a general officer, he could obtain only the honorary colonelcy of an infantry regiment, on the plea that he had not served in the cavalry as a field officer! That was carrying routine rather far in the case of a man who had always served in the cavalry, English or Allied; and to whom Lord Wellington had, towards the close of the Peninsular War, entrusted 6,000 Spanish horse for complete organisation!

On the 23rd October, 1813, Lord Wellington writes to Sir Henry Wellesley:

The Cortes have acted in respect of the resignation as they have on every other subject. (Lord Wellington had, in disgust, sent in his resignation of the command of the Spanish Army). The delay is a matter of indifference to me; and things may go on as they are, as long as they choose to delay. In the meantime, the

197

Minister of War has written me a most impertinent letter, of which I shall take no notice.

Lord Wellington adds:

> I would recommend you, if you find the new Cortes act upon the same democratical system as the last, to quit them, and travel about to amuse yourself.

Lord Wellington had little reason to be pleased with the democratic government of the Cortes, which continued most of the abuses of Old Spain, without the responsibility or regularity of the monarchical rule.

It cannot, therefore, be surprising, that General Whittingham shared the feelings of his chief; and that, though (unlike the latter) his antecedents were not likely to make him otherwise than liberal minded, he was not pleased with the very republican form of government now established in Spain; for which that country was then, as it is now, quite unfit, for want of sufficient education and civilization. It is necessary to take these facts into consideration, in judging of the future proceedings of General Whittingham in Spain; and also to bear in mind that, as a foreigner in command of troops, he deemed it his duty to take no part whatever in any political intrigues or changes of government; unless, at the request of the English Ambassador, when his services were deemed necessary.

To his Brother-in-law.

Saragossa, 28th December, 1813.

As a proof how much more easy it is to feel the extent of the sacrifices which one may be called on to make, than to carry that sentiment into execution. Lord Wellington himself—in spite of his admirable system of forbearance—sent in his formal resignation of the supreme command of the Spanish armies, not long since; and in the discussion in the Cortes, whether it should be accepted or not, the point was only carried in his favour by a majority of four votes!

He is, however, thank God! again firmly seated; and I hope and trust, that when all the members of the Cortes have taken their seats, we shall see a new Regency, and a new Ministry of War—without which, believe me, things cannot go on long. The cavalry under my command is composed of nine regiments. The division of Majorca is under my command as before. The artillery fifteen pieces, horse.

The Inspector-General of Cavalry wrote to me the other day, to say that I might consider myself as possessing all his powers; and that I had nothing to do but to propose whatever arrangements might appear to me good, in the certainty that they would be approved of by him. The inspector general wished to have placed all the cavalry in the kingdom under my orders; and he did me the honour to assure Lord Wellington that the only cavalry worthy of the name would be that which I should form!

May I hope that these flattering circumstances will aid and assist my anxious desire to be placed at the head of a British regiment of cavalry? (As Lieutenant-Colonel commanding). Several officers of no great interest have lately been put at the head of cavalry regiments at home. M——, of the 13th, has got the Inniskilling Dragoons.

You would be delighted to see how extremely well eighteen of my squadrons manoeuvre. I am fearful to say all I think of them. But I doubt whether I have seen anything better in any country. I cannot tell you what Lord Wellington means to do with my cavalry. I hope to God he will attach it to his army. It is really good. I am capitally mounted, though half ruined with the expense. I have now seven nags fit for the field. The harmony and union which reign in all the corps of cavalry under my command is the admiration of all! I shall write to Lord Wellington to request that he will allow me to send an officer to England for the clothing.

Torrens has already made me an effective lieutenant-colonel from the 30th May, 1811. (An effective infantry lieutenant-colonelcy, being a matter of rejoicing to a general commanding 6,000 horse, forms here an amusing incident).

I have been elected a member of the Royal Academy of Arts and Sciences of San Luis, established in this town; and the flattering distinctions that I have received here are beyond description. My route to and from the Sunday parades appears more like a Roman triumph than anything else; and the whole population of Saragossa appear to vie one with another in doing me honour! Yet in the midst of all the brilliancy of parade and distinction, my heart beats to return to the scenes of love and affection which await me in your beloved society; and the happiness I enjoy is only the anticipation of the blessings which await me at home!

Alas! for the enthusiastic pride and hopes of the warrior. At length he had obtained a rank and position, and a command sufficiently large to give him sanguine hopes of being able to serve his country (through its allies) on a larger scale and in a more effectual manner than ever. But peace was rapidly approaching, and with it was to disappear the last chance of the re-establishing in the field the lost character of the Spanish cavalry. 'Tis not in mortals to command complete success; but it is at least something to have deserved it, not only by the testimony of his own conscience, but by the approval of that great and fortunate man who, besides securing his own renown, had acquired authority to stamp deserving merit with the seal of his invaluable and durable recognition.

CHAPTER 11

1814

To his Brother-in-law.

Alumnia, 12th February, 1814.

Convinced that peace must soon take place, I am doubly anxious to secure at home such a situation as may enable me to live amongst my best and dearest friends, with the respectability which I conceive necessary, after the command which I have held in this country.

In my campaigns in this country I have the singular satisfaction to be able to state that all my Spanish commissions have been gained in the field of battle; and have been granted to me as a reward of service, without the slightest intervention on the part of any person. In the case of Baylen, I was made effective colonel of cavalry. In Mora and Consuegra brigadier, (no accounts of the combat of Consuegra have reached the editor's hands. It was one of Alburquerque's successful actions). In Talavera, Mariscal de Campo. Still, however, I long to return to the service of my own country; and I would not hesitate a moment between being a British Colonel, or a Lieutenant-General in any other service. If, however, circumstances should render this impossible, I must, I fear, give up those hopes which have ever been most cherished by my heart; and continue my services here.

I confess to you that I have not the best opinion of the future state of things in this country. I enclose a gazette containing the peace treated of by Buonaparte and Ferdinand the Seventh; and the decree of the Cortes in consequence. We expect the king to return here soon. It is not easy to imagine what Buonaparte's motives can be for sending him. I fear much that disputes will occur between the king and the Cortes, which may lead to a civil war; or at least to differences, which the Corsican may know too well how to avail himself of. All will depend upon the class of men in whom the king may place his confidence, God grant that he may choose well! (This prayer was not heard). I enclose also another gazette of a review of my fourteen squadrons of cavalry, and of one of artillery given by me to the authorities of Saragossa.

To the Same.

Saragossa, 20th March, 1814.

Nothing can be more grievous than the uncertainty and delay of our correspondence! I only yesterday received your letter of the 31st January!

I enclose the state papers which have been published here relative to the mission of the Duke of San Carlos. (Friend of, and Minister to, Ferdinand VII.).

In this country I have no idea of remaining. The republican party is every day gaining ground; and civil war must ultimately decide the contest.

Lord Wellington is finally arranging the form and number of the Spanish armies. This will determine when and how, and where I am to be employed. In the meantime my cavalry continues to improve and is very fit for any service.'

★★★★★★

By a Return of 1st April, 1814, in Spanish, General Whittingham's force at Saragossa consisted of nine regiments of infantry, eleven regiments of cavalry, and 18 pieces of horse -artillery: a large command for a British Lieut.-Colonel,—See list following.

Return of Corps of different Arms of the Spanish Army under the Orders of Lieutenant-General Whittingham, when only Lieutenant-Colonel in the British Army.

Saragossa, Head-quarters, April 1, 1814.

Regiments of Infantry	Regiments of Cavalry	Horse Artillery
5th Battn. of Grenadiers	The Prince's Regt. of Horse	Squadrons 5th
1st Regt. of Cordova	Santiago do.	and 6th, each
1st do. Guadalaxara	Calatrava do.	squadron con-
1st do. Grenada	Queen's Dragoons	sisting of 3
2nd do. Majorca	Almanza do.	troops, each
2nd do. Burgos	Madrid do.	troop 4 pieces
2nd do. Murcia	Soria do.	of 8, and 2
1st do. Nueva Creacion	Olivenza Chasseurs	howitzers of
Cazadores of Majorca	Ubrique do.	5¼ inch.
Company of Sappers	La Mancha do.	
	Ferdinand VII.'s Hussars	

Total:—9 regiments of infantry; 11 regiments of cavalry; 18 pieces of artillery.

Military College at Majorca, founded by General Whittingham, and under his direction.

General Cavalry Depôt, established by General Whittingham, and under his orders.

******

Lord Wellington writing to his brother the ambassador on the 22nd March, 1814, says:

I am very much afraid that the real mischief is only now beginning in Spain. I was always certain that the conduct of the people of Madrid towards the Cortes would, after a short time, be the same as that of the people of Cadiz. No popular assembly can exist if it opens its galleries under any other system than that in use in England, unless the press is restrained. I heard at Tarbes the other day that the king had passed Toulouse on his return to Spain.'

Again on the 27th March, Lord Wellington writes:

You will have heard that King Ferdinand passed Toulouse on the 18th on his way to Spain.

On the 30th April from Toulouse Lord Wellington writes to his brother:

I shall be very anxious to hear of the king's decision and conduct in regard to the constitution.

Major-General Whittingham to his Brother-in-law.

Madrid, 21st, May, 1814.

I enclose copies of all the official papers which have passed relative to my march here; and I shall now attempt to give you some idea of what took place from the time of my going to meet the King in upper Aragon.

On the 12th of March, we received advice at Saragossa, that the king had determined upon taking that route, instead of going direct to Valencia; and that he would be at Seville on the following day. I immediately pushed on about 300 dragoons; with orders to station themselves by troops on the route, and to advance as far as possible; and myself taking post, (travelling post by relays of horses was then the mode of quick travelling in Spain), set off immediately in the same direction. I met the king at —— , (at the moment of writing, he appears to have forgotten the name of the place—perhaps a small village—where he met the king), where my cavalry relieved that of the first army. As soon as I approached the king's carriage, His Majesty said to me '*Como va? Tiempo ha que tenemos mucha gana de conocerte.*' (How do you do? For a long time, we have much desired to know you.'). From that day, I received the most marked attention from His Majesty, and the Prince, Don Carlos. The king's entrance into Saragossa, and, in short, into all the towns of Aragon, was such a triumph, as it is impossible to express, and not easy to conceive, except by those who witnessed those happy scenes. But if the marks of joy and exultation were strong beyond measure at the king's return, the expressions of dislike and detestation of the Constitution were not less general and strong: and His Majesty, from his entrance into Aragon till his arrival at Madrid, never heard any language that could induce him for a moment to believe that the Constitution had merited the approbation of his subjects.

Nor is this to be wondered at. In the fury of their republican zeal, the rulers of the Cortes had attacked, openly and in the most violent manner, the nobility, the clergy, and the army; and consequently had made the whole of these respectable classes their enemies. They had also, in the plenitude of their financial ignorance, done away with all the old duties, and revenues of Spain; and established, instead, what they called '*la contribucion unica y directa*'; a tax exactly similar to our income tax. You will recollect with what reluctance this tax was admitted in England, although it was only to meet a small part of our expenditure, and although England from her commerce, interior and exterior, has so large a circulating medium, that disbursements must be to her, compared with Spain, of little burthen! You will easily, therefore, conceive the effect of such a tax on the Spanish peasantry, and to an extent sufficient to meet the whole expenditure of government. (It appears that in Spain, no income, however, small, escaped the tax in question—a law that would never he tolerated in England).

The mind of the Spanish nation was in a state of ferment; and the presence of the king produced an immediate explosion.

Had the king found the nation in general attached to the new Constitution, he would undoubtedly have sworn to it. But never was a national opinion more decidedly, or more openly pronounced. Not a shadow of doubt could remain upon the king's mind.

The king staid four days at Saragossa; reviewed my cavalry; and was pleased to say everything that was kind and flattering. I accompanied him, with relays of troops, as far as the frontier of Aragon, where I met my commander-in-chief, General Elio. On my approaching the king to take leave, he said '*No te vayas. Tengo mucho gusto en que me accompañes. Ven conmigo á Valencia.*' (His brother-in-law being a good Spanish scholar, the original alone is in the letter. His Majesty said, 'Don't go. I have much pleasure in your accompanying me. Come with me to Valencia.')

At Valencia, I remained two days, and on taking leave, the king made me a present of a beautiful mosaic snuffbox, which he desired me to keep in remembrance of him. (See note following). The remainder of the details of my march you will be perfectly acquainted with by the enclosed official correspondence. Many of the leading people were arrested the night before the king arrived at Madrid, by the Captain-General Eguia, and there is no longer a shadow of doubt, from the republican papers that have been seized, and the secret correspondence with France, that had the king sworn to the Constitution, he would have gone to the scaffold in less than six months.

★★★★★★

Note:—This box Sir Samford, some nine or ten years later, gave to his beloved and respected friend, the Hon. Sir Edward Paget. This not very valuable gift was all Sir Samford ever received from King Ferdinand.

★★★★★★

From this letter, a great deal in praise of King Ferdinand has been here omitted, as General Whittingham at a later period reluctantly discovered that the amiable and plausible but fickle and weak-minded prince was very far from being the promising sovereign he had mistaken him for in the first excitement of His Majesty's return to his loving and enthusiastic subjects, for such were at that time the great masses of the Spanish nation. Shakspeare confesses that there is '*a Majesty that doth hedge a King,*' but a king smiling, flattering, grateful, plausible, affable, is surrounded by a double hedge of Majesty. No wonder that for a time the Englishman in his service should have imbibed a personal partiality for a sovereign, who on his part displayed so flattering an appreciation of his foreign general.

★★★★★★

If General Whittingham erred in his opinion of King Ferdinand, and of his popularity at this time in Spain, he erred in good company. In a letter dated 'Madrid, 25th May, 1814,' and addressed to Sir Charles Stuart, the Duke of Wellington writes, 'you will have heard of the extraordinary occurrences here, though not probably with surprise. *Nothing can be more popular than the king and his measures, as far as they have gone to the overthrow of the Constitution.* The imprisonment of the Liberates is thought by some, I believe with justice, unnecessary, and it is certainly highly impolitic; but it is liked by the people at large.' In the same letter the duke writes, '*I entertain a very favourable opinion of the king,* from what I have seen of him, but not of his ministers.'—*Wellington Dispatches*, vol. xii.

★★★★★★

To his Brother-in-law.

Madrid, 23rd May, 1814.

The King of Spain continues to distinguish me by every possible mark of attention. I expect daily the commission of Lieutenant-General.

The king and the Infante Don Carlos, are anxious that I should remain in their service: but they know not of what materials my heart is composed, and that I prefer the love of my best and dearest friends to all the glory in the world!

Lieutenant-Colonel Whittingham, for he now usually reverts to his British rank, determined to return to England; but before leaving he desired to obtain from the great duke, '*never prodigal of praise*' some more decided opinion as to the merits of his services in Spain than was to be gathered from the many strong but indirect proofs of confidence which had been hitherto vouchsafed to him.

The result was the following letter, and, considering the character of the illustrious writer, a more comprehensive testimonial can scarcely be imagined, than the words now placed in italics:—

The Duke of Wellington to His Royal Highness
the Duke of York.

Madrid, 4th June, 1814.

Sir,—Colonel Whittingham (Mariscal de Campo, in the service

of Spain) having informed me that it would be necessary for him to return to England in a short time, and having expressed a desire that I should lay before your Royal Highness my sense of his services and merits, I beg leave to inform your Royal Highness, that he has served most zealously and gallantly from the commencement of the war in the Peninsula; and that I have had every reason to be satisfied with his conduct in every situation in which he has been placed.

I have the honour to be, &c.

Wellington.

His Royal Highness the Duke of York.

★★★★★★

Had this letter been delayed a little longer, instead of 'Mariscal de Campo' (that is Major-General), the Spanish rank would have been Lieutenant-General, that is the highest; for Captain-General was (then at least if not now) rather an appointment than a rank, and for it all Lieutenant-Generals were eligible.

★★★★★★

His Grace probably styled Lieutenant-Colonel Whittingham, Colonel by courtesy, but he may have known that on that very day, the *London Gazette* was publishing his promotion.

To his Brother-in-law

Madrid, 4th June, 1814.

I have had a long and very satisfactory conversation with the Duke of Wellington. He is decidedly of opinion that I should by no means think of giving up the British service, although he believes that there will be no objection to my continuing in this part for the moment. He has promised to speak to the Duke of York upon the subject of my commission being dated in the year 1809, which he seems to think may be done with perfect propriety.

He also gave me a letter of recommendation to H.R.H. the duke, "although" as he kindly said "that will not prevent my speaking to H.R.H. as I shall see him before you."

Castaños has given me a letter to General Gordon, reminding him of the king's (George III.] promise, and begging him to submit my case to H.M.'s consideration. I hope also to obtain from the King of Spain a strong letter of recommendation to the Prince Regent.'

Meantime, the conduct of the King of Spain had made him very unpopular in England, and that unpopularity was destined later to extend to General Whittingham, as if he could have in any way interfered in the political government of Spain, or had the least authority for so doing.

The Duke of Wellington wrote from London, (20th July, 1814), to Sir Henry Wellesley:

It is not easy to describe the unpopularity attached to the king's name, from the occurrences at his return to Madrid. The newspapers afford some specimens of it: but at a late dinner at Guildhall, I recommended to the lord mayor to drink the King of Spain's health, and he told me that he was become so unpopular in the city, he was afraid that, if the toast were not positively refused, it would at least be received with so much disgust as to render it very disagreeable to me and to every well-wisher to the Spanish Government.

To his Brother-in-law.

Madrid, 8th June, 1814.

I march this evening to Alcala, where I have directed sixteen squadrons of cavalry, and one of horse-artillery, to assemble. They are to manoeuvre under my direction, fifteen or twenty days previously to their being seen by His Majesty. This will occasion a small delay in my return home.

To the Same.

Madrid, 1st July, 1814.

I have seen by the *Gazette* (of the 4th June) that I have had the high and distinguished honour to be appointed *aide-de-camp* to his Royal Highness the Prince of Wales! It would be indeed difficult to express my feelings on this occasion.

The King of Spain has promoted me to the rank of Lieutenant-General, (this commission as Lieut.-General was dated 16th June, 1814); and H.M. assured me the other day, in a manner truly affecting from its kindness, that nothing could grieve him more profoundly than my quitting his service; an event which he hoped and trusted would never take place.

To the Same.

Madrid, 14th July, 1814.

My dear Davis,—This night I begin my march for Bourdeaux,

through Saragossa.

I had scarcely taken the pen in my hand, when I received an official summons to attend Sir John Murray's court-martial at Tarragona. This will create a considerable delay. Mrs. W. will remain at Saragossa; and I shall proceed on to Catalonia. I have written to you fully, under cover to Torrens, a few days since. I send this to Bilboa.

Yours ever most truly,

Samford Whittingham.

Before leaving Madrid, the English Ambassador added his testimony to the services of General Whittingham, entering into more details than his illustrious brother had done:—

Sir Henry Wellesley to Viscount Castlereagh.

Madrid, 22nd July, 1814.

My Lord,—Lieutenant-General Whittingham being about to embark for England, I have taken the liberty of giving him this letter of introduction to your Lordship.

'The services of General Whittingham, from the period of the breaking out of the general war against France, have obtained for him the approbation of his Royal Highness the Prince Regent, as well as that of the Spanish Government. He was with General Castaños, as a military agent at the Battle of Baylen; and, in the following campaign, was severely wounded at the Battle of Talavera, while leading a Spanish corps into action.

During the period of his residence at Cadiz, he was employed in the formation of a corps of cavalry: and he afterwards formed the division, which, under his orders, behaved with the greatest gallantry at the Battle of Castalla; where it repulsed the attack of nearly the whole of Suchet's corps, and where General Whittingham was again wounded. (It was at Concentayna—an action that took place a little before that of Castalla—that General Whittingham was the second time wounded in the face. The editor can find no record of his having been hit at Castalla).

I have before informed your Lordship that General Whittingham had the good fortune to receive the King at Saragossa, at the head of a division of cavalry, of which he undertook the formation, at the desire of the Duke of Wellington. This division has since been reviewed at Madrid by the King, and was so highly approved by His Majesty, that immediately after the review he conferred upon General Whittingham the rank of Lieutenant-General.

I have thought it my duty to mention these circumstances, so honourable to an officer whose conduct during his employment in Spain has entitled him to general respect and esteem.

I have, &c.,

H. Wellesley.

The following letter, as being also a testimonial to General Whittingham's services, (whilst he was still in Spain, in spite of the peace, English as well as Spaniards still called him General; but on the part of the English this was now only by courtesy); equally flattering, is here inserted a little out of its place, to complete the estimate of his military services at this period:—

The Earl of Fife to General Whittingham.

Paris, 31st December, 1814.

My dear Whittingham,—As you know my friendship for you, and everyone who served in Spain is aware of the great regard and high opinion I always entertained of you, it will not be surprising when I inform you how much pleasure I had in hearing your praises from the *highest authority*, concerning your conduct in the last two campaigns.

I was particularly anxious to know from the French officers who had served in that part of Spain where you were latterly employed, their opinion of your merits and exertions; and, believe me, yourself, or your warmest friends, could not have wished more favourable answers.

The Duke of Albufera, Marshal Suchet, spoke to me a long time about you, and told me that he was surprised at the perfection you had brought your division to, and that they were in as high a military state as any of his own troops, and, he believed, as any other soldiers in Europe; that he had had frequent occasion to admire your conduct in the field; and his opinion of you was that of a most meritorious officer.

I was witness to a great part of your exertions in the cause, and was aware what difficulties on all sides you had to encounter. Nothing can be more satisfactory than the result; and I most heartily congratulate you, on your having so steadily persevered in a contest which has gained you a reputation even among your former enemies, of an excellent officer. With every good wish, believe me, my dear Whittingham,

    Your very sincere friend,

Fife.

(See *Preface*, for Lord Fife's letter to the editor, in confirmation of the above testimony, in 1845).

Such a letter, written by one of the bravest of Englishmen, who courted danger as a volunteer, almost for its own sake, is valuable in itself; but as conveying also the more important approval of one of Napoleon's cleverest marshals, it must ever be treasured by the descendants of General Whittingham, as an invaluable testimony to his merits and exertions; second only to the comprehensive certificate of the Duke of Wellington.

(All extracts from letters, where the writers are not named, are from the letters of General Whittingham).

To Major-General Sir Henry Torrens.
(Extract.)

Saragossa, 2nd August, 1814.

My dear Torrens,—Your letter of the 12th *ultimo* I received here on the 21st July; and am most particularly obliged for the leave you have obtained of His Royal Highness the Prince Regent, and His Royal Highness the Commander-in-Chief, for me to continue my services in this country.

I had come thus far on my route to Tarragona, to attend the court-martial of Sir John Murray; but on my arrival at this town, I received intimation that it would not take place at Tarragona, but was transferred to London.

Previous to the return of my division of Cavalry to Aragon, we had a field-day before the king, at Madrid, who was pleased to express his highest satisfaction. Immediately after the review, His Majesty said to me, "In proof of how much I esteem you, and how highly penetrated I am with a sense of your merit, you will receive to-morrow the commission of Lieutenant-General."

When I waited upon His Majesty to inform him of the honour His Royal Highness the Prince Regent had been pleased to confer upon me, and to ask leave to return to England for eight or twelve months, His Majesty expressed much satisfaction at my appointment. At the same time, he did me the honour to say, "I hope that you do not mean to quit my service. Be assured

it would be a matter of great grief to me that you should do so."
Many things have taken place since the arrival of His Majesty at
Madrid which will, I fear, produce much discontent; and most
particularly the re-establishment of the Inquisition! The army
at least has received this measure with decided disapprobation.
The question of the Inquisition was long and warmly disputed.
The Duke of San Carlos; Macanar, Minister of Gracia and Justi-
cia; Lardizaval, Minister of the Indies; Escoiquez, the priest who
accompanied the King to France; were decidedly against it: and
His Majesty had said that he would take no determination till
the reunion of the Cortes, when he would submit the question
to their decision. But the weight of influence of the Infante
Don Antonio; of Ostalara confessor to the Infante Don Carlos;
of the Minister of War, Eguia; of the Marquis of Palacio; and the
representations in favour of its re-establishment, of very many
towns; at length prevailed, and the king was induced to reau-
thorise a tribunal of secret despotism, and to legalise tyranny of
the worst class.

The greatest, or at least the most pressing evil, however, which
affects this country is the deranged state of the finances.

Under these circumstances. His Majesty ascended the throne;
and although orders were given to do away with the income
tax, and to re-establish the old duties, yet a very considerable
time must elapse before any beneficial consequences can be
expected. (These details having been mentioned in a previous
letter, are not repeated in this extract).

As in his letter to his brother-in-law, so in his letter to Sir Henry
Torrens, his personal attachment and partiality to King Ferdinand, is
very conspicuous. That plausible and personally popular monarch, by
his gracious smiles and by his really friendly appreciation of the Englishman who had served him so well, had thrown a temporary veil
over his real character and vices; which after all were those of a weak
and timid, rather than of a depraved and wicked nature.

To Sir Henry Torrens.
(Extract.)
Saragossa, 30th September, 1814.

My dear Torrens,—I was on the point of beginning my journey to England to appear as a witness on the trial of Sir John
Murray, when I received a letter from Sir John, dated Barce-

lona, stating that he was still in hopes, in consequence of his representations, that the trial would take place in Catalonia; and requesting that I would await at Saragossa the final determination of H.R.H. the Regent. I have now received a letter from him saying that he has received the final answer, and that the trial is to take place in London, to which place he returns by land to France.'

As Sir John travels through France with his own horses and carriage, I hope to be in England as soon as he can. At all events, the difference cannot be great.

Could I have avoided quitting Spain at this moment, I have been given to understand, I should have been appointed Inspector-General of Cavalry. But these unlucky huts must at times happen to all men.

General Mina, on receiving the order of the Government to deliver up the command of his troops to the Captain-General of Aragon, Palafox, has refused to obey, and is at present in open rebellion. He has, however, few followers: most of his battalions have come over to the Captain-General. He still, however, keeps the field between this and Pampeluna. In the present instance, it would not be possible for me to take that route to England. I trust, however, that a few days will put an end to his wild enterprise.

The following account of Ferdinand the Seventh's return to his kingdom is taken from the often quoted *Recollections*, and is confirmed by the letters written at the period in question.

Upon the King's return to Spain, I advanced to the frontier of Aragon to meet him, distributing a sufficient force of Cavalry to form His Majesty's escort on the road, and to furnish his guard at night.

The charge of the king's person, as well as of his brother Don Carlos, and of his uncle Don Antonio, was made over to me on the frontier of Aragon, by General Copons, then commanding in Catalonia. My reception by His Majesty and the Royal family was infinitely gracious and most flattering. Our marches were twenty or thirty miles a day. The coach or rather landau in which H.M. travelled was English built. The roads were tolerably good, and the royal party suffered little or no fatigue. I rode always at the side of the carriage, and we generally arrived at our resting-place between three and four in the afternoon, having started at about half-past nine. I always dined with the king during the march, and the whole route was one continued scene of triumph. I never saw such a wild expression of joy as the Spanish people universally gave way to on the return of their king from his infamous captivity. His Majesty, during the journey, was constantly occupied in studying the Constitution which he was required to swear to.

As I rode close to the side of his carriage, he often entered into conversation with me. One day he said, "Santiago, you will hardly imagine what book I am reading. It is the new Spanish Constitution, formed and published by the Cortes during my absence. I find much that is good in it, but also many things quite inadmissible. Notwithstanding, if the refusal of my sanction is to cost one drop of Spanish blood, I will swear to it tomorrow." (*Lo juraré mañana.*—In the *Recollections* all the royal speeches and his own answers are given in the original Spanish, followed by the English translations).

Such were then the sentiments of Ferdinand. His Majesty remained three days at Saragossa, and did me the honour to inspect the two thousand cavalry and sixteen pieces of artillery, at my head-quarters. I commanded the field-day. We manoeuvred in two lines: and I did everything in my power to give it the appearance of a real action. The king was quite enchanted, and thanked me most warmly for all the services that I had rendered him during his absence.

On arriving at the frontier of Aragon, I dismounted, and requested His Majesty's orders, previously to making over the charge of his royal person to General Elio, who commanded in Valencia. "I desire," said His Majesty to me, "that you accompany me to Valencia. I am much pleased with you, and you must come on with me."

At Valencia, the plot began to thicken, General Elio was a violent ultra-royalist; and was too well supported by a host of fanatical priests and grandees; and hence the first false impressions were made on the king's mind.

General Zayas was sent to sound me: for the general commanding so large a body of cavalry and horse-artillery was too important a person to be neglected at such a crisis. "If," said I to Zayas, "you are sent by order of His Majesty to obtain my real opinion upon the present state of affairs, I shall be happy to submit them frankly and fully, for I conceive the measures now to be adopted of infinite importance to the well-being of His Majesty and of the Spanish Nation.

"In my opinion, there is much that is good in the new Constitution; but as there is also much which requires to be modified, it is not in His Majesty's power to swear to it in its present form; especially, on account of the article which requires His Majesty to swear that no change, alteration, or modification shall take place for eight years.

"Still, however, it must be kept in mind, that the Cortes have rendered the royal cause good service; and that they deserve the gratitude of the king and of the Spanish Nation. On his arrival at Madrid, I humbly conceive, His Majesty should in person thank the Cortes for all their good services, and express his intention to invoke the ancient Cortes of Spain, for their opinion and advice; and having thus announced his royal will, that His Majesty should forthwith dissolve the present Cortes."

It would seem that my opinions were not approved of; for, the next day, I received orders to return to Saragossa, with the escort which I had furnished for the king's guard, and there to await further orders.

In the meantime, orders were despatched to General Eguia, at Madrid, to arrest a number of the leading members of the liberal party; and the charge of the king's person was made over to General Elio.

A few days after my arrival at Saragossa, I received orders to march upon Madrid with the cavalry and horse-artillery under my orders. On my arrival at Guadalaxara, I was directed to halt until further orders; and I did not enter the capital till the morning of the king's entrance; and then only to line the streets in parade order. The arrests had all taken place several days before.

Nothing can give a true picture of the enthusiastic joy manifested by the people of Madrid, on seeing their beloved sovereign once again amongst them. A young and handsome *manola* came close to the head of my charger, and shouted with a most audible voice, "May'st thou be blessed, Ferdinand of my soul; Thou shalt be an absolute king, and thou shalt always do whatever may be thy royal pleasure; and if it be thy will to tread us under thy royal feet, thy will and pleasure shall be our only law!"

This anecdote brings to my mind a circumstance, which occurred during my march from Saragossa to the frontier of Aragon, to meet the king. I had received my billet in the house of a most respectable yeoman, and after supper, he stated his utter incapacity to comprehend the meaning of the doubts and difficulties which seemed to be generally felt. "Whilst the master was absent," said he, "I understand very well that his head servants, *(los criados de confianza)*, must act in his name; but now that the master has returned home, what have the servants to do but to obey his orders?"

As soon as the king had entered the palace, at Madrid, the troops were dismissed; and I retired to my lodgings. A few days afterwards, I had the honour of giving His Majesty a field-day of the cavalry and horse-artillery, which so highly pleased him that he made me a Lieutenant-General on the field. (From the correspondence of the period it would appear that King Ferdinand only took that graceful occasion to announce the reward already intended for his services).

My favour at court was every day increasing; and I had it in my power to be of service to Sir Henry Wellesley, as he has been pleased to state in his letter to Lord Castlereagh. But Tatischeff, the Russian Minister, was too cunning for the straightforward dealing of English diplomatists; and he obtained from Ferdinand the *Toison d'or,* which had been refused to Sir Henry Wellesley. At this time I spent almost every evening, from eight till ten, in the king's private apartment. The queen often joined us; and conversation was as free and as general as could have been the case in the house of any private gentleman. His Majesty never took offence at anything that I said. "I cannot comprehend," said I to him one evening, "the interest which your Majesty takes in the affairs of Russia! Your respective countries are placed in the opposite extremes of Europe; and they have not, nor ever can have, any community of interests. On the other hand, England offers to your Majesty her most advantageous friendship, which you appear to despise."

"What an excellent Englishman thou art, Santiago!" said the king; "would to God all my subjects were as good Spaniards!"

Some time afterwards, (this may mean any time between 1815

and 1819 that he passed in Madrid), His Majesty proposed to make me his Minister of War. I submitted the proposal to Sir Henry Wellesley; and he referred it to Lord Castlereagh, who declared its acceptance to be incompatible with the duties of a British officer; and particularly with those of an *aide-de-camp* of the King of England.

Shortly after this, I announced to the king my intention of returning to England. His Majesty and the Infante Don Antonio were full of expressions of grief at my departure; and the king was pleased to say, "Santiago, tell me what you wish, and on condition that you do not leave me, there is nothing in my power that I will not do to please you." ("*Santiago, dime lo que descas, y con tal que no te vayas y te quedes en mi servicio, no hay cosa en mi poder que no haré por complacerte.*"). But the day of confidence was passed; and I could not make up my mind to give up friends and country, on so unstable a base as the caprice of a weak mind. I pledged myself, however, to return to Spain, should His Majesty call for my services.

They were destined to meet again; but the history of that reunion must be deferred for a time, and form part of the following chapter.

CHAPTER 12

1815

At the commencement of 1815, Colonel Whittingham for the second time in his life had to perform the disagreeable duty of giving evidence on the court-martial of a commander under whom he had served. But in the case of Sir John Murray, Baronet, his task was light compared to what it had been on the trial of General Whitelocke in 1808.

Lieut. General Sir John Murray was tried by a court-martial that sat in London from the 16th January to the 7th February. He was tried (for his conduct in June 1813) on three charges; the first implying imprudence in his plans; and the second, disobedience of orders. But of both these charges he was fully and honourably acquitted. The third and last charge was for his hasty embarkation after raising the siege of Tarragona, although no enemy was near; whereby he unnecessarily lost guns and stores. He was found guilty of 'an error of judgment,' (his errors in judgment were numerous, but Lord Wellington acknowledged his abilities, and he was otherwise a worthy man), in regard to these losses, as specified in a part of the last charge; and he was sentenced to be admonished. But the Prince Regent thought it needless to admonish for an error of judgment, and the result was a virtual acquittal.

Soon after this trial. General Whittingham, (for so he was styled on this occasion) became the object of a parliamentary calumny, which might be termed atrocious, had it not been too ridiculous to merit so strong a denunciation; and he sent to his friend. Sir Henry Torrens, a Bristol newspaper, giving an account of an exciting scene in the House of Commons, in fuller details than were inserted in the London press.

It is needless to reproduce the details of this calumny. It is sufficient to say that Mr. Whitbread in fact argued as if General Whittingham, (as his services for the greater part of the war had been performed in the rank of General it was natural he should be so called in Parliament), were responsible for all the pecuniary assistance which *the English Ambassador, and the English Commander-in-Chief had with the consent of the English Government, given to their Spanish allies!* But not satisfied with this absurdity, he was not ashamed, in the hope of shaking a ministry, to accuse an English officer of distinction of having received more than 50,000*l.* as a bribe to place Ferdinand VII. on a despotic throne; the fact being that the accused officer had lately returned to England a far poorer man than when he had left it; having spent a considerable part of his private patrimony on his commissions and in the public service! But the waves of party spirit then ran mountains high; and even the great duke himself did not escape their fury; as he has recorded in his immortal *Dispatches.*

Mr. Hart Davis, member for Bristol, the affectionate brother-in-law of the calumniated general, a man of high character, naturally retorted with spirit on the privileged calumniator, and a duel appeared imminent. The affair is thus recorded by the Bristol journal. (After Mr. Whitbread's motion had been made and rejected)

> The House had proceeded to the order of the day, when the gentlemen above named retired. The *speaker* felt it to be his duty on the instant, to call the attention of the House to the conduct of two of its members, and to require that the individuals to whom he referred should be immediately called back, to give the House their assurances that no further proceedings should take place in consequence of what had fallen from them in the course of debate.

(The members were brought back, and the gallery was cleared).

> Strangers were not again admitted, but we understand the Hon. Gentlemen readily gave the assurances required, and the business was in a few minutes satisfactorily adjusted.

The Bristol paper which had warmly taken the part 'of our gallant townsman, General Whittingham,' ends its article by stating: 'General Whittingham is at this time at the house of Mr. Davis at Clifton;' one of the brief and rare visits, that he paid to his native country.

Whilst he was thus calumniated in England, in Spain on the contrary—let it be said in justice to the Spaniards—his merits were still appreciated.

The following letter was written by an excellent officer and brave man, who was also a most estimable gentleman in private life:—

Colonel Patrick Campbell to General Whittingham. (He was then Major in the British, and Colonel in the Spanish, service)

(Extract.)

Madrid, 25th March, 1815.

Whatever failings or vices I may have, ingratitude is not amongst them: and truly ungrateful should I be, were I to forget one to whom I owe so very much, and who has shown me so many acts of friendship. Most heartily do I rejoice at the very handsome reception you have received from the Prince Regent. I would to God that you were here again. A. at present is the only countryman of ours at this moment in the peninsula, who has any reputation. B. and C. are only spoken of in derision. D. is never mentioned at all. (A. B. C. D. These letters are used to conceal real names).

You, however, are always mentioned both with respect for talents, and instruction, and with enthusiasm for your gallantry. An army of 8,000 men is ordered to be formed on the frontier, in consequence of the escape of Buonaparte. Who is to command is yet a secret. Castaños has offered his services; and some say he is to command. Others say, the Infante Don Carlos is to go there: but the present deranged state of the finances will not bear that additional expense.

My business of Brigadier is not yet decided. Sir Henry (Wellesley) however, has done whatever he could; and in consequence Ceballos wrote to Eguia. But he is such an enemy to everything English, that he tries all he can to delay it. I have got the supernumerary cross of Charles III. I do not think old Herasti will ever go to Barcelona. I would you were here, as that is the best Government in Spain; and, as you know, if one is not on the spot nothing is obtained. I wish much you would speak to Sir Henry Torrens for the rank of Lieut.-Colonel for me. You were my commander-in-chief; and consequently, the only one who can recommend me.

It is the step of the greatest importance to me. How does Mrs. Whittingham like England? What an infamous, shameful, and lying attack Whitbread has made! I saw it here in the English papers. He talks of 52,000*l*. as given to you for your own purposes; and you above all men; *who, it may he said, never even saw the public money, much less handled it.* (See note following). I wish you could tell me, how we serving here are to be considered, particularly *Don Patricio Campbell*, as I am much interested about him, Castaños and Zayas are well, Giron is in Seville, Serrano is in Badajos.

✶✶✶✶✶✶

Note:—General Whittingham had had the responsibility, had negotiated the bills, and conducted the correspondence; but until Paymaster Foley was appointed, Colonel Campbell performed the actual payments required.

✶✶✶✶✶✶

Colonel Patrick Campbell was in Spain usually styled 'Don Patricio Campbell' to which he playfully alludes. As Lieutenant-Colonel of the Light Infantry Regiment of the Majorca division, as well as on the Staff of General Whittingham, he had always distinguished himself greatly by zeal, intelligence and courage, and, as usual with all who served under the General, was devotedly and permanently attached to his Chief.

Meantime the escape of the great Napoleon had again aroused to arms the greater part of Europe; and reopened prospects of fresh, distinction to all soldiers:—

To Major-General Sir Henry Torrens.
London, 28th May, 1815.

Sir,—I have the honour to inform you, that I received by last mail my appointment of Lieutenant-General employed in the army of Catalonia under the orders of General Castaños. I have therefore to request you will be pleased to submit this appointment to the consideration of H.R.H. the Commander-in-Chief; and at the same time that you will express my hope that H.R.H. will condescend to allow me to proceed to Spain immediately. *Having failed in my solicitations for employment in Flanders,* I am anxious to join the army in Catalonia with as little delay as possible; and as my appointment there has taken place, I cannot, I conceive, use too much expedition in getting to my post. I have the honour to be. Sir,

Your most obedient servant,
Samford Whittingham.

★★★★★★

Till perusing the words now placed in Italics, the editor was wholly unaware of the fact of such applications. No doubt their refusal had been too sore a subject to mention, in spite of the flattering terms in which they had been couched.

★★★★★★

This letter establishes the fact, that he had previously desired rather to serve under Wellington as a colonel, than with the Spaniards as a lieutenant-general. Had his request been granted, he would doubtless have justified himself to the King of Spain, under the sound plea that there was no danger to be immediately apprehended in Spain from Napoleon, as was well-known to be the case.

The word solicitations being in the plural, there rests a strong suspicion in the editor's mind, that Colonel Whittingham, not only applied direct to the Duke of Wellington, but did so also through His Royal Highness the Duke of Kent. In short the editor has some reason to believe that the letter of the Duke of Wellington dated 'Bruxelles, 14th April, 1815,' and addressed to Her Majesty's illustrious father, refers to Colonel Whittingham. Colonel Gurwood having unfortunately left this name in blank, and none of the original applications having reached the editor's hands, the matter must remain for the present doubtful. To desire eagerly to serve under the Duke of Wellington was sufficiently praiseworthy to have justified Gurwood in printing the name of the rejected applicant, especially as the rejection was coupled with the flattering words; 'he knows that if I could have gratified him I would have done so, without the aid of your Royal Highness's powerful influence.' (Vol. xii. of *Wellington Dispatches*).

There can be no question, however, that besides merit, some high aristocratic connection was required at that moment, to obtain a place on the Staff then ambitioned by hundreds of meritorious officers. It was no disgrace to fail in such an application, but rather a high honour when accompanied by an observation, which so plainly and strongly implied that no want of merit occasioned the writer's non-compliance with the request. If a list were made of all those who served on the great duke's staff throughout his life, it would be found that birth or rank had ever the strongest claims on his favour; and that the kind of liberality which was so frequently displayed by kings and royal dukes, was never one of the traits of the essentially aristocratic as well as illustrious Duke of Wellington.

It appears, however, that though to serve under the duke, Sir Samford would have retired from the Spanish service, this was before his services had been called for by the Spanish king. For he declined (subsequently) the offer, of the post of British Commissioner to the Austrian Army, when offered to him by Lord Castlereagh. Now that he was once more going to serve in Spain, he became again a general even at the Horse-Guards. He had also been made C.B. and knighted. (At that time no one could be made K.C.B. under the rank of Major-General; but distinguished officers, who had earned the C.B. were sometimes knighted).

To Lieutenant-General Sir Samford Whittingham.

Horse-Guards, 2nd June, 1815.

Sir,—I have not failed to lay before the commander-in-chief your letter of the 28th *ultimo*, communicating to me, for His Royal Highness's information that you had received your appointment of Lieutenant-General employed in the army under General Castaños; and requesting permission to proceed to Spain to join the same in Catalonia.

I have His Royal Highness's commands to acquaint you that as circumstances do not admit of your talents and experience being rendered available to the services of the British army itself, in a manner adequate to your claims and pretensions, he can have no objection to your being employed in the general cause, by assuming the duties in the Spanish army to which you have been called in so flattering a manner by His Catholic Majesty. I am therefore charged by the commander-in-chief to apprise you, that you have the Prince Regent's leave of absence to proceed to Spain without delay; and likewise His Royal Highness's *special* permission to absent yourself for the same purpose from your situation in the household. I have the honour to be, Sir,

Your most faithful and obedient humble servant,

H. Torrens.

Lieutenant-General Sir Samford Whittingham.

The reference at the close of this letter, to the duties of *aide-de-camp* to the Prince Regent, gives occasion to state that in this capacity Colonel Whittingham appears to have been very successful. It is to be regretted that he did not write of George IV., similar recollections to those he has left of Ferdinand VII. The English monarch, there is reason to believe, treated him with scarcely less kindness than did the Spanish sovereign:—and he used when on duty, to be called into the royal private apartment, to be consulted as to the equipment and clothing of the cavalry. At the levees also, owing to their rarity, and consequent crowding, the post of Royal *aide-de-camp* would appear to have been no sinecure at that period; and physical strength was quite as needful a qualification as courtly manners and bearing. At the royal drawing-rooms especially the crush was tremendous. There also the King alone receiving the ladies, it sometimes happened when some bashful young persons were to receive the *royal lip salute*, that they required to be almost forcibly propelled up to the dreaded spot.

We revert to the *Recollections*:—

Not long after my return to England, Napoleon reseated himself on the throne of France; and a general war was the consequence. I received a letter from (Count) Montenegro, written by order of the King of Spain, desiring me to return immediately to take the command of the cavalry, under General Castaños, who had been appointed commander-in-chief. (His old patron and friend had been created Duke of Baylen, in honour of the first victory gained over the French in the Peninsular War).

I accepted the offer, and was preparing for my departure, when Lord Castlereagh sent for me to inform me, that he purposed sending me as British commissioner, with rank and pay of brigadier-general, and 1000*l. per annum* extra allowance, to the headquarters of the Austrian army, about to advance upon Lyons.

I stated to him the position in which I stood to the King of Spain, should His Majesty call for my services. His Lordship gave it as his opinion, that under all the circumstances, he thought I was bound in honour to return to Spain.

General Whittingham took with him on his return to Spain, for which he embarked from Falmouth, with part of his family on the 30th June, the following letter, for the English Ambassador:—

The Duke of York to Sir Henry Wellesley.

Horse-Guards, 14th June, 1815.

Sir,—Colonel Sir Samford Whittingham having been called to a command in the Spanish army according to his rank of Lieutenant-General in the service of His Catholic Majesty, I have to acquaint you that the Prince Regent has been graciously pleased to approve his acceptance of the same: and I cannot permit this deserving and distinguished officer to take his departure from this country without making him the bearer of my desire that you will be pleased in your diplomatic as well as in your private character, to show him all the countenance and attention which a British officer in a foreign army may frequently require from a person in your high position.

It may be necessary to add, that a sense of Sir Samford Whittingham's merits would have made me desirous of affording him employment in the British army now in the field; and it has only been in the impracticability of making an arrangement suitable to his pretensions, that I have been induced to facilitate the permission he has received to serve in the Spanish Army.

I have, &c.

Frederick.
Commander-in-Chief.

★★★★★★

Being only Colonel in the English Army, he was not eligible to a high command with the troops of his own country, by the then inexorable laws of routine, though he had for so many years commanded in the field as a general officer to the full satisfaction of the Duke of Wellington.

★★★★★★

His return to the Peninsula is thus described in his *Recollections*:

On my arrival in Spain I found the war at an end; for the Battle of Waterloo had taken place, and I had not only lost the opportunity of being present at that memorable action, but I had also deprived myself of the advantage of forming part of the army of occupation commanded by the Duke of Wellington, whose field-days at the head of the principal armies of Europe formed the best school for grand military operations.'

He here alludes to his rejection of Lord Castlereagh's offers, which, however, was under the circumstances unavoidable.

To Sir Henry Torrens.
(Extract.)
Madrid, 8th August, 1815.

Ill health and bad spirits have made me delay writing to you till I am almost ashamed to take up the pen. It appears to me very doubtful whether I shall go to Catalonia or not. The minister of war, Ballasteros, has recommended me to wait for General

Castaños's answer.

It has been determined, (by the Spanish Government), that the division of Majorca, which I had the honour to command during the late war, and which consisted of eight battalions of infantry, two regiments of cavalry, and two troops of horse-artillery, formed a separate *corps d'armée*, and that the cross which I received as General of Division, should have been the grand cross of a commander of a *corps d'armée*. In consequence I have received the grand cross, and kissed the king's hand upon this new honour. (See note following).

★★★★★★

Note:—The *London Gazette* of the 28th November, 1815, sanctions the wearing of this order 'with which His Catholic Majesty has been pleased to honour him, as a signal testimony of His Catholic Majesty's approbation of the distinguished services rendered by that officer on the field of battle, during the Peninsular War.'

★★★★★★

Now in the true spirit of chivalry, I pray you to lay the grand cross at the feet of Lady Torrens, and to assure her that all my knightly services are at her command.

I assure you, we often talk of our trip to Cheltenham; and look back with delight upon the gaiety and constant good humour of our *quartetto*! Alas! what a contrast did our journey from Coruña to Madrid form. Galicia, naturally poor and wretched and now desolate by the late war, is miserable beyond expression. Nor is it possible that anyone could form an idea of want and woe equal to what you meet with from Coruña to Madrid. The state of the finances is so very shocking that I can only convey to you an idea of it by saying that many, very many, meritorious officers would ere this have perished from absolute want had they not received their daily food, and even a room to sleep in, from the charity of the convents! How long this can last, God only knows. In any other country in Europe it could not have subsisted so long; but even here the discontent, particularly of the army, is great, and sooner or later evil must arise. This is a sad picture, my dear Torrens, and would to God it were not so very true; still resources might be found; but the good and amiable Ferdinand is surrounded by men of little, miserable minds, incapable of doing good, but very well disposed to do evil.

To his brother-in-law, he had written, on the 7th August, a long letter to the same effect, adding that he received no Spanish pay as Lieutenant-General owing to the state of the finances.

The great affability of the king, and his flattering partiality for Sir Samford Whittingham, inclined the latter, for some time, to regard his weaknesses with indulgence, and to throw the blame of his conduct upon his ministers. Indeed, Ferdinand does not appear to have been a man of bad natural disposition, and he was certainly very amiable in private life. But his narrow and bigoted education and his want of discernment, incapacitated him from being a good ruler, and his reign was mainly tolerated on account of his personal popularity amongst the mass of his subjects, especially the lower orders. This feeling the king appears to have cultivated in a manner resembling that of our Charles II.; *minus*, however, the immorality, for His Majesty was a very good husband. Sir Samford used to relate how Ferdinand, when handing his beautiful Queen Christina into the royal carriage, would turn round smilingly on the loyal crowd, and observe familiarly to them, '*Is she not a fine woman?*' or some similar remark.

By desire of the King of Spain, General Whittingham wrote a long Spanish paper on the reasons that should induce His Majesty to abolish the Slave Trade. This request was the result of a conversation with His Majesty, for Sir Samford now felt it his duty to use what influence he had with the king, in favour of civilization and good government, reluctant though he was as a thorough soldier to embark in matters which savoured of political intrigues. But ample proofs exist of the noble and patriotic manner in which he exercised his influence with the Spanish King, and especially in the letters of His Britannic Majesty's representatives at Madrid.

Meantime, as the war was over and his active services were no longer required for the safety of the country, the jealousy regarding the employment of an Englishman, (who as such could not but be too partial to liberty in royal eyes,) in a high military command, coupled with the intrigues of courtiers in Spain and the calumnies propagated at home, all combined to deter General Whittingham from either seeking for, or obtaining, a high command. If, indeed, he would have consented to abandon his own service, (in which, for want of military rank, he could expect for many years only a very subordinate position) there is every reason to believe that a fine career was before him; but to this idea he never could resign himself, though sometimes tempted to it by natural ambition of distinction, and by the laudable desire of commanding armies for which he felt himself fully capable.

His voluminous correspondence from 1815 to 1820 shows but too clearly how his active mind revolted from the compulsory idleness, in a military point of view, to which he was at this period condemned by uncontrollable circumstances, however useful he frequently was to the embassy at Madrid. Brief extracts of his correspondence are all that can be laid before the reader.

The following relates to his claims for a small pension from the British Government, afterwards granted to him on the same terms as other officers similarly situated. He had now no salary except his half-pay as a British lieutenant-colonel, and was involved in difficulties.

To his Brother–in–law,

Madrid, 15th September, 1815.

I was, as you know, employed by Mr. Pitt on a secret mission to Portugal. My expenses were, as you also know, very great; but notwithstanding Mr. Pitt's generous offers of remuneration upon my return to England, I declined receiving any re-imbursement of my expenses, and felt happy at being able to render what was then thought a good service, without the possibility of having my motives misinterpreted.

In the Spanish service, I never received any pay as Colonel, Brigadier, or Major-General, till I was appointed to the command of the cavalry in the Island of Leon, and the scale of my expenses in consequence unavoidably increased.

Would to God I could follow the same system at present! but the diminution of my private fortune by unavoidable expenses, and the increase of my family, have placed me in a situation, in a pecuniary point of view, very different from that I have heretofore enjoyed.

General Whittingham endeavoured to counteract by his influence with the King the overbearing influence of the Russian Ambassador and the Holy Alliance principles which the latter warmly advocated. In a letter of the 24th November, he writes to his brother-in-law:

I have been able to render some good service of late. (He means *to the British Embassy*). The king continues his decided partiality towards me; I have frequent interviews and conversations with him. I have had many opportunities of studying Mr. Vaughan lately, (the minister, Mr. Charles Vaughan, acting as such in the absence of the ambassador); I do not think our affairs could be in better hands.'

But King Ferdinand could not forgive the evident sympathy of England with his revolted colonies, and threw himself the more readily into the arms of Russia.

To detail all the circumstances that occurred between King Ferdinand and General Whittingham during the time, (nearly four years,) that the latter resided in Madrid, would swell this work far beyond its intended limits, and being of a diplomatic and commercial rather than military nature, forms no necessary part of a military memoir. But it will be requisite to establish hereafter on incontrovertible testimony the fact, that even in matters of diplomacy, in which he had no official business, he did good and recognised though unrewarded service to his own country.

To his Brother-in-law.
Madrid, 8th December, 1815.

Mr. Barthelemy Frere, brother to John Hookham Frere, went to Constantinople, as Secretary of Embassy to Mr. Liston. Mr. Listen is now at home, and B. Frere will of course have remained there as Minister Plenipotentiary, in the same manner as Vaughan has remained here, as Minister Plenipotentiary in consequence of the absence of Sir Henry (Wellesley). Mr. B. Frere is going to be married immediately. (To Donna Barbara Creus, sister-in-law to the general).

The year 1816 was a gloomy one in Madrid; the king from his despotic and Russian proclivities becoming odious to all men of liberal opinions in Spain, and the recovery of the Spanish American colonies being already nearly hopeless. Sir Samford Whittingham was now thankful that he held no responsible post in Spain, and in spite of his low rank in the English army desired, more and more, employment under the English Government; turning his thoughts meantime to a residence in the south of France. For he writes to Mr. Davis, (in January 1816) alluding to his poverty, '*it is impossible for me to live in England.*'

★★★★★★

It is not superfluous to record such a fact in this *Memoir*, when it is borne in mind that others similarly situated had undoubtedly enriched themselves, and that he had calumniated. Many people are slow to believe this when a man *can*, he *will not* enrich himself.

★★★★★★